# D-DAY SHIPS

# D-DAY SHIPS

## The Allied Invasion Fleet, June 1944

### by Yves Buffetaut

*Frontispiece:* Near to Ver-sur-Mer, on Gold Beach, a very wet group of Royal Engineers emerge on the sand trailing a rope they have used to help a wading recovery tank (this is the square box - replacing a turret - with the helmeted driver's head emerging from it, a few yards out immediately below the ramp of LCT 858 on the right of the picture). Further out are a group of LCT (4)s, plus the characteristic flat bow pierced with oval holes of an LCM(1). On the beach on the left of the picture, numbered 300, is the inflated waterproof skirt of a DD (amphibious) tank.

First English Language Edition published in Great Britain in 1994 by

Conway Maritime Press
The Chrysalis Building
Bramley Road
London W10 6SP
www.conwaymaritime.com

An imprint of **Chrysalis** Books Group plc

English translation
© Conway Maritime Press 1994

*Reprinted 2004*

First published in France 1994 under the title
*Les Navires du Débarquement*
by Marines Edition, Bourg en Bresse

*British Library Cataloguing in Publication Data*
Buffetaut, Y.
    D-Day Ships
    I. Title II. Lyon, David
    623.8

    ISBN 0 85177 639 6

Translated by David Lyon
Printed and bound in Singapore

# Contents

'The question of landing in the face of an enemy is the most complicated and difficult in war.'

SIR IAN HAMILTON,
GALLIPOLI DIARY, 1920.

*But:*

'A Military, Naval, Littoral War, when wisely prepared and discreetly conducted is a terrible Sort of War. Happy for that People who are Sovereigns enough of the Sea to put it in Execution! For it comes like Thunder and Lightning to some unprepared Part of the World.'

THOMAS MORE MOLYNEUX,
CONJUNCT EXPEDITIONS, 1759.

# Introduction: Recent Precedents

View of a quay in Suvla Bay, just before the Allied evacuation of Gallipoli in 1916. During the six months they were established here the British had built a port. The craft in the foreground and middle distance appear to be the specialised armoured landing craft of the First World War - the X craft or 'Beetles'. These powered barges arrived too late for the initial landings, but then proved their worth in landing supplies, etc. (D.R.)

As a MARITIME and colonial power Great Britain had a tradition of amphibious operations and landings in force. However, modern war had changed from the era of Nelson, when the comparative lack of efficiency of weapons had given an undeniable advantage to the attack.

The Royal Navy paid the dues of progress in this matter during the disastrous Dardanelles operations. Without entering into the details of the unlucky attempt to force the Straits, which does not concern us directly, it is interesting to stop a moment to consider the landings themselves, principally carried out on the peninsula of Gallipoli, on 25th April 1915. In the employment of force and the mobilisation of naval effort they involved, these landings were the predecessors of those of the following war.

What is most striking is the lack of anything specifically intended for such operations. The infantry were put aboard ships' boats, most of them unpowered, which were towed in groups towards the coast. If the steam or motor boat acting as tug was damaged or sunk, the boats in the tow drifted under enemy fire. The use of a coaster modified for the occasion to an infantry landing ship turned into a disaster. The SS *River Clyde* was beached at the intended spot, but the disembarking of soldiers by two ramps projecting on either side of the bow turned into a slaughter, to the extent that all attempts to carry on were suspended until nightfall. The lesson of Gallipoli was not lost. In the next war all major landing operations, bar one, were carried out with specialised equipment.

Dunkirk, June 1940. Photo of the beach of Malo-les-Bains taken by the Germans just after the end of the evacuation. The lack of specialised equipment shows in the steel-built ship's lifeboat in the foreground, the bow of what appears to be a small motor cruiser behind, and the improvised jetty formed by a line of abandoned lorries and other vehicles in the background. The latter was useful in allowing men to get out to the deeper draught boats waiting offshore. (Bundesarchiv)

## Dunkirk: a landing in reverse

The exception, of course, was the evacuation of Dunkirk, a landing in reverse, the lessons of which are of the greatest interest. Certainly it was not a matter of attacking an enemy coast, but the logistic problems were nearly the same, if not worse, since 350,000 men of a defeated army (or, rather, two armies) had to be evacuated under air attack in a very few days. From the first hours of the operation, bombing by the Luftwaffe made the use of the port of Dunkirk impossible, though not the mole. Therefore the operation had to be carried out from the beaches which extended from the town itself to Bray-Dunes, via Malo-les-Bains. Warships could not close the shore across these vast expanses of sand without the risk of being grounded. This is why ships' boats were supplemented by numerous pleasure craft to ferry troops between the beaches and the destroyers, cross-Channel steamers and other vessels, then made the voyage back to Dover. In the absence of all but a very few specially adapted craft, the boats and yachts experienced difficulties in loading. Large emergency jetties were improvised, with hundreds of vehicles piled one on another.

In spite of these difficulties, the evacuation proceeded almost according to plan, thanks, above all, to the continual intervention of the aeroplanes of Fighter Command, which managed to keep the Luftwaffe bombers relatively at bay. This lesson was, of course, well learnt.

In the months which followed Dunkirk, Britain began to equip herself with a specialised fleet for the inevitable return to Europe. This was to be a colossal task, because the future invasion would demand a veritable armada. The British armaments industry was torn between so many requirements, each one as urgent as the other; for aircraft, especially four-engined bombers to take the war to Germany, for tanks, for escort ships for the Atlantic convoys, etc. Moreover, on top of all this, it was necessary to design new vessels for landing. Production was therefore slow, and at the moment of the August 1942 Dieppe raid, the number of vessels available limited the forces which could be used.

## Fiasco at Dieppe

Operation Jubilee foresaw the landing of the 2nd Canadian Division and about a thousand commandos (not forgetting fifty or so American Rangers). The aim was to capture the town of Dieppe and some coastal artillery batteries situated on either side of it. It was in no way an attempt to invade, since it was intended to re-embark the troops on the same day. In fact, the operation did not last out the time between tides. This very short period did not prevent the use of the respectable total of 252 vessels of all kinds. Amongst them were nine LSIs (large infantry carriers), twenty-four LCTs (tank landing craft) and numerous wooden infantry landing craft, notably LCP(L)s.

From the start of the landing, in the early hours of 19th August 1942, it was met by opposition too strong for the means used by the attacker. In default of adequate naval support - the most powerful ships used were small Hunt class destroyers with 4in guns - the German shore defences were not muzzled and, nearly everywhere, the landings met a bloody check. In the air the result was mixed, support by bombers and fighter-bombers being insufficient to open a way for the infantry and tanks. On the other hand, air cover of the ships was more successful, and only one destroyer, HMS *Berkeley*, fell victim to the Luftwaffe. The loss of 106 machines to the RAF was also significant. The use of two main types of craft in the landings themselves, LCTs and LCP(L)s, produced little in the way of significant lessons, for different reasons.

The first LCTs (Landing Craft, Tank) began building at the beginning of June 1940, on the demand of Churchill himself. They were intended to transport a troop of three tanks apiece. Their bow ramps and flat bottoms made it possible to disembark tanks directly on to beaches. Their cellular bottoms served as ballast tanks which could be emptied when approaching or leaving the beach. The sides of their hulls, also cellular in construction, were used to contain fuel tanks, various store-rooms and a washroom for the crew. During the operation the Mk II LCTs used were hampered by their combination of flat bottoms with the windage of the superstructure aft, which rendered them difficult to handle. This, combined with a current which swept them westwards, delayed the landing of tanks, which were then rapidly put out of action on the pebble beach, with no support from the already more-than-decimated engineers.

Aboard the LCP(L)s (Landing Craft, Personnel (Large)), the problems were different, but even worse. Machine-gun fire was accurate and heavy, and the wooden sides of these boats offered no protection. Frequently, all of the occupants were dead or wounded before reaching the beach. Even when this was not the case, the craft themselves were very vulnerable and much equipment was lost, whilst many men could not re-embark.

The balance sheet for Operation Jubilee was

An LCT(2) beached and abandoned on the beach at Dieppe. The basic, flat bottomed form, the simple ramp and its equally basic lowering mechanism are all evident, as is the corpse of one of the unfortunate assault troops, mowed down in this attempt at a landing. (ECPA)

disastrous. Out of 305 officers and 4,658 Canadian soldiers embarked, 214 officers and 3,153 men were lost, of whom 805 were killed and the rest taken prisoner. The commandos suffered less (and achieved more), with 132 killed or taken prisoner out of 1,075. The Royal Navy lost 550 out of 3,875 men. German losses on the ground were proportionately insignificant: 121 dead, 201 wounded and 11 missing. The Luftwaffe admitted the loss of some 50 aircraft against the RAF claim of 170.

## Operation Torch: the Americans join the party

Fortunately for the Allies, other landings had already avoided disaster. The British had landed with carrier and battleship support at Diego Suarez, Madagascar, in May 1942, going on to seize that island from Vichy France. This was the first major Allied amphibious success, and provided the first trial for the prototype LSTs (Landing Ships, Tank). Soon afterwards the US Marines began to turn the tide of Japanese victory by their landing at Guadalcanal. Also, much experience of operating landing craft had been gained by the British in numbers of commando raids, small and large, from Bruneval to Vangso and from the Lofotens to Saint Nazaire.

The North African landings of November 1942 were on a much greater scale, and were equally successful. The plan was

This scene taken on 9th November 1942 during Operation Torch, shows an American scout car being pulled out of the sand by a small bulldozer, which also seems to be having some difficulties. Partly obscured in the mist behind is an LCM(3), recognisable by its ramp, with its perforated upper part, and by its narrow wheelhouse. (IWM)

impressive. It foresaw a triple assault on the coastline of Morocco and Algeria. The Western Task Force, coming directly from the USA, would land on the Atlantic coast of Morocco and take Casablanca. At the same time, the Centre Task Force would disembark at Oran. Algiers was the objective of the Eastern Task Force; the last two convoys coming from Britain. The American war effort was already making an enormous addition to Allied strength.

More than 2,000 ships were involved, from battleships and aircraft carriers down to Landing Craft, Assault (LCAs). Artillery support was provided by 200 surface warships, including a multitude of destroyers. The assault forces were aboard 110 troop transports, all of which carried numbers of small landing craft.

The landings began on 8th November 1942. The way things went depended on the location. The army commander in the West, Patton, had placed his sights very low, having little confidence either in the navy or, perhaps, in his own troops, and declaring, 'Never in history has the Navy landed an army at the planned time and place. If you land us anywhere within fifty miles of Fedhala and within one week of D-day, I'll go ahead and win'.[1] Patton's fears were only in part groundless. Though the first assault waves landed only an hour late and in the planned place, there were an incredible number of wrecks because of the

inexperience of the landing craft crews. Thus eighteen of the twenty-five craft of the first wave sank before reaching the coast. Happily, the number of boats present meant that the majority of the infantry-men were saved. That having been said, accidents multiplied during the course of the day, and by midnight nearly half of the 347 landing craft had been lost, very few of them because of the French defence.

Contrary to what the Americans had hoped, the Vichy forces resisted after momentary dithering, thanks to contradictory orders. The French fleet even attempted a sortie with the cruiser *Primaguet* and six destroyers against vastly superior American forces, including three battleships. After a long combat all the French ships were either sunk or disabled; *Primaguet* ran herself ashore.

Ashore, progress was fairly slow, once again owing to the inexperience of the combatants. If the sailors were able to land a sufficient quantity of supplies on the beach, those supplies did not reach the front line. The advance was feeble although French resistance grew steadily weaker and ceased totally on 11th November.

At Oran the landing operations went rather better. The tanks of the 1st Armoured Division were put ashore at the same time as the infantry, thanks to the three 'Maracaibos' - the ancestors of the LST - which were actually shallow-draught oil tankers built for use on Lake Maracaibo in Venezuela, transformed into tank landing ships and just back from their first use in Madagascar.

The landings at Algiers were still more rapid, with only localised French resistance on one beach, and the repulse of an attempt to 'bounce' the harbour defences of Algiers itself (both ships involved sank from the damage they suffered). Once again, however, the chief problems were due to the sea state and the inexperience of the crews. Several craft capsized in the passage of the bar at Sidi Ferruch, and the men of certain American units were scattered over more than thirteen miles.

On 11th November all French resistance ceased

[1] S.E. Morison *History of U.S. Naval Operations in World War II* Vol.2, OUP 1947.

in North Africa. Operation Torch therefore ended in an undeniable victory, even if Allied exploitation of this success was slow enough to allow the Germans to take over Tunisia without opposition.

## Landings in the Mediterranean

The success of Torch left unanswered a number of questions about amphibious operations, primarily that of knowing what would happen against a well defended and fortified coast. The landings in Sicily, Southern Italy and then Anzio began to provide an answer, as well as giving the Allies first-hand experience.

Another, more general, view of Surcouf Beach on 9th November 1942. Three LCVPs laden with infantry can be seen beaching. Behind them is an LCM(3), slewed round by the waves on the beach, and doubtless difficult to get off. Behind that still is an visibly abandoned LCP(L), recognised by the absence of a landing ramp. (IWM)

Operation Husky, the landing in Sicily, was a complete success. It was, moreover, the largest amphibious operation yet. In all, 160,000 men, 24,000 vehicles, 600 tanks and 1,800 guns were brought into action. The Allies took the Axis forces by surprise, and in a few hours success was assured. On the morning after the landings (11th July 1943) the Germans counterattacked with the panzers of the Hermann Goering division. They were stopped in their tracks by the formidable effect of naval gunfire. The British, in fact, sent in six battleships. Aerial support was equally impressive, both by carrier aircraft and by some 670 machines massed on the airfields of Malta and Cape Bon in Tunisia. The campaign itself lasted five weeks, and provoked the fall of Mussolini. However the Allies showed themselves incapable, thanks to excessive prudence, of interrupting the German evacuation to mainland Italy.

On 3rd September 1943 the first landings on the continent of Europe happened, by crossing the Straits of Messina. Because of the narrowness of those straits and the total absence of opposition, this operation taught the Allies no new lessons.

This was not the case with the landing at Salerno, south of Naples, on 9th September 1943. A new tactic was tried, landing the troops without any preliminary bombardment, either from the sea or the air. This was to produce complete surprise whilst permitting

minesweepers to go as close inshore as possible, for the Gulf of Naples was heavily mined. Whilst the landing itself was effected according to plan, its exploitation was soon seen to be impossible. The intact German positions proved to be untakeable. Still worse, the Germans counterattacked in force on 12th September with the 16th Panzer Division. For a short while the position was critical because shore-based air support was too far from its bases to intervene efficiently. The strategic air forces, and especially the powerful guns of the fleet, were needed to stop the enemy. It was principally the 15in guns of *Warspite* and *Valiant* which broke the attacks of the panzers. This provoked massive attacks by the Luftwaffe against the two battleships. For three days the raids all failed, but on 16th September, at the beginning of the afternoon, a glider-bomb launched from a German bomber hit *Warspite* and put her out of action. She was towed away by two American salvage tugs and survived to participate in the Normandy landings.

On 1st October 1943 Naples was finally captured, and the Germans began to withdraw towards the mountain chain where they continued to block the Allies, notably before Monte Cassino. To break the stalemate a landing was made close to Rome, at Anzio, on 22nd January 1944. Enormous resources were not

Still on Surcouf beach, three jeeps set off inland, looking down on a
beached LCVP.(IWM)

used, because it was above all a diversion, and the principal forces were in action in the Apennines. Once again, the amphibious operation was perfectly successful, but its exploitation did not meet expectations and made no difference to the strategic situation in Italy. The position of the troops ashore became critical from the end of January, whilst the fleet suffered badly from air attacks whilst maintaining the bridgehead. The cruisers *Spartan* and *Penelope* were lost, besides other less important vessels. Once again German counterattacks were only stopped with the support of the fleet.

## Pacific experiences

From the purely tactical point of view, amphibious operations in the Pacific bore scarcely any relation to those in Europe. The distances which separated ships from their bases were enormously greater, and the scale of the objectives very much smaller. The capture of an atoll needed far fewer resources than landing in Sicily or Italy. However, the concept of the landing ship (already developed by the British for both tanks and infantry) came into its own in the immense spaces of the Pacific, as did the American development of the tracked, amphibious LVT or 'Alligator'.

At the beginning of 1944 the Allied navies were therefore both technically and tactically prepared for landing in France. There was a lack of some types of vessel, but American industry accomplished wonders in filling these gaps.

However, the success of the Allied plan did not depend solely on adequate landing techniques and equipment. In the end, the Germans had to be defeated strategically. It was not long before Allied staff discussions led to a definitive plan.

# 1    The Plan for Operation Overlord

The professional heads of the Royal Navy and the RAF come to see the operation from the bridge of a British motor launch. On the left, with both hands on the side of the bridge, is Admiral Sir A.B.Cunningham, the First Sea Lord, with, on his left, Air Vice Marshal Portal; both men seem very happy with events. In the foreground are twin Vickers 'K' machine guns. (IWM)

WHEN THE UNITED States went to war in 1917, the general staff had no developed plan for the engagement of the American army. Its newly formed divisions were first used under French or British command. From the outbreak of the Second World War President Roosevelt took to heart the need to foresee a military strategy for the USA. The fall of France in June 1940 only reinforced the President's opinion, and from January 1941 officers of the American and British general staffs met in Washington to develop a common strategy. The first plan was adopted on 27th March 1941. That was nine months before the attack on Pearl Harbor, whilst the USA was still officially neutral. The essence of the plan was that the Americans foresaw the priority of attacking and defeating Germany, seen as more dangerous an adversary than Japan. If Japan also entered the conflict, the priority remained the destruction of Germany.

## The difficulty of finding a common strategy

At the 'Arcadia' conference, held at Washington, DC, two weeks after Pearl Harbor, Churchill detailed his views, which did not receive general agreement from the Americans. It suited him to weaken Germany by blockade, air raids and limited attacks on weak points before launching a massive and decisive attack. The Americans did not believe Germany could be defeated by these indirect means. For them, only a direct attack could be decisive. For two months the two views were in confrontation. The Americans complained of the pusillanimity of the British, of their propensity to discuss and modify existing plans; whilst the British reproached the Americans for their inflexibility and rigidity of thought. In fact, the Americans needed a precise date for the final offensive against Germany in order to launch the whole American industrial effort towards clearly defined objectives, with limiting dates and so on.

A group of four American LSTs moored bow to stern show their particular features to advantage, the comparatively simple shape, somewhat varied armament (the nearest vessel has a quadruple Bofors 40mm mount on the poop, the next one two single Bofors, one superimposed forward of the other), and the 'clamshell' bow doors, opening in No 64 to show the bow ramp lowered almost to water level. The above-water propeller guards, designed to keep smaller craft away from their screws, can also be seen. The nearest LST has been fitted with a powerful crane, not a normal piece of equipment for these vessels. (IWM)

In the end, the long and often acrimonious debate between British and American staffs seems to have produced the best possible result, an invasion which occurred at probably the most favourable time, with adequate preparation and with the best possible chance of success. The British (influenced by the memory of the fearful bloodletting of 1914-18 and conscious of their dwindling manpower resources) were probably right in thinking that the Americans had insufficient experience and underestimated the sheer difficulty of defeating the highly efficient German soldier. The Americans were, however, right in thinking that an invasion of northwest Europe had to come, and in pressing for it to happen sooner than the, perhaps over-cautious, British wanted. It must also be remembered that the arguments were over precise means and exact timing, not over ultimate aims. The British wished to invade Europe just as much as the Americans did, though they sometimes gave the latter a somewhat different impression.

The British had been investigating the means of getting back on to the Continent of Europe from the time of Dunkirk. The Combined Operations organisation, especially under its third head, Lord

Louis Mountbatten, was extraordinarily fertile in producing techniques, training and devices, many of which will feature in the following pages. It also collected an enormous amount of intelligence about beaches and harbours of the invasion coast, which would prove vital. Some of this was done in libraries and by collecting old snapshots, some by much more direct methods. The lonely bravery of the men of the COPP (Combined Operations Pilotage Parties) who reconnoitred enemy-held beaches by night was a vital element in the success of D-Day. So was the immense and ultimately hugely successful series of deception operations which played a major part in persuading the Germans to deceive themselves over the location of the main landings, even after they had actually happened. There is insufficient space to do more than mention this background to the D-Day plans, but the sheer scale and variety of the efforts of many thousands of people who never crossed the Channel, but contributed to the success of those who did, must not be ignored.

The first American invasion plan was drawn up in March 1942 by Eisenhower, at that time head of the plans division in the War Department. Having examined all the possible landing places in occupied Europe, Eisenhower declared in favour of attacking the northwestern coast of France, since the British Isles were the only possible launching pad for such an ambitious undertaking. The invasion could be launched in spring or summer 1943. The US Navy met this plan with little enthusiasm, for it would be very difficult to build a sufficient number of landing craft in time. Having said that, an ambitious plan for the construction of specialised vessels and for the training of their crews was launched on this occasion.

On 27th March 1942 General Marshall, the Chief of Staff of the US Army, presented a memorandum to Roosevelt. It foresaw, amongst other things, the possibility of a landing in the Cotentin peninsula in 1942 if the collapse of the USSR seemed imminent. This was called Operation Sledgehammer. The principal invasion would occur the following year, with a landing between Boulogne and Le Havre, Operation Roundup, which was to be the origin of Overlord/Neptune.

On 14th April 1942 the plan was adopted by the British Chiefs of Staff. However, their reservations were numerous and were soon apparent. Churchill soon proposed an attack on the periphery, in North Africa, which pleased Roosevelt but not Marshall, for whom Germany would never be destroyed if the Allies dispersed their resources in operations of this type. The acceptance of intervention in North Africa automatically implied the postponement of the landing in France for a year.

For several weeks the English and American strategists argued heatedly. The latter even threatened to remove the American troops already in Britain and send them to the Pacific if the British failed to accept Sledgehammer. Finally, Roosevelt ruled in favour of Churchill and accepted the principle of Operation Torch, the landings in Algeria and Morocco, which offered evident strategic advantages. However, this meant that the Americans were entangled in the Mediterranean theatre of war and could not avoid the landings in Sicily and Italy which may have delayed the final assault against Germany, though they may well also have contributed to its success. These latter destinations were in Europe, they did provide much needed experience of both landings and of fighting a fierce and competent enemy, and they put considerable and continuing pressure on that enemy. The Italian theatre was a disappointment to the Allies; more could have been achieved, but its role in wearing down the Wehrmacht should not be underestimated.

## The establishment of a common general staff

In January 1943, at the Casablanca conference, the Allies agreed to the foundation of an Anglo-American staff charged with the task of preparing plans for future operations on the continent. On 13th March 1943 the British General Morgan was designated as Chief of Staff to the Supreme Allied Commander, and the acronym of this title (COSSAC) was used to designate the staff which worked with him. Installed at St James's Square, this staff soon included 489 officers, of whom 215 were Americans.

Work started in April, and a month later, at Washington, Churchill and Roosevelt agreed a date for the landing in Europe: 1st May 1944. COSSAC, after

Another view of a group of American LSTs a little before the invasion. There are LCVPs in the davits on either side of the superstructure. Another pair of these smaller craft can be seen in the water on either side of the nearest LST. (IWM)

an intensive study of European coastlines from Portugal to Norway, placed its choice on two French shorelines, the Pas de Calais and the coast of Picardy from Gravelines to the Bay of the Somme on one hand, and the Bay of the Seine from Caen to the Cotentin Peninsula on the other. The short crossing from England to the Pas de Calais, and the closeness to Germany, militated in favour of the first alternative, but aerial reconnaissance and other intelligence showed that this part of the coast was heavily defended. The other option of the Normandy coast had the advantage of presenting shallower defences. On 26th June 1943 COSSAC decided in favour of the second alternative.

The first months of COSSAC's existence were not easy, as two grave problems hampered its activity. Firstly, no general was yet nominated as the chief of the invasion force. Secondly, the British were still reluctant to commit themselves to an immediate all-out attack. They hoped that the Germans might become so exhausted that the operation might become a simple walk-over. This hypothesis was not envisioned by the Americans. Not only would public opinion in the USA not understand such inaction, but the USSR, if not too exhausted, would be left free to occupy a good part of Europe.

However, an increasing proportion of British officers, notably Lord Mountbatten argued for a rapid landing in Normandy. By July 1943 the majority opinion of the British general staff was that the time to act had come.

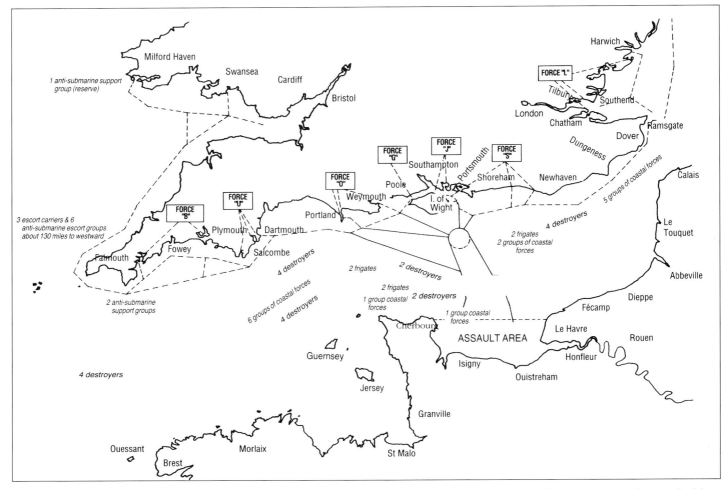

Map of convoy routes and location of naval protection forces for
Operation Neptune. (After Roskill *The War at Sea* Volume III part 2,
HMSO, London 1961)

At the Quadrant conference, held at Quebec in
August 1943, it was finally decided to make the
Normandy landing the first priority. Churchill even
proposed a 25 per cent increase in the force committed
to the operation, with a landing on the southeast coast
of the Cotentin. The date of May 1944 was maintained.
However, all of this did not prevent Churchill once
again proposing a peripheral action against Norway
as an alternative to the invasion of Normandy.

## Stalin puts an end to the hesitations

There is no space here to go into the details of the
arguments over the choice of a supreme commander
which raged in Washington in 1943. Was it to be
Marshall or Eisenhower? For essentially political
reasons Roosevelt hesitated for some months, torn
between Churchill's wishes, political pressures and his
own desires.

In November 1943, at the 'Sextant' conference held
in Cairo, Churchill raised more obstacles to the invasion
of France by proposing a new calendar, with the taking
of Rome in January 1944, of Rhodes in February,
bringing Turkey into the war in the ranks of the Allies
and transforming the Aegean into a supply line to
Russia, and only then unleashing Overlord. If all these
conditions were met, this could take place in the
autumn of 1944. These ideas for dispersing efforts
towards secondary objectives such as Rhodes stupefied
the Americans, and were the despair of Churchill's own
professional advisers.

At the Teheran conference, Stalin ensured agreement.
He claimed to be astonished that no-one had yet been
appointed to supreme command. It was out of the
question to venture on diversionary operations which
would delay Overlord. He also supported the idea of a
landing in the south of France. Stalin's firmness had
immediate results. On 30th November the British
confirmed the May 1944 date for Overlord. Roosevelt
finally took his decision, and on 3rd December he
named Eisenhower as the supreme commander. The
latter arrived in London on 14th January 1944 and

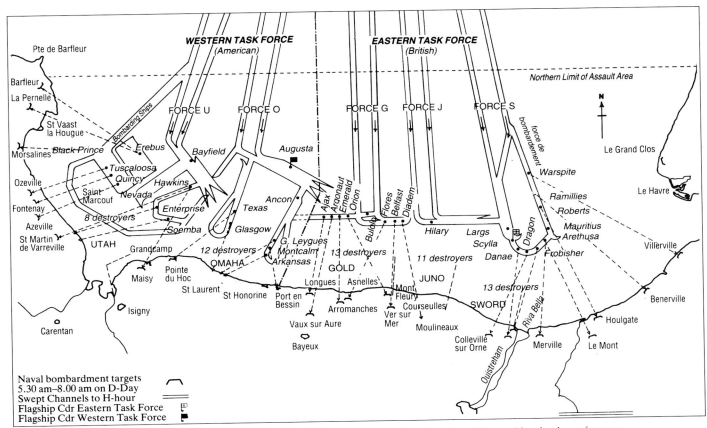

Swept channels and location of the naval bombardment forces on D-Day. (After Roskill *The War at Sea* Volume III part 2, HMSO, London 1961)

absorbed COSSAC into his own staff, now called Supreme Headquarters Allied Expeditionary Force, or SHAEF.

At the centre of SHAEF the three principal commands were given to British officers; Ramsay at sea, Montgomery on land and Leigh-Mallory in the air. Ramsay was undoubtedly the admiral who knew the coasts of the Channel best, and he was also the most experienced in amphibious operations. During the First World War he had served in the famous Dover Patrol. Retired in 1938, he was recalled to service a year later, at the age of fifty-six. Once again posted to Dover, he was the chief organiser of Operation Dynamo, the evacuation of Dunkirk. He was then the author of the plans for the Torch landings in North Africa and, in the following months, initiated the plans for the landings in Sicily and Italy. He had therefore already worked with Eisenhower and was certainly the 'right man in the right place' in SHAEF.

## Operation Neptune/Overlord

Overlord describes the entire landing operation, whilst Operation Neptune was only its naval aspect. Both titles will be used, as Overlord as a whole cannot be separated from its purely naval aspects.

Even before Eisenhower arrived in London,

COSSAC's initial plan of landing on the coast of Calvados with three divisions had been enlarged. It was felt vital to increase the scale of the initial attack to five infantry divisions by extending the assault to include the southern Cotentin up to the river Orne, and one airborne division was also included in the first wave. Eisenhower approved this new plan on 23rd January 1944. However, this increase in numbers posed the problem of where to find the necessary landing craft to transport an extra American division to the Cotentin coast. SHAEF estimated that this would require six more assault transports, plus 47 tank landing ships (LST), 71 infantry landing craft (LCI) and 144 tank landing craft (LCT). These ships did not exist, and there was only one way of obtaining them; give American industry an extra month for their production, and reduce the importance of the projected landing in the south of France, Operation Anvil.

This last necessity produced a new skirmish between the British and Americans. The former wished to concentrate on Overlord and the operations in Italy, and felt (probably rightly as it turned out) that Anvil was an unnecessary diversion of effort. The Americans

The products of American industrial might arrive in a British port. GMC and Autocar lorries are offloaded from a Liberty ship, using the ship's own derricks. The dockers are American black soldiers. The odd angled shape just in front of the bridge is a liferaft on an angled ramp, designed for easy release when a rapid abandon ship became necessary. (IWM)

felt that Anvil was needed to hold down German forces which might otherwise threaten the success of Overlord. Finally, after much discussion, it was decided to reschedule Overlord for the beginning of June and (much later) to postpone Anvil until 15th August 1944.

On 28th February the initial planning was definitively brought to a conclusion. Dempsey's Second British Army was to be landed between Arromanches and the mouth of the Orne at Ouistreham, on three beaches code-named Gold, Juno and Sword. The First US Army (Bradley) would be landed on either side of the Carentan estuary, on two beaches initially called 'X' and 'Y' and later named Omaha and Utah.

The naval plan proper, Ramsay's responsibility, was ready on 10th April 1944. All of the operational orders, down to the least detail, were included, so that with its twenty-two appendices the plan totalled 1,100 printed pages, to the great astonishment of the Americans. They were used to the higher command only giving broad outlines of requirements, with details relegated to lower commands. However, as Ramsay put it, the operational orders had to be voluminous because the operation required the movement of more than 4,000 ships and varied craft during the first three days.

## An improvised port and PLUTO

Given their naval and air superiority, the Allies were fairly sure of success in the actual landings. However,

both the Dardanelles and Anzio showed the catastrophic results of failure to exploit that success. Clearly, rapid reinforcement was needed to prevent the loss of tactical initiative, and this meant the use of a port. The invasion coast had no ports of a suitable size. Furthermore, the tragic example of Dieppe had shown the difficulty of frontal attack on any well defended port, whilst German skill at demolition held out little hope for rapid utilisation of such a port even after capture.

The only large port near the landing beaches was Cherbourg, but its capture would not be possible in the first days, let alone the first hours, of the assault. It was therefore necessary to find another solution. By the end of 1941 the British had already begun work on this. They had set in train the design and construction of an artificial port, moving with the tide, protected by caissons, and linked to the shore by floating jetties, like the catwalks of present-day marinas. In July 1943, during a meeting of COSSAC which was confronted by the impossibility of capturing Cherbourg fast enough, Commodore Hughes-Hallett of the Royal Navy (a leading light of the Combined Operations HQ) surprised his American questioners by declaring, 'Well, all I can say is, if we can't capture a port we'll have to take one with us'. On the following day he showed his colleagues the British project which was soon to be codenamed 'Mulberry'. The details of its construction will be described later. Two examples were to be built, each with as much quay space as the port of Gibraltar. Starting as a British idea, all the necessary equipment was British-built.

PLUTO was another British invention. This was the acronym of 'pipe line under the ocean'; a flexible pipeline laid like a cable from specially-fitted craft across the bottom of the Channel. Through it fuel would be pumped to the armies fighting in Normandy. This would relieve the strain on port facilities, as well as that on the available tankers, the favoured targets of German submarines and aircraft.

## A powerful protecting fleet

Allied naval forces were heavily drawn upon to escort the vast numbers of landing vessels required for the operation. The other naval commands, in the Atlantic, the Mediterranean, and (to a lesser extent) the Pacific were proportionately weakened. A total of 286 destroyers, sloops, frigates and corvettes formed the escort. The majority of the Allied nationalities were represented: principally Britain and the USA, but also the Netherlands, France, Greece, Poland and Norway. Seventy-nine per cent of the warships, excluding transports and landing craft, were British, 16.5 per cent were American, and 4.5 per cent were from the other nations.

Apart from the escort, larger warships were provided to lay on fire support at close, medium or long range (see the accompanying tables for their allocation). The mobilisation of forces for the landing itself did not prevent resources being allocated to certain linked missions. Thus four anti-submarine support groups were based on Plymouth for patrols in the northeastern Bay of Biscay to attack U-boats off their bases of Lorient, Saint Nazaire, La Rochelle and Bordeaux. In addition, three escort carriers were to patrol off the entrance to the Channel.

Coastal Command set up an unprecedentedly thorough 'spider's web' system between Lands End and the Breton coast to the north of Brest. Every part of this large area would be swept every half hour, day and night. It was of prime importance to prevent U-boats endangering the invasion fleet, and the effort worked. Out of the twenty-one submarines spotted on the surface on 3rd June, seven were sunk and the others were forced to proceed submerged and exhaust their batteries.

## An overwhelming concentration of vessels

A great deal of careful planning went into the allocation of vessels of the invasion armada to individual British ports. The five assault forces, each intended for a particular beach in Normandy, were assembled in the south coast ports between Plymouth and Newhaven, to give the shortest possible voyages to the French shore. The second wave forces were spread amongst rather more distant ports, whilst the back-up troops and supplies were in vessels moored in the Thames and the Bristol Channel. The warships of the covering forces were concentrated at Plymouth, Dartmouth, Portsmouth and Dover. The battleships, cruisers and other more powerful units were based beyond the usual range of the Luftwaffe, at Belfast and in the Clyde. The mass of ships was so great that they overflowed the ports and 130 'hards' (loading ramps) were constructed along the southern English coast to permit direct loading of tanks and lorries from the beach.

From east to west the assault forces were divided as follows:

For Sword Beach, in the Ouistreham sector the ships transporting the 3rd British Division loaded men and matériel at Newhaven, Shoreham and Portsmouth,

| Allocation of Warships for the Assault phase | | | | | |
|---|---|---|---|---|---|
| Type | Western Task Force | Eastern Task Force | Home Command | Reserve | Total |
| Battleships | 3 (US) | 3 | - | 1 | 7 |
| Monitors | 1 | 1 | - | - | 2 |
| Cruisers | 10 (3 US 2 French) | 13 (1 Polish) | - | - | 23 |
| Gunboats | 1 (Dutch) | 2 (1 Dutch) | - | - | 3 |
| Fleet Destroyers | 30 (US) | 30 (2 Norwegian) | 20 (4 US & 2 Polish) | - | 80 |
| Hunt Class Destroyers | 5 | 14 (2 Polish, 1 Norwegian, 1 French) | 6 | - | 25 |
| Sloops | - | 4 | 10 | - | 14 |
| Fleet Mine-Sweepers | 56 (6 US) | 42 | - | - | 98 |
| Other Sweepers | 62 (16 US) | 87 | - | 40 | 189 |
| Frigates etc | 12 (6 US & 2 French) | 19 (2 French) | 32 | - | 63 |
| Corvettes | 4 (2 French) | 17 (2 Greek) | 50 (3 Norwegian & 1 French) | - | 71 |
| Patrol craft | 18 (US) | - | - | - | 18 |
| A/S trawlers | 9 | 21 | 30 | - | 60 |
| Minelayers | - | 2 | 2 | - | 4 |
| Coastal craft (all types) | 113 (81 US) | 90 (30 US) | 292 (8 French, 13 Dutch, 3 Norwegian) | - | 495 |
| Seaplane carrier | - | 1 | - | - | 1 |
| Midget submarines | - | 2 | - | - | 2 |
| A/S Groups | - | - | 58 | - | 58 |
| | | | | TOTAL : | 1213 |

NB: all British or Commonwealth except where noted.
[Taken from Roskill, *The War at Sea*, Vol III part 2 p18, HMSO 1961]

which were also (with the anchorage of Spithead) the assembly points.

For Juno Beach at Courcelles-sur-Mer the 3rd Canadian Division embarked at Southampton and Portsmouth, with the vessels concentrating in the Solent.

For Gold Beach at Asnelles, the 50th British Division's port of embarkation and assembly was Southampton. The 1st US Division, destined for Omaha Beach at Saint-Laurent, assembled at the neighbouring ports of Portland, Weymouth and Poole, having embarked at the first two.

Utah Beach was the destination of the 4th US Division, which loaded at Torquay, Brixham, Dartmouth and Plymouth; assembling at Brixham, Dartmouth, Salcombe and in Torbay.

American soldiers in full combat gear wait to embark on LCVPs, four of which can be seen to the left of the picture, to be ferried out to larger vessels offshore. The ramp they are standing on is one of those recently purposely built for the invasion on the south coast of England. In the middle background are two American YMSs - small coastal minesweepers. (IWM)

A row of loaded American LCT(5)s in an English port. The soldiers almost conceal the two rows of half-tracks in each tank hold. (IWM)

## Aerial and naval protection

As has been shown, this armada was protected by 1,200 warships. Also, more than 2,000 fighters from 171 squadrons would form an aerial umbrella above it. Five squadrons of twelve aircraft apiece were permanently assigned to the protection of the maritime approach routes, whilst ten squadrons were detailed off to provide permanent cover for the invasion beaches. Initially these would be under ground controllers based in England, but three specially modified LSTs would then take over the control of these fighters.

Meanwhile, heavy and medium bombers would weaken the defence. During the night before the invasion the 'heavies' were to attack the ten principal coast defence batteries, while six others would be bombed by 'mediums' at daybreak. Finally, in the 45min before the infantry assault, all the available heavies and mediums were to drop some 4,200 tons of bombs on the beach defences.

To ensure that the assault forces landed in the right place, particularly after this obliterating air attack, a complex buoyage system was prepared. This was both to mark the swept channels through the German minefields and to indicate the access routes to the beaches themselves. Besides motor launches and bell-buoys laid for the purpose, two midget submarines, X20 and X23, were navigation marks for Juno and Sword beaches.

Thousands of mines had been laid by both sides in the waters of the Channel, so sweeping operations were particularly vital. Four channels were cleared to a concentration zone 5 miles in radius about 8 miles to the south of the Isle of Wight. From this circle eight routes (collectively known as 'the Spout') led directly south towards the huge minefield laid by the Germans to the south of the 50th parallel. Ten channels, varying in width from 400m to 1,200m, were swept through this barrier and marked with the aid of lighted buoys. Finally, a number of zones were cleared off the beaches to allow the bombarding ships to manoeuvre during their contest with the shore batteries, whilst channels were swept through to the beaches themselves. It was obviously important that vessels of all sorts could move about without the danger of hitting a mine.

The role of the battleships, cruisers and monitors was equally of first importance. It was not just a question of silencing the powerful German shore batteries, but also of supporting the infantry ashore. Several times in the battle for Normandy naval gunfire stopped attempted counterattacks dead in their tracks. The big warships would arrive in position just before daybreak, divided into five groups, one for each beach (see accompanying table). Naval gunnery spotters were trained to fly Spitfire or Mustang fighters, 102 of which were allocated to fly in pairs, one to spot for the guns

American troops, lorries, half tracks and jeeps on the upper deck of an LST. (IWM)

of the big ships, the other to act as escort. Also other gunnery controllers, titled Forward Observers, Bombardment (British) or Shore Fire Control Parties (American) would land with the first waves. Both groups of men were trained to communicate with ships of either navy.

Finally, it should be added that artillery support during the final minutes before the landings was reinforced by rockets fired from converted landing craft, and tank guns fired from specially adapted LCTs.

## Consolidation

The role of the navies did not cease with the D-Day landing itself, since what was at stake was the invasion of an entire continent. The bridgehead had to be consolidated by the transportation of thousands of men and hundreds of tons of equipment, then feeding and supplying the Allied divisions whilst the decisive breakthrough was being obtained. All was foreseen for this enormous task.

The second phase, that of consolidation, began at the moment of the second high tide of D-Day, in the evening, with the arrival of Forces B and L coming from Plymouth and the Thames estuary. The convoys of cargo ships and coasters followed. These were essential to the consolidation, and from them the best results would be obtained with the coming into use of

| Beach | Battleships | Monitors | Cruisers | Destroyers |
|---|---|---|---|---|
| Sword | 2 | 1 | 5 (1 Polish) | 13 (1 Polish 2 Norwegian) |
| Juno | - | - | 2 | 11 (2 Canadian, 1 French, 1 Norwegian) |
| Gold | - | - | 5 (1 Dutch) | 13 (1 Polish) |
| Omaha | 2 (US) | - | 3 (2 French) | 12 (9 US) |
| Utah | 1 (US) | 1 | 6 (2 US 1 Dutch) | 8 (US) |
| Reserve | 2 | - | 3 (1 US) | 17 (US) |

NB: British unless otherwise stated. From Roskill Vol III pt 2, p 32

An aerial view of part of the invasion armada taken from Admiral Ramsay's personal plane, possibly over the Solent. Just above the wingtip is a liner converted to a troop transport, and some way behind her is an LST. Most of the nearer smaller vessels are salvage tugs of different kinds. (IWM)

the artificial ports. During this period all the large landing vessels, LSTs, LCTs and LCIs, began a ferry service from England. A special staff, called Build-Up Control Organisation (BUCO), was in charge of ensuring the smooth running of these ferries. The English coast was divided at Southampton (which was shared); the eastern ports were requisitioned for supplying the British expeditionary force, whilst those of the west were used by the Americans. This certainly limited the possibilities of confusion.

On the other side of the Channel the offloading of transport vessels, and particularly the MT ships (mechanised transport - vessels carrying lorries and other vehicles) was effected by landing craft, by the amphibious lorries known as DUKWs, and by the outboard motor powered pontoons called Rhino ferries.

## The assault itself

The plan opposite depicts the position of the ships responsible for landing a brigade at 20min before 'H' hour (the moment of the first landing). At about 7 miles from shore the HQ ship and the large LSIs anchored and lowered the small LCAs (Landing Craft Assault), intended to transport the infantry. Meanwhile, the numerous other variety of landing craft got under way, the slowest starting first to ensure synchronisation.

At H minus 2hr the first LCTs moved towards the beach and at 7,000 to 8,000yd from the coast launched the amphibious ('DD') tanks, which had to be on the

beach five minutes before the infantry. At the same time the fire support landing craft and other short-range bombardment vessels moved into position and began to smother the German defences, most dramatically with the rockets of the LCT(R)s. Behind the DD tanks came a wave of landing craft carrying the AVREs (Armoured Vehicles, Royal Engineers) and other specialised armour, fitted with mine-clearing devices, bulldozer blades, bridging devices and the like. Shortly behind came the infantry in LCAs, and then it was the turn of the self-propelled guns (Priests and Sextons) and Royal Marine manned tanks, all fitted to fire whilst still aboard.

On the flanks were the destroyers, ready to fire on targets of opportunity. Out to sea the cruisers and battleships engaged the coast defence batteries at long range. Out of the field of view the two following brigades of the division were approaching in nine separate groups of LCIs and LCTs. Behind them, for the next tide, came the ships dedicated to the period of consolidation, the LSTs, LSIs and so on.

## The German defensive plan

The Germans began to consider the possibility of an Allied invasion during the month of December 1941, when the first grave reverses in Russia showed, against all expectations, that the war might last for a long time.

In March 1942 Hitler named Feldmarschall von Rundstedt commander-in-chief of the Western Front. After the raid on Dieppe the work on the construction of the Atlantic Wall was speeded up. No fewer than 15,000 concrete strongpoints occupied by 300,000 men were supposed to be completed by 1 May 1943. This gigantic task was impossible to complete in so short a time, and despite the efforts of propaganda the Atlantic Wall was never as strong as Hitler wanted. Von Rundstedt recognised, after the war, that it would have taken ten years to achieve Hitler's target. In October 1943 he actually admitted in a report to the Führer that the defences were inadequate, the troops too dispersed, and that his men were only theoretically capable of encountering the enemy.

Hitler took this well. He had a great admiration for the old soldier. In consequence he decided on 3rd November 1943 to further reinforce the defences, principally in the Pas de Calais, which seemed the most probable target because of its proximity to England. He forbade any troop transfers from west to east despite the difficult situation on the Russian front. Better still, he gave von Rundstedt what the latter had long desired;

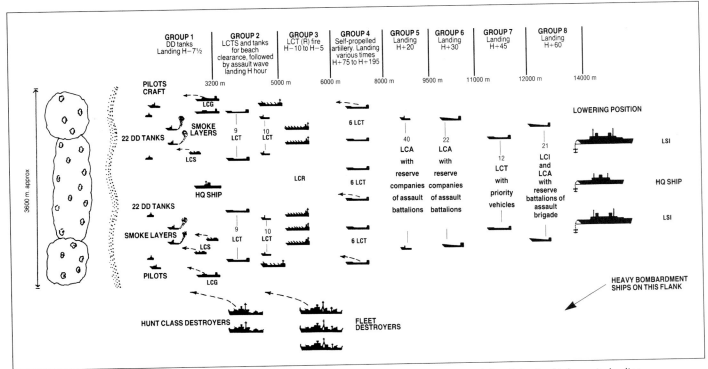

Diagram of the assault on a beach by a brigade of infantry, its landing vessels and their supporting warships. (After Roskill *The War at Sea* Volume III part 2

armoured divisions to form a strategic reserve capable of throwing back the invader. Hitler also decided to give tactical command to Feldmarschall Rommel by naming him chief of Heeres Gruppe B (Army Group B) and therefore placing 7th and 15th Armies under his command. This created an extra layer of command, as von Rundstedt retained his position at the head of all the Western Front.

Thus Rommel only commanded a coastal band some 30km wide. Most, but not all, of the panzer divisions were under his orders. These were together in a Panzergruppe commanded by General Geyr von Schweppenburg. Add to this the total autonomy of the navy and Luftwaffe, and the fact that the Waffen SS was ever more strongly influenced by the orders of Himmler, and one can appreciate how difficult it was for the German generals to exercise command efficiently.

This was even more the case because the two principal chiefs, von Rundstedt and Rommel, had contradictory ideas of what needed to be done. For the old head of the Afrika Korps the enemy had to be beaten the day he landed, if possible on the beach itself. He also thought in terms of a layered defence. First sea mines would be encountered, then beach obstacles followed by the Atlantic Wall itself with its concrete strongpoints and artillery batteries. Finally, if needed, infantry and armoured divisions would counterattack on the day of the landing itself. This implied that they would have to be positioned no more than ten or so miles from the coast. But how could an area as extended as the French coast be covered by the reduced number of divisions available?

Von Rundstedt felt that the chances of stopping the enemy on the beaches were minimal, and he had little confidence in the Atlantic Wall. For him, the only way to push the enemy back into the sea was to have a powerful strategic reserve. This would be located far enough inland to avoid losses to naval gunfire, and above all to be able to intervene in force wherever the enemy landed.

Rommel felt that this was a bad plan, because it neglected the importance of Allied air superiority and the consequent risk of the divisions being blocked before they could reach the Allied beachhead. Today it is obvious that Rommel was right, though he, in turn, seems to have underestimated the danger from naval gunfire. Basically the Germans were in a 'no win' situation – whichever choice they made would be wrong.

The final plan was rather closer to Rommel's ideas, except insofar as von Schweppenburg withdrew his armoured divisions from the coastline, persuaded as he was that gunfire from warships would prevent any serious armoured counterattacks. This was based on his own experience in Sicily and Italy, and certainly was not wrong. However, the compromise plan adopted could only be a botch and therefore deficient.

These three motor gunboats (MGBs) are returning from a patrol off Cherbourg to screen the invasion armada from attack by S-boats. They are of the British Power Boat design, 71ft 9in long and capable of 39 knots. Their main armament was one power operated 2-pdr forward and a twin power operated Oerlikon aft. They could also carry two 18in torpedoes and operate as MTBs. (IWM)

in the Cotentin, where the 'bocage' (hedgerow) country would forbid the deployment of tanks and strengthen the defence.

During an important meeting held on 20th-21st March 1944 with his principal commanders in the west, Hitler showed more clairvoyance than his generals. It seemed probable to him, given the enemy's naval and aerial superiority, that the latter would strike where he chose. The need for the rapid capture of a large port would push him towards a landing in Brittany or the Cotentin to take Brest or Cherbourg. As the commanders in France were not of the same opinion, but could not disobey Hitler, the result was that the entire shoreline of the Channel was reinforced, with a special effort in the Pas de Calais, the Channel Islands (which had no strategic value) and the Normandy coast, where the Allies were indeed preparing to land.

Rommel was overtaken by a veritable frenzy of minelaying. He demanded the delivery of ten million per month, an astonishing figure. His target was to lay 100 million before the landing. In fact, on 6th June, the Atlantic Wall had only four million, and in the chosen landing zone naval gunfire would set off a good many of them.

Other methods were employed to obstruct the landing. 'Chevaux de frise' and other anti-tank obstacles had little real value. Rommel also placed beach obstacles, iron or wooden stakes with mines placed on them in order to destroy landing craft before they beached. Because of the range of the tides, no fewer than four rows of these were lined along the beaches.

In the hinterland, areas suitable for the landing of gliders were covered by stakes, nicknamed 'Rommel's asparagus'; whilst zones which could be flooded were put under water. This was particularly the case with the marsh of Merderet behind Utah beach.

As the American historian Samuel Elliot Morison remarked, it is somewhat strange that the Germans were not able to obtain any information on the Japanese experience of the numerous landings already made by the Americans in the Pacific. However, as he added, the Red Army had not passed on any information on German tactics to its allies either.

## Where would the Allies land?

It seems that certain German naval officers based on the French coast had, in the early months of 1944, guessed that the landing would take place in Normandy. This was thanks to a simple observation. The British, who had laid mines along all the occupied coastline, had 'forgotten' the Bay of the Seine. But the fears of these men 'on the ground' were scarcely listened to in Berlin, where the opinions of the army took precedence. Von Rundstedt was persuaded that the landing would take place between Dunkirk and Le Havre, because the Allies would be able to deploy rapidly on the plains of Picardy in order to strike towards the Ruhr. Rommel thought on the contrary that the invasion would take place further west, though without any idea of a landing

## The artillery of the Bay of the Seine

All these passive obstacles were by themselves incapable of preventing the landing. The whole of the Bay of the Seine was protected by a series of coastal artillery batteries, with particular concentrations around the

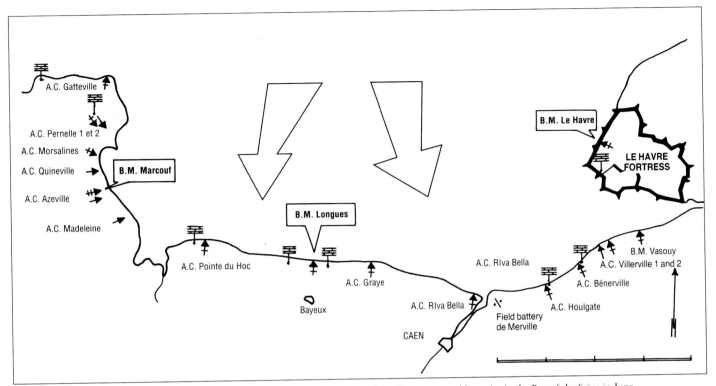

Map of the German coastal batteries in the Bay of the Seine in June 1944. (After Bertil Stjernfelt). [Key: AC = Coastal artillery; BM = Naval battery; ↑ = light battery; ‡ = medium battery; ‡ = heavy battery; Radar = Radar.]

approaches to Cherbourg and Le Havre. The guns were often of French origin, though also Czech and German, had a ranges of between 9km and 24km. Of the eighteen batteries with seventy-five guns of a minimum calibre of 105mm which protected the Bay, thirteen were protected by concrete bunkers, often of imposing dimensions.

## The divisions of the Wehrmacht

After the end of the war, some German accounts said that the infantry divisions holding the coast consisted of elderly or convalescent men, or simply those unfit for normal service. This is certainly an exaggeration. It is, however, true that of the fifty-eight divisions available in the west, thirty-three were static. In other words they were not provided with adequate transport. This was of little importance, though, because they were the ones destined to hold the Atlantic Wall. The twenty-five other divisions were of excellent quality, and seven of these were armoured. It is well to recall that the firepower of a German division was greater than that of an American one. Also, the majority of German tanks were generally superior to the American Shermans and the British Churchills and Cromwells.

Numerical superiority would be simply a question of rapidity of reinforcement. At the beginning the Allies benefited from a double advantage. They had mystified the Germans by a complex and subtle deception policy, reinforcing their delusions by making them believe in a phantom army, commanded by Patton, ready to invade northeast France from Kent. As has been shown, the Germans were already prepared to believe that this area would be the main target, and they placed the larger part of their forces north of the Seine; nineteen infantry divisions and six Panzer divisions. There were only fourteen divisions, only one of them armoured (the 21st, partly equipped with old French tanks) to cover the west coast, Brittany and Normandy.

On D-Day the Allies had a net numerical advantage at the bridgehead. But which side could bring up its reinforcements the faster? If all the available effectives in France could be taken into account, the Germans would enjoy an advantage over the next two weeks. After this, according to SHAEF's plan, the Allies would have landed more divisions than their enemy had in the west.

There were two remaining uncertainties on the eve of the invasion. Could the Germans counterattack with force in the first fortnight, and how long would it take them to get reinforcements, particularly in tanks, from the Eastern Front?

The Batteries of the Bay of the Seine in June 1944 (after Bertil Stjernfelt)

| Battery (Coastal = CA, Naval = NB) | Number & Calibre of guns | Type of gun | Origin | Range in Km | Rate of fire per min | Thickness of concrete metres |
|---|---|---|---|---|---|---|
| CA Gatteville | 6 x 155mm | Field piece M/16 | French | 18.6 (15) | 1¹/₃ | 4 |
| CA Pernelle 1 | 6 x 105mm | Field piece M/13 | Franco/German | 11.5 (9) | 1¹/₃ | 6 |
| CA Pernelle 2 | 3 x 170mm | modern field piece | German | 29.6 (15) | 2 | none |
| CA Morsellines* | 4 x 155mm | Field piece M/16 | French | 18.6 (15) | 1¹/₃ | none |
| CA Quinéville | 4 x 105mm | Field piece M/13 | Franco-German | 11.5 (9) | 1 | 4 |
| NB Marcouf | 3 x 210mm | Skoda guns | Czech | 27.5 (22) | 1¹/₃ | 2 |
| CA Azeville | 4 x 105mm | Field piece M/13 | Franco-German | 11.5 (9) | 1¹/₃ | 4 |
| CA Madeleine* | 4 x 105mm | Field piece M/13 | French | 11.5 (9) | 1¹/₃ | 0 |
| CA Pointe du Hoc* | 5 x 155mm | Field piece M/16 | French | 18.6 (15) | 1¹/₃ | 0 |
| NB Longues | 4 x 152mm | Naval guns M/28 | German | 22 (17) | 6 | 4 |
| CA Graye | 4 x 122mm | Field piece M/31 | German | 18.5 (14) | 1¹/₃ | 2 |
| CA Riva Bella* | 6 x 155mm | Field piece M/16 | French | 18.6 (15) | 1¹/₃ | 0 |
| CA Houlgate | 4 x 155mm | Field piece M/16 | French | 18.6 (15) | 1¹/₃ | 2 |
| CA Bénerville | 4 x 155mm | Field piece M/16 | French | 18.6 (15) | 1¹/₃ | 3 |
| CA Villerville 1 | 4 x 105mm | Field piece M/13 | Franco-German | 11.5 (9) | 1¹/₃ | 4 |
| CA Villerville 2 | 4 x 155mm | Field piece M/16 | French | 18.6 (15) | 1¹/₃ | 1 |
| NB Vasouy | 4 x 152mm | Naval piece M/28 | German | 21 (17) | 6 | 4 |
| NB Le Havre | 3 x 170mm | Modern field piece | German | 29.6 (24) | 2 | 1 |

\* = Guns installed on temporary emplacements which were unable to go into action on 6th June for technical reasons.
Figure given in brackets in the 'Range' column is effective range.

## Growing weakness

The incredible degree of aerial superiority which the USAF and RAF had won over the Luftwaffe was an encouraging factor in reducing the uncertainties of battle. We have already seen that 2,000 fighters were available to protect the invasion fleet. If one adds over 2,000 bombers of Bomber Command and the Eighth US Air Force, and great numbers of other aircraft (reconnaissance, Coastal Command, transport aeroplanes, etc) the total reached well over 6,000.

Against this, the 3rd Luftflotte could only place 481 aircraft, of which about 100 were fighters. In other words the Luftwaffe was suffering from growing weakness and would be quite incapable of protecting German units trying to reach the front. Obliged to move only by night, von Rundstedt's divisions arrived terribly late to be thrown into battle higgledy-piggledy and in disorder. German naval weakness was, if anything, even more lamentable (see a later chapter for details).

# 2    Landing Craft and Ships

This stern quarter view of LCA 873 shows both flat bottom and shallow draught. The wooden construction and steel bullet-proof plating on the sides and steering shelter forward are clearly visible. The loops along the side are lifelines for men in the water, whilst the reinforced eyes to take hoisting can be seen at either end of this line of loops. (IWM)

WHEN THE CRISIS of the summer of 1938 came to an end with the Munich agreement, the British realised that war with Germany was inevitable in the near future. Rearmament, already commenced in the mid-1930s, was speeded up. This included the navy, and prototype landing craft were designed, which served as models for hundreds of descendants built in Britain, and of thousands more built in the USA.

Given the multiplicity of fronts on which the Allies were operating in early 1944 it is almost miraculous that Eisenhower had enough landing vessels for the June landings. The Americans called the period leading up to the invasion 'the battle for the landing craft'.

## A battle against time

It is very interesting to trace the incredible development of the fleet of landing vessels in the year preceding the invasion. When the headquarters responsible for the American naval participation in Operation Neptune established itself at Falmouth on 15th July 1943, it had not even a barge of its own. On 1st September of the same year the IX Amphibious Force was created at the same port. At that stage it had five LCTs and ninety-five smaller craft, all LCVPs.

This insignificant total exasperated the British who accused the Americans of favouring their effort in the Pacific to the detriment of the agreed priority task of defeating Germany. This was both true and false. In April 1942 at the time when the Allies for the first

A maritime review before King George VI a little before D-Day with columns of LCAs struggling to keep formation, a difficult task with speed differences threatening collisions. They are escorted by what look like a couple of MLs (Motor Launches), and are seen from an LSI with an LCP(L) visible in her davits. (IWM)

| Theatre | LST | LCI(L) | LCT | LCM | LCVP | LCA |
|---|---|---|---|---|---|---|
| USN - Britain | 168 | 124 | 247 | 216 | 1,089 | 0 |
| RN - Britain | 61 | 121 | 664 | 265 | 0 | 646 |
| TOTAL -Britain | 229 | 245 | 911 | 481 | 1,089 | 646 |
| US - Mediterranean | 23 | 59 | 44 | 185 | 395 | 0 |
| RN -Mediterranean | 2 | 32 | 64 | 95 | 0 | 138 |
| US - Pacific | 102 | 128 | 140 | 1,198 | 2,298 | 0 |
| RN - S.E.Asia | 0 | 4 | 2 | 67 | 0 | 46 |
| East Coast (USA) | 95 | 89 | 58 | 57 | 341 | 0 |
| West Coast (USA) | 0 | 41 | 1 | 60 | 181 | 0 |

US = US Navy, RN = Royal Navy. The ships on both coasts of the USA were presumably mostly new construction - the ones on the east coast including vessels for the RN as well as the USN.

It is interesting to note how many more USN landing vessels were in the Pacific than in England, though with a different pattern of types. It has been argued that the insatiable demands of the Pacific commanders for landing craft, even more for shipping resources, and their tendency to retain both whenever possible; lengthened the war in Europe by several months.

## I Vessels for landing infantry

Allied nomenclature for landing vessels was divided into three major categories:
- Ships longer than 350 feet and capable of crossing oceans by themselves.
- Large landing craft capable of reaching the area of operations by short stages under their own steam, but which could be transported by LSD or LST over long distances.
- Smaller craft which would be launched just off the landing beaches.

Besides these horizontal divisions there was a basic vertical division between vessels of all sizes whose primary purpose was to transport men, and those chiefly intended to carry tanks or other vehicles. A source of mild confusion is the fact that the early British craft had their designations given in a different order than later became the practice. LCAs were originally ALCs, LCTs started as TLCs, whilst the original LCMs were initially MLCs. The change in designations was made soon after the Americans entered the war.

## The saga of the LCA

The LCA was the smallest landing craft employed by the Royal Navy for the landing of infantry. This was not a type used by the US Navy, which had the LCVP instead.

The origins of the LCA go back to 1938. After the Munich crisis it was decided to order a vessel of less than 10 tons capable of carrying thirty-two fully-equipped infantrymen and drawing less than 2½ feet.

time were considering a landing in France, the US Navy had given absolute priority to the construction of landing ships and craft, to the detriment of the programme of destroyers and escort carriers. With British hesitations and the increasing involvement in the Mediterranean, the Americans decided to send their landing craft to the Pacific rather than convoying them to Britain with the invasion deferred. From June 1942 the Pacific had priority as the destination for American landing craft production.

On 3rd September 1943 Admiral King promised to furnish his allies with the following for Overlord: 110 LSTs, 58 LCIs, 146 LCTs, 250 LCMs and 470 LCVPs. These numbers were in fact quite inadequate, particularly after the inclusion of the Cotentin coast had been agreed on.

An important conference was held in London on 13th February 1944 in order to determine the exact number of landing vessels required for Operation Overlord. It was decided to draw to an extent on the number of available craft in the Mediterranean, not easy to do as at that stage the final decisions had not been made on Operation Anvil, the landing in Provence. Finally on 21st March Eisenhower decided to put back the date of Anvil, which allowed for an appreciable reinforcement of the main invasion fleet.

The table below gives the total number of landing craft available to the two main Allied navies on all fronts on 1st June 1944:

The earliest, and rather rudimentary, American landing craft, the LCP is seen in this photograph of No 851. This is one of the British boats supplied under lend-lease, and manned by a couple of British sailors. They had no ramp, no armour and no shelter for the helmsman. (IWM)

The first prototype, built by White of Cowes to a design by Fleming, was not very successful. The second, built by Thornycroft, was much closer to what the navy wanted, with its low silhouette, silenced engines and shallow draught. Designated ALC No 2 (Assault Landing Craft), it was 41ft 6in long over all and driven by two Ford V8 engines of 65bhp each. The design was slightly modified by the Admiralty; some 1,929 were built during the war. In 1944 sixty were being built each month. After the war many were converted to houseboats by the addition of a cabin.

The LCA was reasonably seaworthy, so long as waves were less than 5ft high. In a heavy sea the situation could become critical and a number of LCAs converted to support craft, and therefore heavier than normal, disappeared in the choppy seas of 6th June.

The first LCAs were used at Narvik where four of them landed 120 French Foreign Legionnaires. They were later to be found at Dieppe, then taking part in Operation Torch and all subsequent British landings. In effect these craft were lightly armoured troop carriers, their plating being only sufficient to withstand rifle bullets and located on the sides (³/₄in), the side decks alongside the troop space (giving a little overhead protection to the troops sitting on benches on each side), over the machinery room (¹/₄in) and as a forward bulkhead forward just behind the disembarking ramp. The helmsman's position, originally placed aft but soon moved forward to the starboard side of the ramp, was also armoured. So was a corresponding machine gun position to the left of the ramp.

Apart from the support craft variants (described separately) there was the LCA (OC), which was fitted to clear foreshore obstructions. Neither the LCA (FT) fitted with a flamethrower, nor the LCA (CDL) appears to have been used in action. The latter was a conversion by the parent firm of Thornycroft to carry an armoured searchlight ('canal defence light') originally developed for use in tanks and intended to blind the enemy in a night attack. Though plans exist of a prototype conversion it is not clear whether it was ever completed. Finally there was even an LCA (Bakery) variant to provide fresh bread!

**Particulars of the LCA**
Length: 41ft 6in oa, 38ft 9in bp
Breadth: 10ft
Draught: 1ft forward/2ft 6in aft
Displacement: 9 tons empty, 11 tons loaded (early craft) 13¹/₂ (later)
Speed: 6 to 10 knots (11 empty)
Range: 90 to 140 miles
Capacity: 35 troops or 800lb of equipment
Armament: positions for three Bren LMGs - one twin and two single mounts and for two 2in mortars (the weapons of the troops carried).
Crew: 4 men (also 1 officer to every 4 LCAs)
Fuel: 64 gal
Losses: 267 in 1944 (out of 371 losses during the whole war)

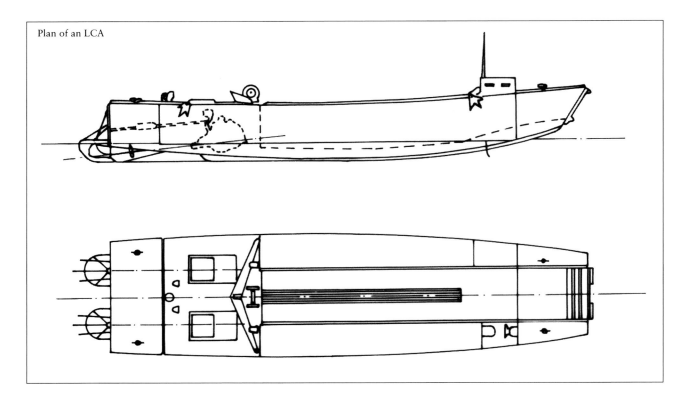

Plan of an LCA

## The LCP(L) - American industry to the aid of Britain

This type was no longer in first-line use during the Normandy landings, but should none the less be included, because it was the origin of the LCVP. Moreover it continued to be used as the loss of 128 in 1944 shows. It was itself derived from a fast motor boat - the 'Eureka' design - produced by Andrew Higgins of New Orleans. This type, capable of 18 knots on its 225bhp engine in its original form, was spotted in 1940 by British purchasing officers. They were looking for suitable craft for use in commando raids and ordered this design in quantity. The first 500 were built to British orders, and were followed by others built for the US Navy.

Built entirely of wood these Landing Craft Personnel (Large) were originally run ashore at speed and the soldiers disembarked by jumping off the bow which was flat in front of the slightly raised helmsman's position. They were normally transported by LSIs and lowered fully loaded from the davits of these ships. Later many were modified to the LCP(R) standard by being fitted with a bow ramp. Both types had a machine gun mounted forward in an emplacement. There were a number of different versions with varying powerplants, Hall Scott 250bhp, or Kermath 225bhp petrol engines, or a Gray diesel of 225bhp. The design then was further modified to become first the LCV and then the extremely versatile LCVP - the latter

becoming very popular and largely replacing its predecessors, especially in American service, by mid-1944.

Conversions which were used on D-Day were the navigational versions; the LCN - used for lead craft for waves of assault craft, and the LCP (Survey) for inshore survey work. Then there were the LCHs which were fitted as ambulances to carry six stretcher cases and ten walking wounded (not to be confused with the LCH converted from the much larger LCI(L)s as Headquarters craft - in this instance 'H' for HQ, not for Hospital). There was also a conversion for fire support - the LCS(S).

Particulars of the LCP(L)
Length: 36ft 9in oa
Breadth: 10ft 9in
Draught: 2ft 6in forward/3ft 6in aft
Displacement: 6 ½ tons light, 9 to 10¾ tons loaded
Speed: 10 to 8 knots loaded
Range: 50 to 320 miles
Capacity: 30-35 men (American), 25 men (British) or 4 tons of equipment (both)
Armament: one or two 0.303in machine guns (Bren, Lewis, BAR, etc)
Armour: (later British and all American types) three ¼in transverse bulkheads
Crew: 3 men (the British usually allocated one officer to every 3 boats as well)
Losses: the Royal Navy lost 88 LCP(L)s and 40 LCP(R)s in 1944 alone, also one LCP (Survey)

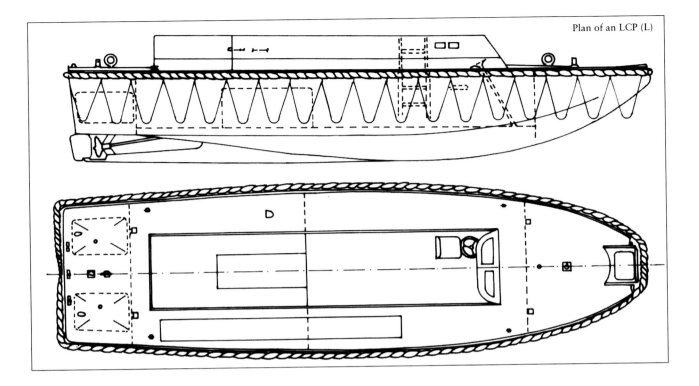

Plan of an LCP (L)

## The LCVP: the boat constructed en masse

As its name (Landing Craft Vehicle Personnel) indicates this was a craft or barge for all purposes, capable of carrying infantry or small vehicles like the Bren gun carrier or Jeep, or even a 3-ton lorry. Its origin was the Higgins-designed LCP(L) described above. The ramped version of this was further altered by giving it a larger armoured ramp forward to enable a small vehicle to be carried as an alternative to troops. This was the LCV (Landing Craft Vehicle). Some 200 were built for the Royal Navy. The chief defect was that the elevated steering position aft was completely unprotected. British experience with this design led to further modifications, including the fitting of side armour, lowering the steering position and placing it within the troop space on the port side aft, and providing machine gun emplacements; this produced the LCVP.

It was capable of being lowered into the water by special davits when fully loaded, and all American examples were fitted with TCS or TBK radios to permit contact with their mother ships or control craft. Used as a floating ambulance it could carry seven stretchers. They were also much in use as tugs for elements of the Mulberry harbour and many other engineering or harbour tasks.

The astonishing total of 23,358 examples of this design were assembled. No other landing craft came near these numbers. The British believed their LCA to be more seaworthy and capable of taking a heavier sea, but the LCVP was more powerful. The Royal Navy acquired numbers of the latter towards the end of the war and forty-five LCVPs (with a similar number of LCMs) were used in Montgomery's crossing of the Rhine in March 1945. No LCAs were present.

A number of LCVs were converted for minesweeping with light sweeps close inshore and designated LCV (M/S). Others, called LCE, were converted for the salvage and repair of other landing craft, carrying extra crew including two mechanics and two shipwrights, plus a salvage pump, a line gun, fire fighting gear and engine spares.

Both LCVs and LCVPs were wooden built.

**Particulars of the LCVP** (LCV given in brackets)
Length: 36ft oa (36ft 3in)
Breadth: 10ft 6in (10ft 9in)
Displacement: 8 (7) tons light, 11½ (11) tons loaded
Draught: 2ft (1ft 6in) forward/ 3ft (3ft) aft
Speed: 9 (9) knots
Range: 102 (-) miles
Capacity: 36 men or 3 (4½) tons of cargo or a light vehicle
Armament: two (one) 0.303in machine guns
Armour: ¼in ramp and sides (ramp only)
Crew: 3
Propulsion: Hall-Scott 250bhp petrol engine or Gray 225bhp diesel
Losses: the Royal Navy lost 3 LCVs, 4 LCEs and 62 LCVPs in 1944

An LCP shows her bare interior when seen from above, stowed inside an LCM(1). It looks rather as if both are on the deck of a British LSG, with the hoisting spans of the gantry clearly seen, as is the winch in front of the steering shelter of the LCM. (IWM)

## The LCI(L)

In early 1942 it appeared to the British that the smaller craft would not suffice for major operations, especially those which took place far away from their bases. They therefore designed a type of landing vessel capable of accommodating 200 men for a period of several days and with a draught shallow enough for beaching. The latter requirement implied a light hull, which would have to be steel-built. As the British had no spare steel ship-building capacity they turned to the Americans to build the type. This the USA did with great success, and by the end of the year LCI(L)s(Landing Craft Infantry (Large)) were crossing the Atlantic under their own power, to participate with great success in all the landings of 1943. All those used in the Normandy landings landed troops from lowering gangways on either side of the ship-shaped bow (a later version substituted a bow ramp). Another feature of later vessels was that the twin screws were variable-pitch.

Normally the 180 to 200 troops to be landed would be transferred to the LCIs about 48hr before the landing. There was a bunk each. In exceptional conditions another fifty men could be placed on the deck without any shelter.

The British relaxed their staff requirements to produce a somewhat smaller woooden-built LSI, which was built in Britain, designed by the Fairmile organisation as their type 'H'. This was known as the LCI(S) with 'S' standing for 'Small'. It had a transom bow, and troops were landed across four moveable 'brows' (bow gangways). Like the larger type it had totally enclosed troop spaces.

The size of the LCIs made them too large targets, and they were too vulnerable, to be used in the actual assault. They were therefore used for landing the reserve and reinforcement units and were organised in flotillas of a dozen boats.

Twenty LCI(L)s were converted to the LCH standard with extra communications gear to act as headquarters and communications vessels for groups of landing craft. Also LCI(L) number 101 was fitted out for the use of press and radio correspondents on D-Day. Some LCI(S)s were converted to support craft as LCS(L)2.

Plan of an LCVP

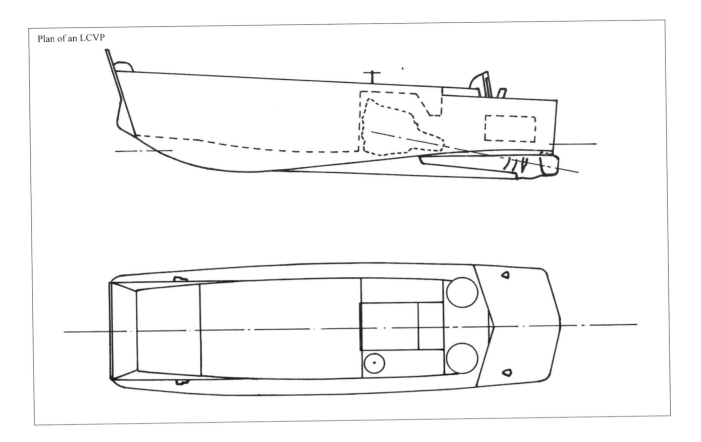

Plan of an LCV

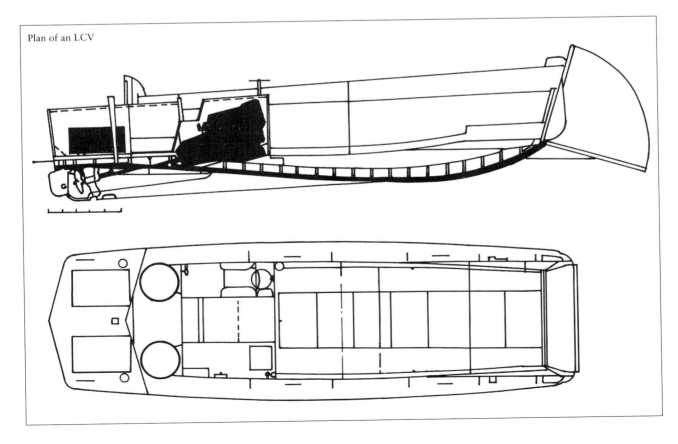

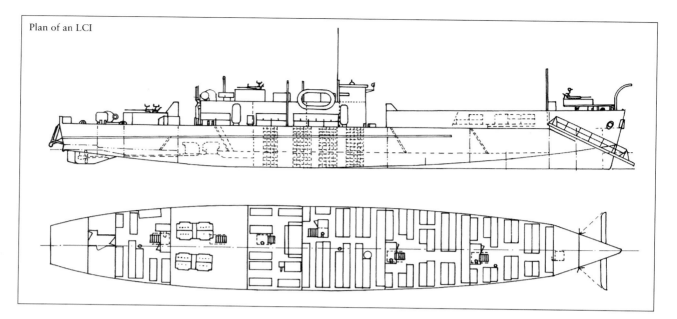

Plan of an LCI

**Particulars of the LCI**
Figures in brackets are for the LCI(S). The figures given for the LCI(L)s are for the earlier models; later ones varied, but only very slightly.
Length: 158ft 6in (105ft) oa, 150ft(100ft) bp
Breadth: 23ft 3in (21ft 6in)
Displacement: loaded 384 (110) tons, light for beaching 234 (63) tons
Draught: loaded 4ft 9in (3ft 3in) forward, 6ft 6in (3ft 9in) aft, light for beaching 3ft (?) forward, 4ft 10in (?) aft
Speed: 14 (14½) knots
Range: 4,000 (?) miles at 12 (?) knots
Capacity: 188 (102) troops or 75 (?) tons
Armament: four 20mm Oerlikons (two Oerlikons plus two machine guns)
Armour: plastic armour on bridge and gun positions (¼in plate on bridge, sides and gun positions)
Crew: 24 including 3 officers (17)
Propulsion: 2 General Motors diesels giving 1,440bhp in total (2 Hall Scott petrol motors giving 1,140bhp total)
Losses: in 1944 the Royal Navy lost 5 LCI(L)s, 8 LCI(S)s, plus one LCH

## The large family of the LSI

The larger troop transports, known as Landing Ships, Infantry were all converted cross-Channel steamers or larger merchant ships. Like those craft not intended to beach, the modifications needed only extended to the superstructure. Life boat davits were strongly reinforced to take the weight of LCAs, LCVPs or LCSs. Because these were merchant vessels they were not grouped in classes, but certain types had common characteristics, and a selection is given here. The main divisions were between LSI(L) - large, (M) - medium, and (S) - small, plus the separate group of small landing ships known as LSI(H). The 'H' stood for 'hand hoisting' because this is the way their davits were operated. Both (S) and

(H) were short sea vessels of small capacity, not intended for transoceanic work. The American equivalent to the LCI(L) was the 'Attack transport' (AK) - which was modified from a commercial hull design and built as a class. Twelve of these (US Maritime Commission C1-S-AY1 type) were transferred to the British under lend-lease and given names beginning with *Empire* as was standard for British war-emergency built merchantmen.

## Examples
**LSI(L) - Glen type**
Tonnage: 9,800.  Speed: 18 knots.  Capacity: 1,087 troops, 3 LCMs, 24 LCAs.  Crew: 280.  Propulsion: 2 diesels, 12,000bhp

**LSI(L) - Keren type**
Tonnage: 9,890 gross.  Speed: 17 knots.  Capacity: 1,500 troops, 2 LCMs, 2 LCP(L)s, 10 LCP(S)s, one LCS(M) and 9 LCAs.  Complement: 297.  Propulsion: 2 steam turbines, 12,000shp

**LSI(L) - American (AK) type**
Tonnage: 11,650 displacement.  Speed: 14 knots.  Capacity: Usually around 500 troops and equipped with LCVPs.  Complement: 250.  Propulsion: Steam turbine, 4,400shp

**LSI(M) - *Queen Emma* (Dutch) or *Prince Henry* (Canadian) types**
Tonnage: 6,900-4,100 gross.  Speed: 23-22 knots. Capacity: 440-370 troops, 2 LCMs, and 6 smaller craft, a mixture of LCS(M)s and of LCAs or LCP(L)s. Complement: approx 200

**LSI(S) - ex Belgian cross-Channel ferries**
Tonnage: approx 3,000 gross.  Speed: 23-24 knots.  Capacity: 250-200 troops, 8 LCAs or similar

**LCI(H) - ex British cross-Channel steamers**
Tonnage: 3,900-1,900 gross.  Speed: 23-16 knots.  Capacity: 830-150 troops, 6-10 LCAs.  Complement: 120-230

A mass of American landing craft. The majority are LCM(3)s. The armoured steering positions can be seen aft, flanked by mountings for machine guns (removed - presumably for maintenance - in this picture). On the top left hand side of the picture is an LCVP and on the right the bow of an LCT. (IWM)

## Other troop transports

Other ships served the Allies as troopships but not in this invasion : the liners that carried reinforcements across the oceans and the APDs, fast transports converted from old destroyers by the Americans, which carried raiding parties landed by the LCVPs they transported. The latter were mainly used in the Pacific.

There were also smaller craft not mentioned yet - the British LCP(M)s, based on the cobles of the northeast coast and used by commando raiders, and the British designed LCP(S) and their successors the LCP(U)s intended for landings which were not under fire. However these 'second wave' landing craft were not used for the intended purpose, but instead were put to work for general utility purposes as harbour craft and the like.

Finally some LSTs were converted for transporting infantry rather than tanks. Re-designated as LST(A) (A for Assault), they carried eight LCAs on davits and 423 troops. Four of these were required for transporting a battalion.

This picture was taken at the Scottish base of Irvine, and shows American-built and British-manned landing craft. An LCV acts as a 'pusher' tug to provide bow thrust for one of the earliest LCI(L)s. The wartime censor has obliterated an antenna of some kind from one side of the bridge. (IWM)

## II Tank transporters

### The LCM - the first tank transport

As in the case of the LCA, the efforts that led to the construction of the LCM began in 1938. They were based on the existence of two prototypes, MLC 1 built in 1926 and MLC 10 built by Rowhedge Ironworks in 1929. MLC stood for Motor Landing Craft. Both were powered by waterjet propulsion (Hotchkiss and Gill systems respectively). This certainly avoided any risk

This converted liner fitted as an LSI(L) is the *Monowai*, built in 1925 for the P&O Line as the *Razmak*, but transferred to the Union Steam Ship Company of New Zealand and renamed in 1930. She is one of a number of liners temporarily converted as LSIs after serving as armed merchant cruisers. The photo was taken at the end of April 1944 during a landing rehearsal off the Isle of Wight. The powerful anti-aircraft armament, the double row of LCAs and the slanted launching ramps for Chipchase liferafts by the foremast and on the poop are all evident. The small gaff-rigged boat in the foreground is a local Solent type known as an Itchen Ferry punt. (IWM).

of damaging propellers when beaching, but resulted in a top speed of under 5 knots. The first was of 16 tons and could carry a hundred troops, but the high ramp system adopted was no good for the disembarking of vehicles because of the small ground clearance of the machines of the period. The enlarged second vessel, 20 tons light and 32 loaded, could carry the same number of men or a 12-ton tank. Four of this type, later followed by another six, were ordered. They were of limited seaworthiness, but were used at Narvik in 1940, where tanks were landed but not recovered. All of these craft used were lost in the operations themselves, through stress of weather, or abandoned before the town was evacuated.

The 1938 prototype, designed and built by Thornycroft, was more seaworthy. It was basically a powered pontoon with twin screws, bulletproof plating

on the ramp and sides, and the helmsman placed aft in a bulletproof shelter with somewhat limited vision. The 44ft long LCM (Landing Craft, Mechanised) MkI was light enough (21 tons unloaded) to be embarked aboard larger ships, but could carry a 14-ton tank. Even before trials were complete another twenty-four were ordered (in February 1940). Until the autumn of 1941 this was the only type of landing craft in the British inventory capable of carrying a heavy tank (Valentine or similar). In the end over five hundred were built, many of them by railway workshops (the Great Western Railway at Swindon and the Southern Railway at Eastleigh). Locomotive works, used to working with steel, were well adapted to building tanks and landing craft.

Even before the Americans entered the war they were very interested in producing craft to transport tanks, both to sell to the British and for their own services. In

The Southampton quay usually used by transatlantic liners is jammed solid with a mass of LCTs, with only the ship-shaped bows and narrower lines of the two LCHs in the second row to break the mass of ramped bows and tank-decks swathed in camouflage nets (to conceal whether they were loaded or not). The LCHs were LCIs modified with extra radio sets to act as headquarters ships for groups of landing craft. The numbers shown on the sides of the bows are the serial numbers of the craft whilst those on the front of the bridge indicate the number of the group or convoy to which they were attached for the crossing. The LCTs are a mixed group of Mk3 (7008) and the visibly broader Mk4 (678, 878). (IWM)

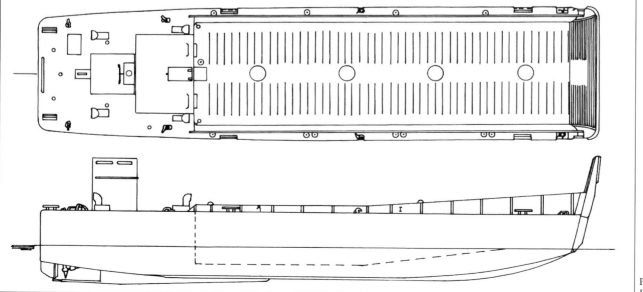

Plan of an
LCM Mk6

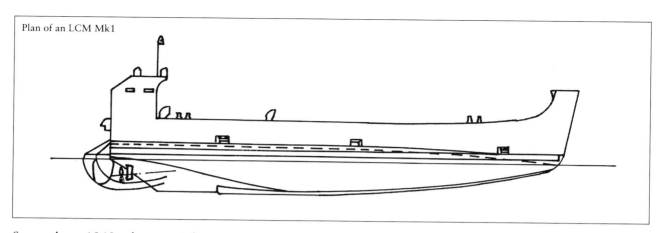

Plan of an LCM Mk1

September 1940 the specialists in amphibious operations, the US Marine Corps, put out a request for designs, one which was fulfilled by the ubiquitous Andrew J.Higgins. He modified the design of a shallow draught tug into what was to become the LCM Mk2. Capable of carrying a 16-ton tank and 45ft long this was promising, but its loading ramp suffered from a water-tightness problem. The British purchasing committee realised that, with slight modifications and a bit more length a vessel could be produced capable of carrying a 30-ton tank, twice the load of an LCM Mk1. Higgins met this requirement and remedied the defects of the original craft with a new 50ft long model, known as the LCM Mk3, and 8,631 examples of this very successful design were built. A slightly longer variant, capable of taking a Sherman tank without dangerously reducing the freeboard, was built as the LCM Mk6, but only for the US Navy. The Mk4 and Mk5 versions were British adaptations of the LCM Mk3 - but few were built. The American LCMs had a better position for the cox'n, in a bullet-proofed steering shelter aft with much better visibility. They were also more powerful and had better lateral stability, the load being placed below the waterline. However the lighter, riveted LCM Mk1 could be lowered or hoisted by the davits of a landing ship with a tank aboard, whilst the welded American craft could not, which was enough to keep the British design in production for some time.

## Multiple loads

The LCMs were true maids of all work. Even the LCM Mk1, the least powerful of all the models measuring only 48ft by 14ft could carry any of the following loads:

- A tank or lorry of less than 16 tons
- Two DUKW amphibious lorries
- One DUKW and a mobile kitchen
- Two 37mm or 2pdr anti-tank guns and their tractors

- A 37mm-gun, its tractor and two jeeps
- Six Jeeps
- A staff car
- Two Bren gun carriers
- 100 troops

However, whilst the listed load was a maximum of 17½ tons, the limit imposed by the strength of davits was more often around 10 tons.

The Mk3 had a more impressive load carrying capacity still - the figures given by the Americans (who, as usual, gave each soldier more space and therefore crammed fewer in than did the British) were:

- A 30 ton tank (such as the Sherman)
- A cargo of 30 tons
- 60 men.

However, it should also be noted that the transport of a Sherman aboard a craft of this type was distinctly limited. No more than 7in clearance was left between the flanks of the tank and the sides of the tank hold. This made loading by crane from another vessel, at least at sea, virtually impossible.

The Americans reckoned that one LCM Mk3 was worth between three and five LCVPs.

The British produced a new design of LCM, the 60ft long Mk7, in 1944, but this was for service in the Far East and was not used in Europe.

**Particulars of the LCM**
**LCM Mk1 (Thornycroft)**
Length: 48ft 6in oa, 44ft 9in bp
Breadth: 14ft
Draught: loaded 2ft 6in forward, 3ft 6in aft, light 1ft 4in forward, 2ft 9in aft
Speed: 7½ knots maximum, 6½ knots cruising
Displacement: 21 tons light, 36 tons loaded
Capacity: see above
Armament: two 0.303in machine guns
Complement: 6 (plus one officer for 3 LCMs)
Propulsion: 2 Thornycroft or Chrysler petrol engines, 120bhp
Losses: 66 in 1944

**LCM Mk3 (Higgins)**
Length: 50ft oa
Breadth: 14ft

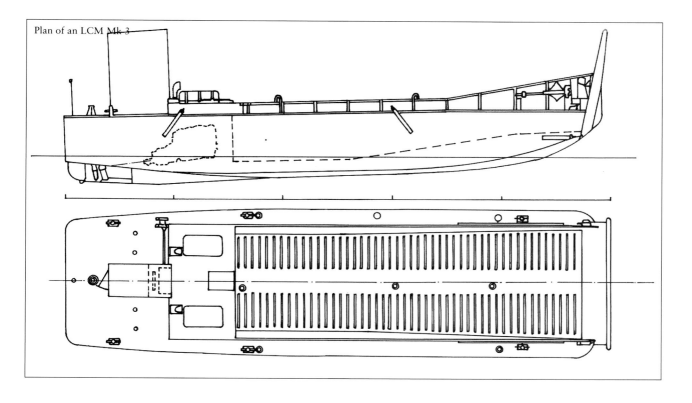

Plan of an LCM Mk 3

Draught: loaded 3ft 6in forward, 4ft 6in aft, light 3ft forward, 4ft aft
Displacement: 22 tons light, 55 tons loaded
Speed: 8½ knots loaded, 11 knots light
Capacity: see above
Armament: two 0.303in or 0.5in machine guns
Complement: 4
Propulsion: 2 diesel motors, total of from 220 to 450bhp
Losses: the Royal Navy lost 78 in 1944

## The extended family of the LCT

With these craft we enter the category of large landing craft of over 120ft in length. Their construction began in 1940 with an Admiralty demand for large landing vessels capable of carrying 40-ton tanks (which did not yet exist), and to cross the Channel with the obvious target of a future landing on the French coast. To do this the vessel should be capable of 10 knots, whilst measuring less than 160ft long. The design was produced by Roland (later Sir Roland) Baker of the Royal Corps of Naval Constructors, responsible for many successful landing craft designs, in only three days. The design was developed for production by the two shipbuilding firms, John Brown and Fairfields. The prototype began trials in November 1940.

Basically it was a large flat-bottomed powered barge. A ramp nearly 12ft high formed both the bow and the main means of landing. Behind this armoured doors shut off the open tank deck, the vehicles on which were

covered only by tarpaulins or camouflage nets. Both the bottom and sides of this deck were of cellular construction, offering both buoyancy and strength. Abaft this on the lower deck was the crew accommodation next to the engine and generator rooms. Here lived ten men in cramped, uncomfortable and noisy conditions. The cabins for the two officers, on the upper deck next to the wheelhouse, were somewhat more comfortable. These craft were built so that they could be split into four sections for shipping overseas.

The first vessel to be tried, LCT No14, demonstrated that she was well fitted to beaching and unbeaching, but also that her flat bottom made her difficult to control as she zigzagged along the river Tyne at constant risk of collision or grounding. This did not prevent the Admiralty placing more orders.

A number were shipped to the Mediterranean and seventeen of these were lost to air attack in the evacuations of Greece and Crete in spring 1941 out of the ninety-nine LCTs Mk1 built. By this time there was already a successor to the Mk1, the Mk2, with a slightly greater capacity. It could embark two rows of 16-ton tanks. Unfortunately the lack of available Hall Scott engines led to the employment of three Napier Lion aero-engines, whose design dated back to 1918. The engines were not robust, and were insufficiently powerful to the extent that the Mk2 only reached 10½ knots instead of the forecast 12.

LCT(3) 465 disgorges Bedford lorries onto a quay. The greater breadth
of the later Mk4 LCT made them more convenient for tanks to
manoeuvre off and on, though the Mk3 was adequate for most other
vehicles, as can be seen here. Single Oerlikons flank the bridge aft, on
either side of the bow are a version of a much less effective weapon,
the Holman projector. (IWM)

After three flotillas had been built with these engines,
steps were taken to replace them with 500hp Paxman
diesels. Despite some failings this engine was more
reliable, an important feature in a vessel with a range
of 2,700 nautical miles and which was therefore
expected to operate far from its base.

The Mk2 was fitted with equipment appropriate to
larger vessels, two groups of generators, a radio and
even an entirely electrical galley, plus magazines,
ammunition hoists, electrical emergency lights, etc. In
order to free shipbuilding firms for other tasks, a plan

of construction involving prefabrication was prepared
so that small engineering firms could take over the
building of the prefabricated parts. Whilst this certainly
increased production (200 of this type were built,
numbered 100 to 299), this was still insufficient to
create a large enough fleet for the invasion of Europe.
Once again it became necessary to fall back on
American help.

Meanwhile the John Brown yard produced a new
version, the Mk3, which was a Mk2 lengthened by
inserting another 30ft section amidships. This actually
improved the speed a little, and made a larger load
possible. The Mk3 could carry five heavy Churchill
tanks, or eleven Valentines or Shermans. First trials
took place on 8th April 1941. These were very
promising, except in showing that the draught of this
version was sufficient to prevent the landing of tanks
on beaches with the gentle slope of those of the Channel
coast. The Admiralty therefore developed a further
type, the LCT Mk4, though two series of the Mk3
design were produced, numbered 300 to 499 and 7001
to 7150.

The Mk4 was a little shorter than its predecessor.
Thanks to its two Paxman diesels this type could
transport nine Shermans at 10 knots, and land them
on the shallow beaches of the French coast. More than
800 were produced, numbered 500 to 1364. These were
entirely built by the structural steel industry and not
shipbuilders. They were also originally intended to be
unarmed, and adopted a flimsier form of construction
than the previous types. Though structural strength
was still adequate, later examples were strengthened
and fitted with armament, and these modifications were
extended retrospectively to the rest of the class.

## The American LCT

The Americans began by constructing an LCT known
in Britain as the Mk5 (or LCT(5)). This was
considerably shorter than the British types, and came
from an idea of K.C.Barnaby's. He was the chief naval
architect of Thornycrofts, a British shipbuilder which
had already played a major part in landing craft
development. This was a vessel intended only for fairly
short voyages, but specially adapted for ferrying
between larger ships and the shore. Capable of being
shipped in three sections all of which floated (which
was the way they crossed the Atlantic aboard cargo
ships), they could also be carried intact aboard an LCT
(2). They were not intended to carry troops, and only
had accommodation for the crew. For an American
type they were built in comparatively small numbers;
a total of 470 were built.

This was mainly because an improved version soon
appeared. This had two ramps, one at either end, like

Three LCT(3)s seen alongside at the Scottish port of Troon in the winter of 1944/1945 have clearly undergone hard service. From here they would be sent out to the Far East. (IWM)

modern car ferries. The bridge was offset to port. This very convenient arrangement made them useful mobile bridges between LSTs and larger LCTs and the shore. According to an American officer at Salerno this type, the LCT (6), was the best way of moving cargoes of tanks or lorries from ship to shore. Nearly all of the 965 built served with the US Navy. Originally twenty-one were to be delivered to the Royal Navy, but in the end only two (Nos 2627 and 2628) were provided, presumably for evaluation purposes.

For the larger LCT(7) see later under its more frequent title of LSM. The British LCT (8) was intended for long-range use in the Far East, but does not concern us here as none of the 200 examples ordered were completed until 1945.

There were many conversions of the different types of LCT for other purposes than the one they were designed for. Most of these are listed later under the support craft, but there were also conversions to carry locomotives and rolling stock, for emergency repairs, for ridding harbours of obstructions and salvage work, or as floating generator stations.

**Particulars of the principal LCTs used in Normandy**
**The LCT Mk3**
Length: 190ft 9in oa, 175ft bp
Breadth: 31ft
Displacement: 350 tons light, 640-625 tons loaded
Draught: light 1ft 9in forward, 5ft 3in aft; loaded 3ft 9in forward, 7ft aft
Propulsion: 2 shaft Paxman diesels 920bhp. 10½ knots

Armament: two 2pdr or two 20mm
Complement: 12
Capacity: five 40-ton tanks, or ten 3-ton lorries, or 300 tons of cargo.
Losses: 16 in 1944

**The LCT Mk4**
Length: 187ft 3in oa, 171ft bp
Breadth: 38ft 9in
Displacement: 200 tons light, 586 tons loaded
Draught: light 1ft forward, 3ft 9in aft; loaded 3ft 9in forward, 4ft 3in aft
Propulsion: 2 shaft Paxman diesels 920bhp=10 knots
Armament: none (later two 20mm)
Complement: 12
Capacity: six 40-ton or nine 30-ton tanks or ten 3-ton lorries or 300 tons of cargo.
Losses: 30 in 1944

**The LCT Mk5**
Length: 117ft 6in oa, 112ft 3in bp
Breadth: 32ft 9in
Displacement: 143 tons light, 311 tons loaded
Draught: light 1ft 6in forward 3ft 9in aft; loaded 3ft forward 4ft 6in aft
Armament: two 20mm
Complement: 13
Capacity: three 50-ton, four 40-ton or five 30-ton tanks or nine 3-ton lorries or 150 tons of cargo.
Losses: 13 in 1944

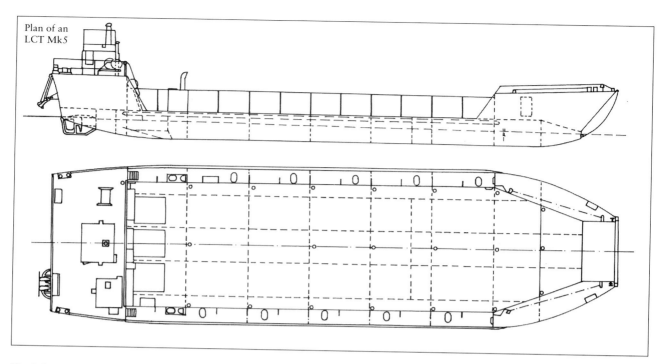

Plan of an LCT Mk5

**The LCT Mk6**
as Mk5 except:
Length: 120ft oa, 112ft 3in bp
Draught: loaded 3ft 6in forward, 4ft aft.

## The LST - the true tank ferry

In 1940, soon after the Dunkirk evacuation, the first demands were made for a vessel capable of landing tanks directly onto a beach anywhere in the world. The ships that came from this had to square the circle. They had to combine shallow draught with ocean-going ability. They needed reasonable speed, yet the best way to land tanks on a beach was by a ramp extending from the bow, which meant that the bows needed to be comparatively bluff. The first step taken by the British was to convert three shallow draught oil tankers built for service to Lake Maracaibo in Venezuela. These worked, and with their engines aft and a ramp built into the bows were visually similar to the later LSTs, but they were not particularly satisfactory. The ramp was long and articulated, they could not beach in shallow water, and their rate of unloading tanks was slow.

Another trio of vessels were being specially built in Britain. These were the Landing Ships Tank (1). They were not much more satisfactory. Their ramp was over 100ft long and complicated. They were reasonably fast, but their turbines and their complicated construction made them unsuited to mass production. They, too, had too much draught to cope with shallower beaches. The name ship of the class (*Boxer*) was converted to a fighter direction ship.

The British Admiralty then took their concept of a cheaper, slower landing ship, suited to mass production, to the Americans, who produced the design of the LST(2). This was all-welded, strongly built and propelled by diesels situated aft. A ballast system which made the vessel more stable at sea, but permitted very shallow draught especially forward, made beaching even on gently-sloping beaches reasonably feasible. Bow doors opened to permit a simple ramp to come down onto the beach.

Over a thousand were built in the USA, and they were a total success. They were an essential element in Allied victory. However the Americans, thanks to the demands of the Pacific War, kept the lion's share to themselves. So the British decided to build their own version, the LST (3). This was basically the same design, but, because of the limitations of British industry, riveted instead of welded, and powered by steam reciprocating engines instead of diesels. This made them somewhat heavier and deeper draughted for an identical load. The British built some three dozen of these, and another couple of dozen were constructed in Canadian yards.

LSTs could actually carry LSTs stowed athwartships on rollers with their ends overhanging the sides. They would be lifted aboard by big cranes for long voyages. Launching at the destination was by the very spectacular but surprisingly safe means of listing the LST using its ballast tanks until the LSTs, unfastened one by one, rolled into the water with a great splash.

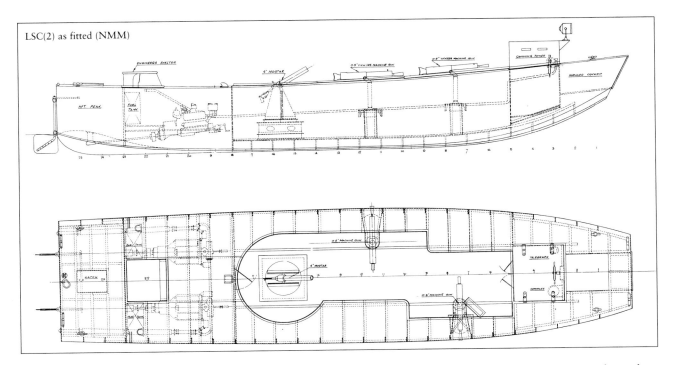

LSC(2) as fitted (NMM)

## Particulars of the LST (1)
Dimensions 390ft bp x 49ft
Displacement: 3,616 tons light for beaching, 5,970 tons deep
Draught: for beaching 5ft forward, 13ft aft
Machinery: 2 shaft turbines
Speed: 17 knots
Range: 8,000 miles at 14 knots
Load: thirteen 30- to 40-ton tanks, (or twenty 25-ton tanks), twenty-seven 3-ton lorries , 193 troops, also one LCM or LCS
Armament: two 4in smoke mortars, four 2pdr, eight 20mm
Complement : 169

## Particulars of the LST (2)
Displacement: 1,435 tons light, 2,100 tons beaching, 3,800 tons ocean
Dimensions: 327¾ft oa x 50ft 1½in
Draught: 2½ft (forward)/6ft 1in (aft) light, 3ft 1in/9½ft beaching, 7ft 1in/13½ft ocean
Machinery: two General Motors 900bhp diesels
Speed: 10-11½ knots
Endurance: 19,000nm at 10 knots (loaded)
Capacity: 2,100 tons, eighteen Churchill tanks or twenty (30-ton) Sherman tanks, or twenty-seven loaded 3-ton lorries plus eight jeeps and 177 men
Armament: one 40mm or one 12pdr, six 20mm
Complement: 60
Losses: the British lost seven in 1944

## The LSS (Landing Ship, Stern-Chute)
An early British conversion of train ferries. They carried loaded LCMs or similar small craft on what had been the train deck, and launched them over a stern slipway. There were only two of these curious vessels, one of which was mined in early 1945.

For Neptune they were adapted to carry locomotives and rolling stock again as well as landing craft, so that the continental railways could be pressed into service as the front expanded.

## Particulars of the LSS
Displacement: 2,680 gross
Dimensions: 363ft 6in oa, 350ft 6in bp x 58ft 9in
Draught: 11ft
Machinery: 2 shaft reciprocating 3,000ihp
Speed: 11 knots
Complement: 200
Capacity: 13 LCM(1)s or 9 LCM(2)s plus 105 troops
Armament: four 2pdr, five 20mm

## The LSG (Landing Ship, Gantry)
These converted fleet oilers were, like the LSS, intended to carry loaded LCMs and other craft. The method of launching here was for an athwartships-mounted gantry crane to pick up the landing craft from the deck, to shift it outboard and then lower it into the water. The LCMs were moved about the deck on rollers. There were three of these ships, one of which had her oil tanks converted to carry water.

## Particulars of the LSG
Displacement: 16,750 tons
Dimensions: 483ft oa, 460ft bp x 59ft 3in
Draught: 26ft 6in
Machinery: 1 shaft diesel, 3,000bhp
Speed: 12½ knots
Complement: 40 plus
Capacity: 15 LCM(1)s plus 215 troops
Armament: one 4.7in, one 12pdr, four 20mm

## The LSC (Landing Ship, Carrier)

These two vessels were simply the type of merchantman known as a 'heavy lift ship', fitted with very heavy derricks to lift such loads as locomotives, boilers, etc. They were merely converted to carry loaded LCMs on deck and use their existing derricks for lowering them.

Particulars of the LSC
Displacement: 14,500 tons
Dimensions: 433ft 6in oa, 416ft bp x 66ft 9in
Draught: 26ft 6in
Machinery: 1 shaft diesel, 2,500bhp
Speed: 11 knots
Complement: 40
Capacity: 21 LCM(1)s plus 295 troops
Armament: one 4in, one 12pdr, six 20mm

## The LSV or AP

An American variety of Landing Ship, converted from naval auxiliaries. Originally either minelayers or netlayers, they were large vessels transformed into amphibious vehicles. They had ramps both fore and aft, but were not intended to approach the beach. Used for DUKWs, another version which carried the LVT ('Alligator' or 'Buffalo'), the tracked landing craft, was only used in the Pacific.

Particulars of the LSV or AP
Displacement: 5,875 tons
Dimensions: 455ft 6in oa, 440ft wl x 60ft 3in
Draught: 20ft
Machinery: 2 shaft geared turbines, 11,000shp
Speed: $20^3/_{10}$ knots
Complement: 564
Capacity: 44 to 29 DUKWs, plus 800 troops, plus 14 LCV(P)s
Armament: two 5in, eight 40mm

## The LSD (Landing Ships Dock), the floating dock

The previous four types of vessel were all more or less satisfactory conversions of existing ship types to carry smaller types of landing craft across the sea to a position

LCT 1169, a brand-new Mk4, leaving the yard that had built her. She was built by a labour force, sixty per cent of whom were women and some of whom can be seen waving. The yard concerned was one abandoned since the end of the First World War, but was now producing one landing craft a week, a faster rate than any other yard in Britain. No doubt this record was somewhat helped by the fact that the yard was merely assembling prefabricated sections built by engineering firms inland. (IWM)

An LST(3) seen in late 1944 (none of this type were completed in time for the D-Day landings). The background looks rather like the Firth of Clyde, a river on which many of these British versions of the American Mk2 were built. Triple expansion steam engines replaced diesels in this type, as British industry could not produce enough of the latter type of engine, and few British yards at this stage could cope with welded construction, which is why the Mk3 LSTs were riveted. (IWM)

close to the invasion beaches. The specially designed type that appeared to do this job was the LSD. This was the brainchild of a young British naval architect, who suggested building an oceangoing ship with the stern half incorporating a floating dock, in which landing craft could be stowed, and out of which they could be floated when the ship 'flooded down' and opened the stern doors. The British had not the capacity to develop the idea at the time, and so passed it on to the Americans who developed the detailed design and built numbers, of which seven were transferred to the Royal Navy. The original reason for building these vessels, the transporting of tanks across greater distances than LCTs and LCMs could manage, and then landing them, was rendered less urgent because of the success of the LSTs, but the LSDs proved enormously useful, nonetheless. These vessels could carry fourteen loaded LCMs, forty-one DUKWs or use their docks for accommodating landing craft requiring emergency repairs up to the size of LSI(L)s.

**Particulars of the LSD**
Displacement: 4,270 tons light, 7,930 deep
Dimensions: 457ft 9in oa, 454ft bp x 72ft 3in
Draught: 17ft
Machinery: 2 shaft geared turbines, 7,000shp
Speed: 16 knots
Complement: 290
Capacity: two loaded LCT(3) or (4) or three loaded LCT(5)s or 1,500 tons of cargo, plus 263 troops
Armament: one 3in, four 2pdr, sixteen 20mm (British), one 5in plus twelve 40mm (American)

## III Support landing craft

Landing craft were not only used for the transport of tanks, infantry and supplies. Some were also fitted for self-protection, to provide the close-in fire to supplement the contributions of the larger warships and of air power. There were therefore a number of specialised fire-support types, the majority British, converted from the various types of landing craft.

## The LCA (HR)

The HR stood for 'Hedgerow' - an adaptation of the 'Hedgehog' anti-submarine spigot mortar, twenty-four of which were fitted in four rows of six in what had been the troop space - which fired a salvo of bombs intended to blast a way through the beach minefields. This would work on the principle of 'countermining' (setting off) the mines both above and below the water's edge, and proved very successful.

**Particulars of the LCA:**
as for LCA, except complement of 4 men and the 'Hedgerow'

## The LCS(M) 'M' for Medium

From the start it was intended to use armed versions of the LCA to provide close support to their troop-carrying sisters, with heavy machine guns and with smoke-firing mortars. The two prototypes were converted for this purpose, and other, similar, conversions became the Mk1 version of the LCS(M). The Mk2 was similarly armed on a similar standard LCA hull, except that the two machine guns were in a twin turret rather than single mounts. As these craft did not need to beach it was more sensible to give them a proper bow, and thereby make them more seaworthy. This process produced the LCS(M) (3) which remained in production for the rest of the war.

**Particulars of the LCS(M)**
as for LCA except armament (see above) and deep displacement of 10½ tons, 12½ tons and 13¼ respectively for the LCS(M)1, 2 and 3

## The LCS(S) 'S' for Small

This was the American version of the previous type, based on the LCVP but with a similar armament to the British support craft.

**Particulars of the LCS(S)**
as for the LCVP except mix of 0.5in and 0.3in machine guns, rocket launchers and smoke pots. Complement: 6

## The LCS(L) (L = large)

These were somewhat larger craft fitted with tank-type turrets to deal at close range with tanks and other 'hard' targets on the beaches. The Mk1 version was too small and unsuccessful, but the Mk2 version converted from Fairmile-designed LCI(S)s was rather better. It was equipped with a 6pdr gun in a turret, a 4in smoke mortar, two 20mm and a twin 0.5in machine gun turret. There was armour protection, but thin, and hardly to compare with contemporary tanks. Three of the ten built were lost in 1944. The Americans also developed

a type with the same designation from the LCI(L) - but too late for service off Normandy.

**Particulars of the LCS(L)**
as for the LCI(S) except for the armament given above and a complement of 25

## The LCG, the Landing Craft, Gun

The idea of having relatively heavy guns close at hand to the landing craft, combined with the success of the LCF (see below) produced the LCG(L)3s - 'L' being for large (the purpose built Medium variety armed with army 25pdr or 17pdr guns did not enter service until later in 1944), and '3' because they were converted from LST Mk3s. These were armed with two ex-destroyer 4.7in guns, manned by Royal Marines, plus three to five 20mm Oerlikons. The type proved very successful, and a more elaborate conversion was made of a number of LST(4)s. These were given a more ship-shape bow, the after 4.7in was in a superimposed position, and ten to fourteen 20mm were fitted in twin mountings. The only real limitation of these powerful little ships, virtually miniature monitors, was that their high velocity guns had a low trajectory and were therefore not capable of coping with targets in dead ground. Five of these craft were lost in 1944.

**Particulars of the LCG**
as the types of LCT they were converted from, except for the armament (see above), extra armour to the gun positions. Complement: 47 (3), 48 (4)

## The LCF Landing Craft, Flak

Early experience in the Mediterranean, especially in 1941 off Greece and Crete, showed the danger posed to landing craft by air attack. Two prototype A/A landing craft were converted from LCT(2)s - one with two twin 4in guns, the other with a mixture of 2pdr pompoms and Oerlikons (eight and four respectively). The latter, close range, armament was preferred, and a number of LCT(3)s were converted to LCF(3)s. The later ones of these changed four 2pdrs for the same number of Oerlikons, which was also the armament for the LCF(4)s. They could put up a formidable barrage of close range fire against surface attackers as well as aircraft. Five of all types were lost in 1944.

**Particulars of the LCF**
as the type of LCT they were converted from apart from armament, extra armour on the gun positions, a speed of 11 knots, and a complement of 62 or 66

The Mk3 LST No 465 is pictured here in the flooded dock of a Landing Ship Dock, probably the *Eastway*, the first LSD completed in the USA for the Royal Navy. (IWM)

## The LCT(R), massed rockets

The simplest support conversions of LCTs (which is why they kept that designation, merely adding 'R' for rocket) were those LCT(2)s and (3)s with their tank decks filled with a massive battery of 792 or 1,080 5in rockets in rows of six. This formidable quantity of missiles could be fired electrically in salvos to saturate a given area of beach with rockets. The idea of this downpour of high explosive (smoke or incendiary heads could be fitted as well) was to pulverise resistance in the 760yd x 160yd which were the target area. It was certainly a spectacle which impressed and encouraged friends and terrified the enemy, especially by night. The rocket frames were fixed so aiming was done by pointing the vessel, and firing had to be at a fixed distance from the beach to reach a given area, so navigational accuracy was important.

**Particulars of the LCT(R)**
as the type of LCT they were converted from

## Other types of landing craft

The need for specialised Headquarters ships was demonstrated during the Torch landings when an American general found himself taken away from his troops in mid-landing because the warship he was aboard was involved in a naval battle. Subsequent landings, with ships specially converted to take the combined services staffs and the communications equipment needed to control the multitude of ships, troops, aircraft and tasks involved, proved the concept. The main LSH (Landing Ships, Headquarters) used in Normandy were medium sized passenger ships converted for the purpose, *Bulolo*, *Largs*, *Hilary* etc.. However there were also smaller ships for lesser headquarters controlling smaller aspects of the battle, converted from small warships: two 'Hunt' class destroyers, three 'Captains' class DEs, five 'River' class frigates, and the *Locust*, an old river gunboat.

The LSF were in many ways very similar to HQ ships, covered as both were by antennae of various kinds, and also converted merchantmen. However their main task was indicated by the 'F' for fighter direction in their designation. They were 'ground' control for

A view of LST 465 and (probably) *Eastway*, with the former discharging lorries onto the deck of the dock, which is flooded down to water level. The LSD's own stern ramp has been let right down. The black parasol-like shapes are of 20mm Oerlikons at full elevation in their mounts and with waterproof covers over them, the usual way of stowing this particular weapon. The LST's weapons are in a similar position, but unshrouded. An LCP(L) can be seen behind the LST. (IWM)

fighter interceptions of potential raiders, and therefore well equipped with radar and radios. They were backed up by the three converted LST(1)s and another three converted LST(2)s which were called FDTs (fighter direction tenders).

Repair ships were also an essential element of the invasion fleet, fleet auxiliaries, old cruisers, Landing Ships Emergency repair (LSEs) and conversions of smaller craft as well. Many craft were salved and repaired to fight another day after being damaged by the enemy, bad weather or just mishandling.

Because of the shortage of landing craft the British made great use of converted swim barges (LB). Many were converted with ramps (LBR, LBV), numbers of these were powered (LBV). LBOs and LBWs were fitted with tanks for oil and water, respectively. LBKs were fitted and stored as mobile kitchens, LBEs carried a workshop lorry. There were two versions which carried army guns which could be fired from aboard - LBGs with 25pdr field guns and LBFs with 40mm A/A guns.

Another way of moving vehicles and stores within the shelter of Mulberries or Gooseberries was on powered pontoons - the so-called 'Rhino ferries' - these were formed by using NL (Naval Lighterage) caissons, which were rectangular steel boxes (Type T6, 5ft x 5ft x 7ft), or pontoons with a triangular end (Type T7, 5ft x 7ft x 7ft). They could be joined together by angle irons, clamps and pins, as were the two types (T8 and T11) which formed the floating roadways. Propulsion was provided by what were essentially large outboards, powered by 115hp Chrysler engines, which could be swivelled vertically for steering. The screw could be swung completely out of the water for beaching. A pontoon made of 4 x 12 units could be propelled at $3^{1}/_{2}$ knots whilst loaded with 100 tons of supplies, whilst two outboards would give a pontoon of 3 x 7 units a speed of $6^{4}/_{5}$ knots.

A column of LCG(L) Mk4s, distinguishable from the Mk3 version by greater breadth and a superimposed mounting for the after gun. The guns behind the seaman in the wing of the bridge are twin 20mm Oerlikons. (IWM)

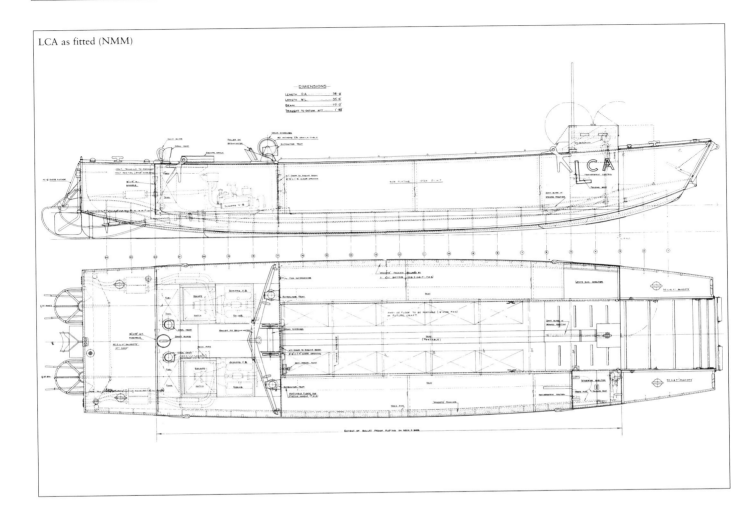

LCA as fitted (NMM)

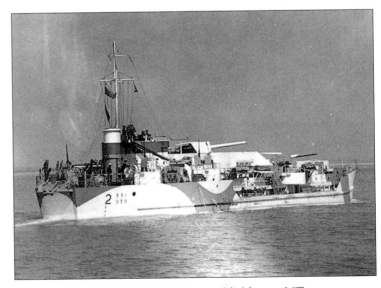

A stern quarter view of an LCG(L) (4) 939, modified from an LCT
(4). (IWM)

Another view of LCG(L) (4) 939, this time from just aft the bow, with her 4.7in guns trained to starboard, and her after 20mm guns in the usual vertical position. Her bow ramp was welded into position. What looks rather like the bow of another LCG is appearing from behind her stern, whilst the craft beginning to cross astern of her on the right of the picture is an LCF. (IWM)

This close-up photo of LCG(L) (4) 939 shows her forward 4.7in gun inside its 'zareba' (protected enclosure - a term coming from the British Army's experience of fighting in the Sudan) with its crew in white anti- flash gear, though most of them have shoved the hoods down to the backs of their necks. The craft in the background would appear to be LCVPs. (IWM)

A bow quarter view, taken on the same occasion of the rehearsal off the Isle of Wight (24-28th Apr
slenderer 20mm Oerlikons. The welded-up bow ramp, no longer capable of lowering, can clearly b

4) as the previous photos of LCGs; this shows an LCF (4), No 32. The four larger 2pdr pompoms with their conical muzzles are clearly distinguishable from the
. Also the 'ghost' of the old, larger, bow number 'F32' can still be made out under the painting-out. (IWM)

Yet another photo taken on the manoeuvres off the Isle of Wight in
late April 1944 shows two LCT(R)(3)s in line ahead. The massed
racks of rockets on their false deck and the cylindrical shield for their
position-finding radar are very evident. It can also been seen that the
ramps are not welded shut, and are ready for use again once the
vessels are reconverted to ordinary LCTs. (IWM)

# 3    The Fleets

The battleship HMS *Warspite* during a visit to the anchorage of Villefranche on the Côte d'Azur in April 1938. This was just after her major rebuild, and this is how she still looked in 1944, though the 6in guns visible just below upper deck level amidships had been removed. The red, white and blue bands on 'B' turret are neutrality markings, for this was the period of the Spanish Civil War. (Marius Bar, Toulon).

THE MAJORITY OF the warships off the Normandy beaches at dawn on 6th June 1944 were of British origin, just as the larger number of landing craft were of American construction. The predominance of the Royal Navy is easy to explain. Even if surpassed in numbers and firepower by the US Navy, it was none the less still the second biggest navy in the world, and much the largest in Europe. Moreover the air-sea struggle in the Pacific had absorbed a large proportion of the American navy.

The two great Anglo-Saxon navies were supported in the landings by those ships of the lesser Allied navies which had survived the disasters of 1940. Two nations which, like the British, still possessed important overseas empires, counted for a little more in the total. Even if the flower of the French fleet had been scuttled at Toulon in 1942, whilst much of the Dutch navy had been wiped out by the Japanese defending Indonesia earlier the same year, both navies still had enough ships to make some difference.

I do not propose to describe here all the vast number of warships forming the armada which took part in

Operation Neptune. Instead I will give a description of every major Allied unit, battleship, cruiser and monitor. Only the French navy will be studied in greater depth, down to the level of its corvettes.

## The major units of the Royal Navy

In order to place the ships in the context of the battle, we will look at them by the task forces they were attached to, going from east to west along the invasion front. It should be noted that, whenever possible, the particulars given are those for the ships as they were on D-Day not as designed or as built - and this means that there are sometimes considerable differences from the usual figures given for the older vessels.

## Force S

At the extreme eastern end of the invasion fleet, Force S was above all intended to knock out the coastal batteries around the Seine estuary. Serving with the *Scylla*, flagship of the Eastern Task Force, were nine major units, plus thirteen destroyers. They were as follows:

### Warspite

We begin with the most famous of the battleships involved. Best known for her period as Cunningham's flagship in the Mediterranean, this 'grand old lady' had also served at Jutland. Her task on D-Day was to silence the German batteries of Villerville (four 105mm guns and four 155mm which were of French origin, their range being 9 and 15 kilometres respectively). It seems that the Allies had not taken the four 152mm German manufactured guns of the Vasouy battery into account, unless (as is likely) they had not differentiated them from the Villerville guns.

This ship was of the *Queen Elizabeth* class, the best balanced and fastest battleships of their day, and the first to be armed with 15in guns. She was built at Devonport Dockyard, launched on 26th November 1913 and completed in March 1915. She joined the other four ships of her class in the Fifth Battle Squadron; which formed a fast wing to the battlefleet capable of 25 knots rather than the 21 knots of previous battleships. This speed also made it possible for the 'QEs' to support the Battlecruiser Fleet, which is what they were doing on the day of Jutland. *Warspite*'s early history was full of accidents, groundings, collisions and the like, and her experience in the biggest sea battle of the First World War was well in character. At one stage the Fifth Battle Squadron was left closest to the advancing High Seas Fleet, and had to turn away. At this critical stage *Warspite*'s helm jammed and she went round in circles under the concentrated fire of the enemy fleet. Her strong construction was fully up to this test, despite being hit by fifteen 11in and 12in shells and another five 6in projectiles, she managed to unjam her helm and stay with her squadron for the rest of the battle.

Her armoured deck had been pierced, and she required dockyard repairs at Rosyth, from which she emerged on 22nd July. In February 1918 she became flagship of the Fifth Battle Squadron. After the Armistice she served successively with the Atlantic and the Mediterranean fleets. Between 1924 and 1926 she had a major refit at Portsmouth, where a number of major alterations were made, of which the most obvious was the trunking of her two original funnels into a massive single one. Ten years later, again at Portsmouth, a new, and much more radical, reconstruction was carried out. In this full modernisation her big guns had their elevation (and therefore range) increased by 10 degrees. The twenty-four old boilers were torn out and six larger ones of a different type fitted. These were served by an entirely new single funnel. The opportunity was taken to fit modernised armour protection, new aircraft and anti-aircraft arrangements and an entirely different and much larger bridge.

Her performance in the Second World War was the material of legend. A dramatic and decisive intervention in the fight between British and German destroyers at the Second Battle of Narvik (1940) was followed by her arrival in the Mediterranean as Andrew Cunningham's flagship. In a series of conflicts with the Italian fleet, culminating with the Battle of Cape Matapan, an effective superiority was maintained. Then came the dark days of evacuations from Greece and Crete. *Warspite* had to go to the USA for repairs to the damage caused by German bombs during this period. She was also fitted with radar. She then went to the Eastern fleet and then returned to the Mediterranean, as we have seen, to be badly damaged at Salerno. For the rest of her life she served with a temporary repair keeping her afloat - a large cofferdam of concrete built into her hull. Her secondary armament of 6in guns was removed at this stage. After Overlord she was again used for bombardment during the Walcheren landings. In 1947 she was under tow to the breaker's yard when she decided to die in her own fashion, broke loose and went ashore on the Cornish coast. For another nine years she was slowly broken up where she had grounded.

**Particulars of the *Warspite***
(in 1944 unless otherwise stated):
Displacement: 36,450 tons deep load (as in 1937)
Dimensions: length 639½ft oa, 600ft bp x 104ft
Draught: 33ft 10in deep (1937)
Machinery: 4 shaft Parsons turbines, 6 Admiralty small-drum boilers
Sea speed: 22½ knots (probably less by 1944)
Armour: 13in belt maximum, 5in decks maximum
Armament: eight 15in (four twins), eight 4in (four twins), four octuple 2pdr pompoms, thirty-five 20mm Oerlikons
Complement: approx 1,200

### Ramillies

Begun two days after the launching of the *Warspite*, this ship belonged to the next class, the 'Rs'. With the same main armament of 15in guns these ships were initially better protected than the 'QEs' but reverted to the slower speed of the main battlefleet. Therefore

when the question of rebuilding the battlefleet was raised between the wars it was the earlier but larger and faster ships that had the major rebuilds, whilst the 'Rs' had only the minimum modernisation. *Ramillies* was refitted in 1934 with new aircraft and anti-aircraft arrangements being the main alterations. During the war she was given increased deck armour and light A/A, whilst the four foremost 6in guns were removed to lighten her.

She had been completed in 1917, and saw no serious action in the First World War. During the following conflict she was present at the Madagascar landings, shortly after which, lying in Diego Suarez harbour, she was torpedoed by a Japanese midget submarine.

After D-Day she moved to the Mediterranean where she provided support for the 'Anvil' landings in the south of France in August. She was sold in 1948. On D-Day itself she had the Berneville battery as a target. This was armed with four ex-French 155mm guns, with a range in practice of just under 10 miles. As was the case with *Warspite* the battleship's 15in guns allowed her to remain well outside the range of the German guns whilst firing upon them.

**Particulars of the *Ramillies***
Deep displacement: 33,390 (in 1945)
Dimensions: length 620½ft oa, 580ft bp x 102ft
Draught: 34ft deep (in 1945)
Machinery: 4 shaft Parsons turbines, 18 boilers

The battleship HMS *Ramillies* off the French Mediterranean coast in 1930. She was little changed; apart from a new bridge, a funnel cap and more A/A guns; when she took on the German batteries on D-Day. This is another photo by the well known naval photographer, Marius Bar of Toulon.

Speed: 21½ knots (probably less by 1944)
Maximum armour: 13in belt, 4in vertical
Armament: eight 15in (four twins), ten 6in, eight 4in (four twins), two octuple plus two quadruple 2pdr pompoms, twenty or twenty-three 20mm Oerlikons
Complement: approx 1,200

### *Roberts*

Designed specifically for shore bombardment, the *Roberts* and her near-sister *Abercrombie* were Second World War adaptations of the *Erebus* class of the previous conflict. They, in their turn, were an improvement of an earlier class of 15in armed monitors, from one of which, the *Marshal Soult*, the turret came which was fitted aboard the *Roberts*. The turret was modified in the same way as those fitted to *Warspite*, so that elevation was now 30 instead of 20 degrees.

Built by John Brown on the Clyde between 1940 and October 1941 she took part in the 'Torch' (where she was damaged by air attack), Sicilian and Salerno landings. Her target for the Normandy landings was the Houlgate battery, another one equipped with four ex-French 155mm guns. Later she supported the

A stern view of the battleship HMS *Rodney* in action off the Normandy coast in the month after D-Day. She and her sister *Nelson* had been held in reserve on D-Day itself, but then took part in supporting the bridgehead. As all their three triple 16in turrets were forward they cannot be seen here, only the twin 6in guns of the secondary armament adding their contribution, but they were the heaviest guns to support the landings. (IWM)

Walcheren landings, and was to survive until sold for scrap in 1965.

**Particulars of *Roberts***
Deep load displacement: 9,150 tons
Dimensions: 373ft 4in oa x 89¾ft
Draught: 13½ft
Machinery: 2 shaft Parsons turbines, 2 boilers
Speed: 12½ knots
Maximum armour: 5in belt, 13in turret, 8in barbette
Armament: two 15in (one twin), eight 4in (four twins), one octuple, two quadruple 2pdr pompoms, fourteen 20mm Oerlikons
Crew: approx 460

## *Mauritius*

One of the ships of the *Fiji* (or 'Colony') class, the last British cruisers designed within the constraints of the naval treaties, she was a slightly smaller version of the earlier 'Town' class, with the same basic armament of 6in guns in triple mountings, but with a transom stern, and a little too crowded as a design easily to take the increases in radar, light A/A and complement made necessary by wartime developments.

She was completed in 1941 and had a relatively undistinguished wartime career. She shared the same D-Day target as *Roberts*, the battery at Houlgate, and like that ship was also broken up in 1965.

**Particulars of *Mauritius***
Deep displacement: 10,736 tons (as built - more in 1944)
Dimensions: 555½ft oa, 538ft bp x 62ft
Draught: about 20½ft deep by 1944
Machinery: 4 shaft turbines, 4 boilers
Speed: 32¼ knots
Maximum armour: 3½in belt and deck
Armament: twelve 6in (four triples), eight 4in (four twins), two quadruple 2pdr pompoms, twenty-four 20mm, six 21in torpedo tubes (two triples)
Crew: 920

## *Arethusa*

The name ship of her class of small cruisers intended for fleet work, the *Arethusa* was basically a smaller version of the earlier *Leander* class (see *Orion* and *Ajax* below), with the two funnels of the intermediate *Apollo* class (all of which served in the Royal Australian Navy), but of smaller dimensions and with only three turrets. The *Arethusas* proved very satisfactory in service and their design was modified for the *Dido* class (see *Scylla* and *Diadem* below). All three of the original class had a very active war, especially in the Mediterranean, and the two others had been sunk by D-Day. *Arethusa* herself had a narrow escape in November 1942 when she was hit by an air-dropped torpedo. She caught fire, had two of her three turrets out of action, and was badly flooded. However she survived to be repaired at Charlestown in the USA. On 6th June 1944 her target was the Mont battery. As this was in fact not in use she was available to fire on other targets.

**Particulars of *Arethusa***
Deep displacement: 7,406 tons (April 1944)
Dimensions: 506ft oa, 480ft bp x 51ft
Deep draught: 18ft
Machinery: 4 shaft Parsons turbines, 4 boilers
Speed: 32¼ knots
Maximum armour: 2¼in belt, 1in deck
Armament: six 6in (three twins), eight 4in (four twins), two quad 40 mm, sixteen 20 mm, six 21in torpedo tubes (two triples)
Complement: 500 (probably slightly more by 1944)

## *Frobisher*

One of the *Cavendish* class (also known as the *Hawkins* class - the 'improved *Birminghams*' or the

A Marius Bar photo of the cruiser HMS *Frobisher* taken in 1920. Twenty-four years later her appearance was not fundamentally different, though the beam 7.5in gun on either side (on either side of the after funnel) had long since been removed.

'Elizabethans'), cruisers designed in 1915 for hunting down commerce raiders in the oceans of the world and armed with the heavier 7.5in gun in order to outrange and overpower vessels armed with the standard cruiser 6in calibre. In fact the 7.5in proved too heavy a weapon for easy hand working, even when allocated crews of the largest and strongest men available.

*Frobisher* was still on the stocks at the Armistice in 1918, and her construction slowed down. Launched in 1920 she was not completed until 1924. In 1939 she had been disarmed as a cadet training ship, but was then re-armed and refitted, recommissioning in early 1942. On D-Day she was allocated the important target of the Riva-Bella battery. This was equipped with four ex-French 155mm guns in open positions with no concrete or other protection.

**Particulars of *Frobisher***
Deep displacement: 12,300 tons (as built)
Dimensions: 604ft oa, 565ft bp x 65ft
Draught: 19¼ft deep
Machinery: 4 shaft Brown-Curtis turbines, 10 Yarrow boilers.
Speed: 30½ knots
Maximum armour: 3in belt, 1½in deck
Armament: five 7.5in, five 4in, two octuple 2pdr pompoms, nineteen 20mm
Complement: 712 (as built - probably rather more in 1944)

### Dragon

The 'D' or *Danae* class cruisers were a lengthened version of the earlier 'C' class cruisers (themselves expanded versions of the *Arethusa*s - the first British light cruisers) in order to incorporate another 6in gun and extra torpedo tubes. They came into service in 1918. *Dragon* served in the Baltic in 1919-1920 against the Bolsheviks. The ships of this class were intended to be converted to anti-aircraft cruisers, but the outbreak of war in 1939 put an end to this, and, apart from the removal of a 6in gun and an increased A/A armament *Dragon* was little altered from her original appearance. On 15th January 1943 she was handed over to the Polish Navy in exile, and so was flying the Polish flag on D-Day, when her target was the German 122mm gun battery at Graye. On 8th July she was torpedoed by a German midget submarine of the *Neger* type whilst off the Normandy coast. Too old and damaged to be worth repair she was scuttled as another part of the breakwater at Arromanches.

**Particulars of *Dragon***
Deep displacement: 5,853 tons (in 1930)
Dimensions: 472½ft oa, 445ft bp x 46ft
Draught: 16½ft (as built)
Machinery: 2 shaft Brown-Curtis turbines, 6 Yarrow boilers
Speed: 29 knots
Maximum armour: 3in belt, 1in deck
Armament: five 6in, two 4in, two quad 2pdr pompoms, fourteen 20mm, twelve 21in torpedo tubes (four triples)
Complement: 450 (as built - will have been more by 1944)

### Danae

Another 'D' class cruiser, like the *Dragon*, she also served in the Baltic in 1919. Basically similar to her sister she had much the same alterations, including the landing of one of her 6in guns, though she appears to have had one twin 4in mount rather than two singles, and rather fewer 20mm. Otherwise her particulars were the same as *Dragon*. On D-Day her target was the Riva-Bella-Ouistreham battery. After the loss of the *Dragon* the Poles were given *Danae* as a replacement in October 1944. She was then renamed *Conrad*. Returned to the Royal Navy in September 1946 she was scrapped a couple of years later.

### Scylla

One of two sisters (the other was, appropriately, *Charybdis*) building as anti-aircraft cruisers of the *Dido* class, which, because of bottlenecks in the supply of twin 5.25in turrets, were supplied with four twin 4.5in mountings instead of five of the former weapons. Naturally they were known as the 'toothless terrors', but proved much better anti-aircraft ships than their sisters armed with the more cumbersome and less satisfactory 5.25in. From her entry into service in 1942 she had an active war. During the Normandy landings she flew Admiral Vian's flag, until badly damaged by a mine. She was laid up without being repaired until broken up in 1950.

Particulars of *Scylla*
Deep displacement: 6,975 tons
Dimensions: 512ft oa, 485ft bp x 50ft 6in
Deep draught: 17ft
Machinery: 4 shaft Parsons turbines, 4 boilers
Speed: 32¼ knots
Maximum armour: 3in belt, 1in deck
Armament: eight 4.5in (four twins), two quad 2pdr pompoms, twenty 20mm, six 21in torpedo tubes (two triples)
Complement: 480

### Largs

This ship was the headquarters ship for this sector, and was a conversion of the French passenger motor ship *Charles Plumier*, built in 1938. She had been an ocean boarding vessel before her HQ ship conversion in 1942. She had a close range anti-aircraft armament of one 12pdr gun, two 2pdrs and fourteen 20mm. She also carried four LCP(L)s.

## Force J

Intended to support the Canadians on Juno Beach, this consisted of eleven destroyers with the mission of suppressing the beach defences. Shore batteries in this sector were left to the cruisers of Force G. The flagship and HQ vessel of Force J was another merchant ship conversion, the *Hilary*.

## Force G

Besides the cruisers described below, this force included thirteen destroyers tasked with dealing with the beach defences of Gold Beach.

### Diadem

A 'modified *Dido*' (or *Bellona*) class anti-aircraft cruiser, this type was armed from the start with only four 5.25in twin turrets, and also differed from the *Didos* in having vertical, rather than raked, masts and funnels. She was very new at this time, having completed in January 1944. Her assigned target on D-Day was the Moulineaux battery. In 1956 she was ceded to Pakistan and renamed *Babur*. She lasted in Pakistani service till the mid-1980s, though in her final years as a harbour training vessel renamed *Jahangir*.

Particulars of *Diadem*
as *Scylla* except:
Deep displacement: 7,350 tons
Armament: eight 5.25in (four twins), three quad 2pdr pompoms, twelve 20mm, six 21in torpedo tubes (two triples)
Complement: 600

### Belfast

This ship, with a sister sunk earlier in the war, was the largest of the British 6in cruisers. A development of the earlier 'Town' classes, the chief difference was the addition of an extra hull section between the mast and forefunnel, which may have been unsightly but permitted a larger A/A armament and heavier protection (originally it had been intended to have quadruple 6in turrets as well). *Belfast* was completed in 1939, only to be badly damaged by a magnetic mine shortly afterwards. The rebuilding of the broken-backed vessel with wider bulges took till 1942, but she then had an active war, playing an important part in the sinking of the *Scharnhorst*. The Ver-sur-Mer battery was her assigned D-Day target. Reconstructed soon after the landings, in 1971 she was the Second World War British cruiser in the best state of preservation, and so was taken over by the Imperial War Museum. She is now a museum ship moored in the Thames opposite the Tower of London.

Particulars of *Belfast*
Deep displacement: 14,900 tons
Dimensions: 613½ft oa, 579ft oa x 66ft 4in
Deep draught: 23ft 2in
Machinery: 4 shaft Parsons turbines, 4 boilers
Speed: 32½ knots

Maximum armour: 4½in belt, 2in deck
Armament: twelve 6in (four triples), twelve 4in (six twins),
two octuple 2pdr pompoms, eighteen 20mm,
six 21in torpedo tubes (two triples)
Complement: 850 (probably more by this stage)

### Flores
See the separate section on Dutch ships for this interesting gunboat.

### Orion
Marked by her single, trunked, funnel, this ship was clearly one of the *Leander* class, the first British 6in light cruisers to be built after the First World War, and completed in the mid-1930s. *Orion* served throughout the war. She was hit by two 500kg bombs in the Mediterranean in 1941, and then repaired in the USA. Her targets on D-Day were supposed to be batteries at Ver-sur-Mer and Mont Fleury, but these do not appear in the German accounts. Probably it was a confusion with the battery of four 122mm guns which the Germans called the Graye battery.

**Particulars of Orion**
Deep displacement: 9,642 tons (in 1940)
Dimensions: 544½ft oa, 522ft bp x 56ft

A *Leander* class cruiser, seen late in the war, quite probably *Orion*. The single trunked funnel was unique amongst British cruiser classes. (ECPA).

Deep draught: 20¼ft (approx)
Machinery: 4 shaft Parsons turbines, 6 boilers
Speed: 32½ knots
Maximum armour: 3in belt, 1¼in deck
Armament: eight 6in (four twins), eight 4in (four twins), two quad 2pdr pompoms, seven 20mm, eight 21in torpedo tubes (two quads)
Complement: 570 men (probably more by this time)

### Emerald
One of a class of two designed to emphasise high speed at the cost of other qualities, designed in 1917 for use against German cruisers, and particularly minelayers, in the North Sea. The 'E' class had a very high ratio of length to beam, and only one more gun than their predecessors of the 'D' class despite being much bigger and more expensive. Begun in 1918 *Emerald* was completed in 1926. Little reconstruction was done on her, her main wartime alterations being the removal of one 6in and the addition of a few light A/A weapons. Her targets on D-Day were German defences around Arromanches.

Marius Bar photographed the USS *Arkansas* when she was new. On D-Day she was the oldest battleship present, and had been considerably rebuilt. She had a single funnel, more superstructure and a different secondary armament. However the 12in guns which battered the German defenders of Omaha Beach were the same.

**Particulars of *Emerald***
Deep displacement: 10,350 tons
Dimensions: 570ft oa, 535ft bp x 54½ft
Deep draught: 18½ft
Machinery: 4 shaft Brown Curtis turbines, 8 Yarrow boilers
Speed: 32½ knots
Maximum armour: 3in belt, 1in deck
Armament: six 6in, three 4in, two quad 2pdr pompoms, twelve 20mm, sixteen 21in torpedo tubes (four quads)
Complement: 572 (probably more by 1944)

### *Argonaut*

A ship of the *Dido* class of A/A cruisers and the last to be completed (August 1942) to the unmodified design with three twin turrets forward. The third ('Q') turret was removed when she was repaired in the USA in 1943. These repairs were needed because she had been hit, simultaneously, by two torpedoes at opposite ends of the ship. On 6th June the battery at Longues was her target.

**Particulars of *Argonaut***
as *Scylla* except:
Deep displacement: 7,515 tons by 1945
Armament: eight 5.25in (four twins), three quad 2pdr pompoms, sixteen 20mm, six 21in torpedo tubes (two triples)

### *Ajax*

Another single-funnelled *Leander* class cruiser, the *Ajax*

is best known for her participation in the battle of the River Plate against the *Admiral Graf Spee*, during which she was hit by an 11in (280mm) shell which put her 'X' turret out of action. Damaged again, she had a major refit in the USA during 1943. Her D-Day target was the four coastal defence guns of 152mm calibre in the Longues battery.

**Particulars of *Ajax***
as *Orion* except
Deep displacement: 9,653 tons in 1942
Armament: eight 6in, eight 4in, two quad 40mm Bofors, twelve 20mm, eight 21in torpedo tubes

## *The American Task Force*

Because of the war in the Pacific the Americans could not assign as many large warships as the British, so Forces O and U included a significant number of non-American warships, British, French and Dutch.

In the list which follows only the ships of the two Anglo-Saxon navies are listed; the Dutch and French follow in a separate section.

### Force O

The area to be covered by this force extended from Port-en-Bessin in the east to Isigny to the west. As the initial indicates it was responsible for Omaha Beach, with twelve destroyers plus the major warships whose names now follow:

## USS Augusta

She was the flagship of the Western Task Force, carrying General Omar Bradley, commander of the First US Army. She was a heavy cruiser of the *Northampton* class, designed in the late 1920s and completed in January 1931 under treaty restrictions. The class differed from the previous *Pensacolas* by having raised forecastles and three triple turrets rather than two triples and two twins. She had extra accommodation to fit her for use as a flagship.

**Particulars of *Augusta***
Deep displacement: 12,150 tons
Dimensions: 600¼ft oa, 582ft wl x 66ft 1in
Deep draught: 19ft 5in
Machinery: 4 shaft Parsons turbines, 8 White-Forster boilers
Speed: 32½ knots
Maximum armour: 3in belt, 1in deck
Armament: nine 8in (three triples), eight 5in, four quad plus four twin 40mm, twenty 20mm, six 21in torpedo tubes (two triples).
Complement: 748 not counting the staff

## USS Arkansas

*Wyoming* class battleship, and the oldest US battleship to serve in the Second World War. Her 12in gun main armament was accepted instead of the proposed 14in one to save time in building. Completed in 1912 she saw service in both World Wars. Because of her age she was not considered as a task force escort, but was well suited to the fire support role. She was rebuilt in

The USS *Texas* photographed by Marius Bar shortly after her 1926 rebuild. Her general appearance, despite a completely new secondary armament, was not essentially different in 1944.

the 1920s with better protection and oil firing. In 1942 she was given a new tripod foremast and a new bridge. Also most of her old secondary armament of 5in guns was removed.

**Particulars of *Arkansas***
Deep displacement: 27,243 tons
Dimensions: 562ft oa, 555½ft wl x 106¼ft
Deep draught: 32ft
Machinery: 4 shaft Parsons turbines, 4 White-Forster boilers
Speed: 20½ knots
Maximum armour: 11in belt, 2in and 3in decks
Armament: twelve 12in (six twins), ten 3in, nine quad 40mm, twenty-eight 20mm
Crew: 1,650

## USS Texas

The *New York* class of two battleships were designed in parallel with the *Arkansas* and her sister, but with 14in instead of 12in guns. They also reverted to reciprocating engines, a decision based on initially unpromising trials and unco-operative suppliers of turbines, but in retrospect an unfortunate mistake. Completing in 1914, *Texas* was rebuilt in the mid 1920s, reboilered and fitted for oil fuel. By D-Day she had lost most of her original 5in gun secondary armament. Her target then was the Pointe du Hoc.

The considerably rebuilt USS *Nevada* off Cherbourg on 25th June 1944. The rebuilt bridge, twin 5in/38 turrets and the assemblage of radar aerials and light A/A mountings, not to mention the funnel cap, make her look much more modern than she really was. It would appear from the chain going down vertically from the bow that she was streaming paravanes from either side of the bow to give some protection from moored mines. (IWM)

She is now the oldest preserved US battleship, a museum ship at Galveston in the state after which she is named.

**Particulars of *Texas***
Deep displacement: 32,000 tons
Dimensions: 573ft oa, 565ft wl x 106¼ft
Deep draught: 31½ft
Machinery: 2 shaft triple expansion, 6 White-Forster boilers
Speed: 21 knots
Maximum armour: 12in belt, 2½in and 3½in decks
Armament: ten 14in (five twins), six 5in, ten 3in, ten quad 40mm, forty-six 20mm
Complement: 1,530

### HMS *Glasgow*

This was one of the first group of 'Town' (originally *Minotaur*, later *Southampton*) class 6in gun cruisers. Powerful, handsome and sturdy ships, they gave good service in the war. *Glasgow* was very badly damaged in 1940, torpedoes fore and aft, her back was broken.

She was under repair for nine months. On D-Day her purpose was to provide fire support to the troops landing at Omaha Beach.

**Particulars of HMS *Glasgow***
Deep displacement: 12,469 tons
Dimensions: 591ft oa, 558ft bp x 64ft 2in
Deep draught: 21½ft
Machinery: 4 shaft Parsons turbines, 4 Admiralty boilers
Speed: 32 knots
Maximum armour: 4½in side, 1¼in deck
Armament: twelve 6in (four triples), eight 4in (four twins), two quad 2pdr pompoms, twenty-six 20mm (eight twins, ten singles), six 21in torpedo tubes (two triples)
Complement: 800+

### Force U

Tasked with supporting the landing at Utah Beach, this force was opposed by an impressive total of eight batteries with thirty-four guns of between 210mm and 105mm calibre. The larger vessels were to cope with these whilst the eight attached destroyers covered the assault waves on the beach itself.

### HMS *Hawkins*

A sister of the cruiser *Frobisher* described earlier. Completed in 1919 she was disarmed under the

provisions of the London Treaty in 1936, but her guns were replaced on the outbreak of war. On 6th June 1944 she had two targets; the German radar station of Grandcamp-Maisy and the battery of St-Martin-de-Varreville (which the Germans called the Madeleine battery). Confusingly there was an American destroyer with the same name in the D-Day fleet.

**Particulars of *Hawkins***
as *Frobisher* except:
Deep displacement: 13,160 tons
Armament: seven 7.5in, four 4in, ten 2pdr (two quads, two singles), nine 20mm

*HMNS Soemba* see under the Dutch section for this gunboat.

### HMS Enterprise

This was the sister of the cruiser *Emerald* described above. Their main difference was that *Enterprise* had a twin 6in turret forward, instead of the two single mounts of her sister. This ship is not, of course, to be confused with the American carrier of the same name, the 'Big E'.

**Particulars of *Enterprise***
as *Emerald* except:
Deep displacement: 10,220 tons
Armament: five 6in (one twin, three singles), two quad 2pdr, sixteen 20mm (six twins, four singles)

This photograph of the heavy cruiser USS *Quincy* was taken postwar by Marius Bar of Toulon, but there is little visible difference from her appearance on D-Day.

### USS Nevada

This battleship was of the class that followed the *Texas* (see above), and is of importance in the history of warship design as the vessel that introduced (or, rather, re-introduced) the 'all or nothing' scheme of armouring - in other words having either thick armour or none at all, rather than a mixture of thicknesses, the thinner of which would only serve to set off a shell and not to stop it. With this ship American battleships returned, this time for good, to turbine propulsion. Laid down in 1912 she completed in 1916 in time to serve in the First World War, but Pearl Harbor (1941) was her first major experience of action, where she was torpedoed and had to be beached. She was then rebuilt with a new secondary battery of dual purpose 5in guns. On D-Day her assigned target was the 105mm battery at Azeville.

**Particulars of *Nevada***
Deep load: 34,000 tons
Dimensions: 583ft oa, 575ft wl x 108ft
Deep draught: 32½ft
Machinery: 2 shaft Curtis turbines, 12 Bureau Express boilers
Speed: 20½ knots
Armament: ten 14in (two triples, two twins), sixteen 5in (eight twins), twelve quad 40mm Bofors, twenty-seven 20mm
Complement: 2,100

### USS *Quincy*

The newest of the bigger American vessels (commissioned in December 1943), the *Quincy* was one of the large class of heavy cruisers known as the *Baltimores*. These shared a common ancestry with the even larger *Cleveland* class of 6in cruisers, which they somewhat resembled, both having evolved via the (8in armed) *Wichita* from the (6in armed) *Brooklyns*. All of these classes were excellent and powerful examples of the American liking for larger cruisers. On D-Day *Quincy*'s 8in guns were opposed to the three similar calibre 210mm guns of the Saint-Marcouf battery. This heavy cruiser, much altered for a new era of warfare, would serve again off Vietnam (she was taken out of service in 1973).

**Particulars of *Quincy***
Deep displacement: 17,070 tons
Dimensions: 675ft oa, 664ft wl x 70¾ft
Deep draught: 26ft
Machinery: 4 shaft General Electric turbines, 4 Babcock & Wilcox boilers
Speed: 33 knots
Maximum armour: 6in belt, 3in deck
Armament: nine 8in (three triples), twelve 5in (six twins), eleven quad and two twin 40mm Bofors, twenty-eight 20mm
Complement: 1,700

### USS *Tuscaloosa*

This heavy cruiser was one of the class generally considered as the best of all the 'treaty cruisers' built between the wars to the 10,000-ton and 8in gun limits by any nation (with the possible exception of the French *Algérie*). The *New Orleans* class were well protected and well balanced fighting ships, whose design began in the year 1929. *Tuscaloosa* was completed in 1934. At this stage of the war she had only had minor alterations, the most important of which, apart from the inevitable increase in light A/A guns, was the replacement of the closed bridge by an open one. Her D-Day mission was to silence the Quinéville battery of four 105mm guns. She would be broken up in 1959.

**Particulars of *Tuscaloosa***
Deep displacement: 13,500 tons (more by 1944)
Dimensions: 588¼ft oa, 574ft wl x 61¾ft
Deep draught: 25ft
Machinery: 2 shaft Parsons turbines, 8 Babcock & Wilcox boilers
Speed: 32.7 knots
Maximum armour: 5in belt, 3in deck
Armament: nine 8in (three triples), eight 5in, six quad 40mm Bofors, twenty-eight 20mm
Complement: 1,200

### HMS *Black Prince*

Another 'modified *Dido*' class light cruiser, this vessel was completed in November 1943. Her target was to be the Morsalines battery with four 155mm guns.

**Particulars of *Black Prince***
as *Diadem* except:
Deep displacement: 10,220 tons
Armament: five 6in (one twin, three singles), two quad 2pdrs, sixteen 20mm (six twins, four singles)

### HMS *Erebus*

With her sister *Terror* (lost in 1941) the last and best of the big gun monitors of the First World War. Basically built round a twin 15in gun turret, with shallow draught and comparatively low speed, and intended purely for shore bombardment. Indeed the ideal type of ship for the present purpose. Her design was used without many major alterations as a basis for another two 15in gun monitors built in the second conflict. She was completed in 1916, and took part in many bombardments of the Belgian shore batteries. During one of these she was hit by an early guided missile, a radio-controlled explosive speedboat. In 1919-1920 she fought both Bolsheviks and German *freikorps* in the Baltic. Rebuilt in 1939 she had a distinguished career in the second conflict, especially in the Mediterranean. On D-Day she was given three targets, the two Pernelle batteries (three 170mm guns and six 105mm) and the six 155mm guns at Gatteville.

**Particulars of *Erebus***
Deep displacement: 9,800 tons
Dimensions: 405ft oa x 88ft 2in
Draught: 11ft 8in
Machinery: 2 shaft triple expansion, 4 Babcock & Wilcox boilers
Speed: 12 knots
Maximum armour: 13in turret, 8in barbette, 4in belt, 2½in deck
Armament: two 15in (twin), six 4in, thirteen 2pdr (three quads + one single), one 40mm Bofors, fifteen 20mm
Complement: 315

## British and American destroyers

As we shall see, the close up fire support of destroyers was very important to the success of the landings - probably vital on Omaha Beach. The destroyers involved are therefore worth a brief word. All the named American destroyers which feature in the following pages are of the similar *Benson* and *Gleaves* classes, which together made the last group of American destroyers to be building when war broke out. They were mostly launched in 1941 or 1942. They were originally intended to be armed with five 5in guns, but those taking part in the landings will all have been fitted with only four, whilst one of the original two quintuple torpedo tube mountings was also removed to make way for the two twin 40mm Bofors mounts

and the seven 20mm Oerlikons fitted as an anti-aircraft battery. They were capable of 35 knots.

The Americans also had numbers of destroyer escorts (DEs), originally designed to a British requirement (quite a few were delivered to the Royal Navy, which called them 'Captains' class frigates). Their gun armament of three 3in guns (there was a version with two 5in, but none were present off Normandy) was inadequate for shore bombardment, but they were useful as escorts, and a number were converted to headquarters or fighter control ships. There were different versions with diesel, diesel electric, turbine and turbo-electric propulsion. Speeds varied between 24 and 19½ knots.

The British used their escort destroyer equivalent,

This US Navy photo of the French cruiser *Montcalm* was taken just after her refit in the USA, on 15th June 1943. The most obvious sign of this refit are the 20mm guns spread over the upper deck and superstructure.

the 'Hunt' class, for inshore bombardment. Presumably this was on the grounds of their smaller size, greater manoeuverability and lighter draught than their fleet destroyer contemporaries. Certainly they performed valiantly on 6th June. Their main armament was two or three twin 4in mountings, according to type. Their top speed was 27 knots.

The bigger fleet destroyers were used more for escort and patrolling work out to sea. Some of these were of the older two-funnelled inter-war destroyers, for

Another photo of the French cruiser *Montcalm* taken in 1943, this time as seen from the bow. The 152mm (6in) guns in their triple turrets, the deck-level single 20mm and the quadruple 40mm Bofors mounts on the bridge wings are all dramatically evident. (ECPA)

example of the 'B' class; some the single funnelled 'war emergency' destroyers, for example the recently-completed 'S' class. In either case the main gun armament was of 4.7in guns in four single mounts, though this was altered in some of the earlier vessels (*Boadicea*, which will be mentioned later, for example, was down to two 4.7in guns but had one 3in and two 6pdrs for anti-S-boat work). We will also later come across the larger 'Tribal' class, which by this time were armed with six 4.7in and two 4in, all in twin mountings, plus a single quadruple mounting of 21in torpedo tubes. Speeds varied between 35 knots for the earlier vessels to 37½ for the 'Tribals' and ¼ of a knot more for the 'war emergencies'.

## The Dutch fleet

The invasion of the neutral Netherlands in 1940 only lasted four days, but a fair number of warships managed to escape to nearby Britain: two cruisers, one destroyer, nine submarines, two gunboats, one sloop and six MTBs. There was also a good-sized fleet in the Netherlands East Indies (the modern Indonesia). However the Japanese invasion culminating with the disastrous battle of the Java Sea in 1942 put an end to that fleet. Only the cruiser *Sumatra*, the gunboat *Soemba* and seven submarines contrived to escape to Australia. The two surface ships both participated in D-Day. The old cruiser *Sumatra* was on her last voyage; she was scuttled as a breakwater for the artificial port of Arromanches on 9th June. However her guns were removed to provide replacements for those of the gunboat and her sister, who played a much more active part.

### The *Flores* class gunboats

The two armoured gunboats *Flores* and *Soemba* were sisters launched in 1925. Their chief mission was to defend minefields, and that was why they were given three cruiser-size guns in single mounts and excellent fire control, also an armoured deck. These features also made them very suited to shore bombardment, despite their comparatively small size. They were originally equipped with an aircraft apiece, though these had been removed and new anti-aircraft armament added some time before. The first of this pair was allocated the German battery at Graye as her target, the second Utah Beach.

**Particulars of the *Flores* class gunboats**
Displacement: 1,734 tons full load
Dimensions: 249¼ft bp x 37¾ft
Draught: 11¾ft
Machinery: 2 shaft triple expansion, 4 Yarrow boilers
Armour: 1in deck
Armament: three 150mm (5.9in), one 3in AA, four 20mm (two 40mm plus two 20mm for *Flores*), four 12.7mm machine guns
Complement: 132

## The smaller Allied fleets

Besides the French, whom we will leave till last, and the Dutch, there were other nations represented at sea on 6th June, but mostly only by small ships.

- The Greeks had two corvettes, provided by the British.
- The Norwegians had two ex-British 'S' class destroyers - the *Stord* and the *Svenner*, the latter of which would be sunk on the first day of the invasion. They also had one ex-British 'Hunt' class escort destroyer, the *Glaisdale*, three corvettes and three MTBs.
- The Poles had an old cruiser, the *Dragon* (see above), two 'Hunt' class escort destroyers, *Krakowiak* and *Slazak*, and two other destroyers employed on protective patrols away from the Bay of the Seine. One of these, the splendid *Blyskawica*, we shall meet later. Designed and built in the late 1930s by the British builder, J.S.White, she was large and powerful, with an impressive single funnel. In many ways a predecessor of the British 'Tribal' class super destroyers, she had had her original seven 4.7in guns replaced by eight British 4in guns in twin mounts after a dramatic escape, with most of the small but well-equipped and trained Polish navy, from the Baltic in 1939. She survives to this day as a museum ship in Poland.

### The Free French Forces

In numbers of ships and men the French navy was the third biggest to participate in the Normandy landings,

with:
- two cruisers
- one 'Hunt' class destroyer
- four destroyer escorts
- two frigates
- three corvettes
- eight motor launches

The old battleship *Courbet* should be added to this total, for she was sunk as a breakwater off Arromanches on 9th June. She and the two cruisers were the only vessels in this list which were designed and built in France.

### The two *La Galissonière* class cruisers

Though built to the same basic design these two light cruisers slightly differed in detail, as *Montcalm* was built by Chantiers de la Méditerranée at la Seyne, and *Georges Leygues* (known to the lower deck of the Royal Navy by the nickname 'Gorgeous Legs') was launched in Brittany by Saint-Nazaire-Penhoët.

These were designed at much the same time as the Royal Navy's rather similar *Leander* class, but, as the official French report on their construction pointed out, took almost twice as long to build as the British ships. Both these ships entered service in December 1937, although *Montcalm* was launched nearly half a year before her sister. They proved to be 'fast, reliable and successful ships ... among the most successful cruisers ever built, and were both fast and well protected'[1]. Three sisters were caught in France and scuttled at Toulon in 1942; our two, with a third which was not present at the landings, were refitted in the USA in 1943. Their aircraft arrangements were removed and replaced by a heavy armament of Bofors and Oerlikons.

Both cruisers formed part of Force O, with the coastal defences of Omaha Beach and Port-en-Bessin as their targets. *Georges Leygues* flew the flag of Contre-amiral Jaujard and was commanded by Capitaine de Vaisseau Laurin, whilst Capitaine de Vaisseau Déprez captained her sister.

**Particulars of the *La Galissonière* class**
Deep displacement: 9,100 tons
Dimensions: 589ft oa, 564¼ft bp x 57¼ft
Draught: 17½ft
Machinery: 2 shaft Parsons turbines, 4 Indret boilers
Speed: 32 knots
Maximum armour: 4in belt, 1½in deck
Armament: nine 6in (152mm, three triples), eight 3.5in (90mm, four twins), twenty-four 40mm (six quads), sixteen 20mm, four 21.7in (550mm, two pairs) torpedo tubes
Crew: 764

## The American destroyer escorts

At the beginning of 1944 the USA delivered six 'DEs' to France, of the diesel-powered *Cannon* ('DET') type,

The 'Hunt' class destroyers, mostly of the Type III variant shown here, and their twin 4in guns, played a major part close inshore in suppressing German beach defences on D-Day itself. This example of the British escort destroyer type was handed over to the Free French before completion (December 1942). Her name, *La Combattante*, was peculiarly suitable, and she had a fine record of successful action by the time she was sunk in the North Sea by a German *Seehund* type midget submarine on 23rd February 1945. (Marius Bar, Toulon)

numbered DE 106 to 111. They were renamed by the French in tribute to various fighting peoples from the French Empire who served in the French armed forces (rather like the Royal Navy's 'Tribal' classes): *Sénégalais*, *Algérien*, *Tunisien*, *Marocain*, *Hova* (a Madagascan people) and *Somali*.

### *La Combattante*, the 'Hunt' class escort destroyer

She was launched as HMS *Haldon* by Fairfields on 27th April 1941, but completed with her new French name. She was one of the torpedo-tube equipped Type 3 'Hunts', with two twin 4in mountings, and a twin 21in torpedo tube set. During Neptune she patrolled off Le Havre, which produced a number of clashes with German minor units. She had a very active wartime career, which ended on 23rd February 1945 when she was sunk by a German miniature submarine of the *Seehund* type (KU 330).

### The French *Flower* class corvettes

In 1939 the French Navy placed orders for four 'Flower' class corvettes in Britain (just as, in the previous conflict, a number of 'Flower' class sloops had been ordered from British yards). After the fall of France they reverted to the Royal Navy. However, between 1941 and 1943 eight other ships of this type were transferred to the Free French forces. Two were torpedoed in 1942, but six remained in 1944. These were *Aconit* (a name of some distinction in the Battle of the Atlantic), *Commandant Détroyat*, *Commandant Drogou*, *Renoncule*, *Roselys* and *Lobélia*. Of these the

[1] H.T.Lenton *The French Navy*, MacDonald 1969, p19 & p102

British 'River' class frigates were prominent in the anti-U-boat patrols in the entrance to the Channel on D-Day, also as headquarters ships and as escorts. This post-war photograph shows one of those transferred to the French Navy in 1943, named *L'Escarmouche*. (Marius Bar, Toulon).

first and the last were part of the anti-submarine escort of Force U on 6th June 1944.

### The *River* class frigates

Six British-built frigates of this class were transferred to the Free French in 1943 and 1944. Two of these, *L'Aventure* and *L'Escarmouche* were part of the escort group of Force O on D-Day.

## The Kriegsmarine

The listing of the fleets present on D-Day would be incomplete without mentioning the disposition of the German naval forces in the West.

By 1944 no surface warships of any importance were left on the southern shore of the Channel, so close to Allied airfields. The biggest there were a mixed group (see Chapter 7 for details) of five of the smaller destroyers that the Germans called torpedo boats based at the port of Le Havre. This also sheltered some fifty minesweepers of all types and twenty-one small patrol craft. In all there were 163 minesweepers, 57 patrol craft and 42 artillery barges based on the Channel coast, none of which were any sort of threat to the immense invasion fleet. The only surface vessels which posed any danger, apart from the five TBs already mentioned, were the thirty-four S-Boote. These were the excellent, seaworthy, sturdy and well-armed MTBs known to the Allies as 'E-boats', whose crews never dreamed of letting things go to pieces, despite the great disparity

of forces. These excellent torpedo craft were disposed as follows: six at Ijmuiden in the Netherlands, five at Ostend, eight at Boulogne and fifteen at Cherbourg.

This light dusting of naval force was hardly reinforced by the fleet on the Atlantic coast of France, whose weakness was extreme. There were 5 destroyers, 1 torpedo boat, 146 minesweepers and 59 patrol craft. The great base of Brest, doubtless because it was so often bombed, only sheltered 1 torpedo boat, 16 patrol boats and 36 minesweepers. The ports of Bénodet, Concarneau, Lorient, Saint-Nazaire and Nantes each held some fifteen patrol boats or sweepers, (the first held only six). South of the Loire there were 20 sweepers at Sables d'Olonne, 1 destroyer at La Pallice and 12 patrol craft at Biarritz. The largest part of the force was in the Gironde: 4 destroyers and 49 sweepers.

In fact the only real menace to the invasion fleet from the German navy was from its submarines. Forty-nine of these were specially allocated for attacking the Allied force when it chose to cross the Channel. The table given below shows the distribution of the U-boats:

| Port | Total | Schnorkel | Unavailable | Ready |
|------|-------|-----------|-------------|-------|
| Brest | 24 | 8 | 9 | 15 |
| Lorient | 2 | 1 | - | 2 |
| St.Nazaire | 19 | - | 5 | 14 |
| La Pallice | 4 | - | - | 4 |
| TOTAL | 49 | 9 | 14 | 35 |

Out of the forty-nine U-boats theoretically intended to oppose the invasion, fourteen were not available, a significant number. The number of vessels with Schnorkels was low. It was only this device, which allowed submarines to proceed using their diesels at periscope depth, which would give the U-boats a chance to win through the massive patrols covering the approach routes, let alone to stay long enough to cause any losses in the invasion area. Electric motors would give neither the speed, nor still less the endurance to begin to attempt this task, and attempting to proceed on the surface would be suicidal given the density of Allied air and sea activity.

The low number for the great submarine base of Lorient is explained by the employment of the larger oceanic submarines (Type XI) based there on other tasks in the Atlantic and beyond. Only the smaller type VII boats would be used against the invasion fleet.

# 4    The Crossing

As 5TH JUNE 1944, the date nominated by Eisenhower, approached, so the activity in the ports of southern England increased by leaps and bounds. All loading was completed on 3rd June. This meant that thousands of men aboard hundreds of vessels were awaiting the moment of departure. The ports were crowded as never before and, without spaces available, many vessels had to anchor in estuaries and other sheltered waters from the Clyde and Belfast Lough round to the Humber. The number of ships actually crossing the Channel was impressive enough; 931 for the Western Task Force and 1,796 for the Eastern Task Force. If the smaller craft are taken into account then those numbers are greatly increased, by 2,010 for the Western and 3,323 for the Eastern force. All these units were grouped in convoys on departure from England. Thus Force U, under Admiral Moon, was divided into a dozen convoys, and Admiral Hall's Force O into nine. The British forces G, J and S were grouped into sixteen, ten and twelve convoys respectively. And even then this was not taking into account anything except the assault forces themselves. It does not include the support groups or the consolidation forces which were also getting ready.

A row of American LCT (5)s loading White half-tracks just before D-Day. They were shorter than other LCTs, but broader in proportion to their length. As can be seen here they could take three rows of half tracks. There are more LCTs behind them, whilst the larger craft in the top right hand corner of the photo are LSTs. (IWM)

## An incredible organisation

To load these thousands of vessels in encumbered ports required first-rate organisation. In fact the flow of vehicles, tanks and infantry was uninterrupted. So long as well-trained troops went aboard ships with well-trained crews there was no problem. For example it took half an hour to load an LCT, whilst at the same time filling fuel and water tanks. Large concrete access ranks were built along beaches, particularly the famous shingle bank of Portland Bill. Landing craft could run up on these and lower their ramps to provide direct loading of supplies and matériel. Men, apart from those embarked by LSIs, would make most of the crossing aboard the big LSIs. There was therefore comparatively little to fear from seasickness. For the last few miles, however, things were very different, since the troops had to go aboard LCAs and LCVPs, with their limited seaworthiness and redoubtable capacity to roll and pitch. With cold and apprehension added to motion

This magnificent wake of a destroyer going at 30 knots is that of HMS *Kelvin*, the ship that took Churchill across the Channel to see the bridgehead, and by this stage one of only two survivors of the magnificent 'K' class, the last pre-war class of destroyers. The destroyer behind is HMS *Scourge*, of the 'S' class. She was one of the latest British destroyers at this time, her hull based on the 'K' class, but with an armament of four single 4.7in guns instead of the six in twin mountings of the 'Ks'. The cylinders on rails on either side of the stern are depth charges.(IWM)

sickness the lot of the majority of the troops was not enviable.

According to the orders all vessels had to be ready for sea during the night of the 3rd or early morning of 4th June, at a time which varied according to the distance of the departure port from the landing beach. Thus 0315 on the 4th was the sailing time from Portland, whilst the ships intended for Utah Beach had already been at sea for several hours.

Several dozen vessels had sailed beforehand; the minesweepers with their essential role in the opening hours of the operation. They were so vital that Admiral Ramsay himself had taken command of the 245 ships involved in this great cleaning-up. They principally consisted of sweepers, of course, but there were also Fairmile motor launches and other vessels responsible for marking the access routes with lighted buoys.

## Bad weather

Starting on 1st June General Eisenhower had organised two daily meetings in order to study the meteorological predictions. On Saturday 3rd, Group Captain Stagg of the RAF produced a particularly pessimistic report. A great depression bounded by the Greenland and Azores anti-cyclonic systems, was advancing across the Atlantic in an east-northeasterly direction. It carried with it strong winds which would raise a difficult sea. Nonetheless Eisenhower confirmed the sailing orders, at least for Force U, which had the greatest distance to cover. However, at the 4am meeting on the 4th, the predictions were even worse. Cloud base would be so low that the majority of aircraft would be unable to complete their missions. The sea would be so rough that the smaller landing craft could not be certain of reaching their beaches. In these conditions the officers of the RAF and the USAAF demanded the postponement of the operation. They were supported by Admiral Ramsay, for whom a landing in a Force 6 wind was an aberration. Only Montgomery supported the maintenance of the planned date. After an hour of debate, Eisenhower decided to delay the landing for 24hr. In consequence all the vessels already at sea were turned back at 5am on 4th June.

The French coast appears in the distance on the morning of D-Day. British soldiers and American sailors are looking at it from the deck of a USN LST(2). The lorries, staff car and ambulances belong to the 50th British Division (the insignia 'TT' visible on the vehicles belonged to that division), which landed on Gold Beach. The coast is that of Calvados, between Arromanches and Port-en-Bessin. (IWM)

As might be expected, this news was welcomed differently by different types of ship. The heavy ships of the bombardment forces had few problems. They merely turned round in the Irish sea and steamed up and down off the Welsh coast all day before resuming their original course.

The news was very discouraging for the wretched infantry, who had already spent an unpleasant night at sea. Besides, because of the radio 'black-out', the recall order could only be passed by visual means, whether the signal came from a destroyer or an airplane. Thus one minesweeping flotilla was only stopped 35 miles from the French coast, whilst a convoy of LSTs and LCMs was not found by the three destroyers sent in search of them. This was finally located by a venturesome *Walrus* amphibian which signalled the order to return.

This apart, all the convoys had got back to their ports of departure by 2240 on the 4th. The unfortunate missing convoy, when it finally returned to Portland found no room in the port and the unfortunate vessels had to spend part of the night at sea in the middle of the storm. Finally a place was found for them in Weymouth Bay, but too late for LCT 2498, with a motor break-down, which was driven ashore and lost.

The return of the ships to port posed another problem. If the bad weather continued it would be impossible to push the landing on to the 7th, because the warships would have to return for revictualling. Any new adjournment implied a postponement to the 8th, and if the weather was still unfavourable, to the 19th, the only possible date because of the tides. It is worth noting that had this happened the landings would have ended in a terrible fiasco, as the Channel was swept by one of the worst summer storms in its history between the 19th and the 21st.

The 4th June was probably the worst moment of Eisenhower's career. The meteorological meeting held at 2115 was heavy in consequences. A short calmer period had certainly been predicted, but would it be long enough? At the beginning of the evening the wind was still at Force 5 on the Beaufort scale, but little by little it would weaken as the next day approached, and

Upper deck view of what is probably an American LST covered with British lorries and ambulances. In the haze in the distance are several LCTs, at least one LST and what look like one frigate and a destroyer. (IWM)

would result in lowering the surf on the Norman shore. Furthermore, the clouds lifted enough to allow the heavy bombers and the parachutists' Dakotas to take off in the night of 5th/6th June. On the other hand it was impossible to predict developments for 7th and 8th June.

Several factors operated in favour of an assault on the 6th. Above all a postponement to the 8th, or more probably 19th, implied all ships returning to port, and the landing of all the troops. They were now all aware of their destination, and the probability of the news reaching the Germans by one means or another was high. The seamen and Montgomery were all insisting on attacking on the 6th, but Leigh-Mallory was firmly against. This was particularly because of the airborne operation, which he had considered from the start to be likely to lead to a 'futile massacre'. This determination impressed Eisenhower, who finally ordered the ships to sea (the limiting time for departure

of the ships furthest from their destinations to reach the beaches on the 6th being 2300 on the night of the 4th) whilst reserving his final decision to go ahead for the morning of the 5th, when there was still time to recall the armada.

The 'met' meeting at 3.30 on the 5th was therefore crucial. The wind was still high and rain seemed to be falling almost horizontally. But the forecast was more encouraging. Group Captain Stagg predicted a 36hr improvement, beginning on the morning of 6th June, with moderate westerly winds veering to south-westerly, and a much calmer sea off Normandy with waves only 60cm high.

In consequence, at 0415 on the morning of 5th June, Eisenhower announced laconically: 'O.K. We'll go.'

## To the Bay of the Seine

The crossing of the Channel is rarely described by historians, who have tended to concentrate on the landings, or the air operations. However this crossing was quite a maritime adventure. There is no need to recapitulate the impressive number of vessels involved. However it is often forgotten that the crossing took place at the height of the storm on the 5th. As a result keeping place in the convoys was quite a business, especially with craft like the LCTs which were difficult to control anyway. Samuel Elliot Morison's official history of the US Navy quotes the account of an LCT officer, Lt Stanley C. Bodell, USNR: 'We were located in one of the inside columns and spent our entire time trying to keep station. We had the misfortune to have a British "lettered craft" behind us which had the ability to go ahead twice as fast as the Americans, but lacked the backing

View from the bridge of a British LCT looking forward. The tank standing clear of the camouflage netting is a 17pdr-armed Sherman Firefly, the red letters on the turret identifying it as a tank of the 13th/18th Hussars destined to land on Sword Beach. Immediately above it is one of the two visible Holman projectors. Four other LCT(4)s steam across the picture, beyond them in the middle of the picture, easily identifiable because of her comparatively insignificant 4.5in mountings, is the cruiser HMS *Scylla*, Admiral Vian's flagship. (IWM)

power we had. We would pound along, the whole boat bending and buckling; then the one ahead would slow down. We would go into full reverse to keep from riding up its stern, then the Britisher would start to climb ours. To avoid collision we would go full speed ahead with full right rudder, and sheer off toward the other column. The vessels of different columns would close to about five feet or less, usually crashing together, then separating with one going full speed at right angles to the course of the convoy. All day there was always someone heading off by himself, having a wonderful time. Sleep was almost impossible, as you couldn't stay in your sack.'[1]

Despite this none of the 2,000-plus ships engaged in the crossing of the Channel sank, which was itself an achievement in the circumstances. Only a few were badly delayed.

On arrival in the Bay of the Seine, the crews were astonished to see the two flashes of the lighthouse on the headland of Barfleur (to be precise, Gatteville lighthouse), whose rotating light, as in times of peace,

could be seen for 29 miles! The Germans, clearly, were not worried about anything. Nothing had been detected by their aerial reconnaissance, though it was of course true that the Luftwaffe had lost the war for aerial supremacy long since. Even more astonishingly the fast torpedo boats, the 'S-boats', had not sortied from the ports of Le Havre or Cherbourg for their usual nightly patrols. They had received orders to stay in port, as bad weather had, for once, ruled out the possibility of invasion. The Germans did not have the advantage of weather stations which would warn them of the temporary improvement in the weather, as the Allies had contrived to suppress the few their enemies had set up.

[1]Morison pp 84-85

Quite possibly the same tank on the same LCT as in the previous picture 'Carole' is a Sherman Firefly of the 13th/18th Hussars. Its 17pdr gun is the only Allied tank gun capable of coping with the frontal armour of the heavier German tanks. In the background are another three LST(4)s 'rafted up' whilst they wait for orders to proceed to the beach. (IWM)

Finally the powerful radar stations of the Normandy coast did not report anything on their screens till 0309, at which stage numerous Allied ships were already been transhipping men to LCAs and LCVPs for over an hour.

## The Germans do not realise what is happening

To state that the Germans remained totally at ease is, to be sure, not entirely true. Certain troubling facts began to arouse their suspicions, but in such a scattered way that nobody could put things together to form a precise opinion. Also numbers of senior men were absent, beginning with Rommel himself.

This can easily be explained by the bad weather. Every afternoon the weather forecasters of Luftflotte 3 reported on the possibility of invasion in the next 24 hours. The deterioration in the weather from the beginning of June was very soothing and on the 4th the meteorological experts stated: 'The enemy has already let three periods of good weather pass without landing, and the chances of new periods of good weather in the weeks to come have come to seem very uncertain.' They added that all airborne attack was ruled out for 5th and 6th June.

This was doubtless why Sepp Dietrich, the

Another view on board an LCT carrying the 13th/18th Hussars into battle. The tank in the foreground with the perhaps unfortunate name of 'Balaclava' is a standard Sherman with the 75mm gun, but in front of this is what appears to be one of the earlier model of a 'BARV' (Beach Armoured Recovery Vehicle) on a Sherman chassis, with a raised bulwark for the crew, and fitted for wading. The purpose of these extremely useful conversions was to tow bogged or swamped vehicles out of the water. Notice the motor bicycles on either side of the wading structure, and the exhaust trunking fitted to this and other tanks to enable them to wade in deeper water without swamping the engine. The ship in the background is a British fleet destroyer. (IWM)

commander of 1st SS Panzerkorps, was at Brussels, far from the future front; whilst Rommel himself was at home in Germany. This was not on leave, as is so often written, but in order to see Hitler at Berchtesgaden in order to get him to give authorisation to put the 12th ('*Hitlerjugend*') Panzerdivision closer to the coast. Here we have yet another proof of the lack of coherence of the German higher command in the West.

German uneasiness began at 2115, when the BBC messages to the French Resistance lasted twice as long as usual - and included messages that the Germans had already cause to believe indicated that invasion was imminent. At 2200 the radar stations situated between Le Havre and Cherbourg began to be heavily jammed, whilst those situated north of the Seine reported hundreds of aircraft and ships proceeding towards the Pas de Calais. This was the famous British deception operation called 'Fortitude'. About a hundred aircraft and several dozen vessels, using varied electronic means deceived German radar operators in to believing that a much larger number were approaching. In consequence at 2215 the Fifteenth Army, based to the north of the Seine, went on full alert and passed the

warning on to the staffs of Rommel and von Rundstedt, who showed no particular interest in these messages!

Between 2200 and 2300 the Luftwaffe's listening service intercepted numerous reports from Allied weather planes at a much later time than was usual and provided proof of an unusual level of activity. The few available night fighter squadrons were put on alert.

At midnight, therefore, the alarm had only partially been raised, and not on the front of the Seventh Army which was the one due to receive the full shock of the Allied assault. A quarter of an hour later the first parachutists were landing. At 0111 the army corps which held the Cotentin put all its units on full alert and, at 0120, warned Seventh Army of Allied parachute landings in the Cotentin and to the east of Caen.

Seventh Army was finally put on alert at 0130. At the same time naval HQ at Paris transmitted a message of full alert to all its units. But the daily log of Marinegruppe West stated: 'We consider here that it is not a question of an invasion on a large scale, and this opinion is shared by the CinC West, von Rundstedt, and by the head of Luftflotte 3.'

After 0200 things became clearer. The coastal defence battery at Saint Marcouf reported parachutists landing and insisted on the probability of an invasion attempt.

At 0215 Seventh Army told Rommel's HQ at la Roche-Guyon: 'Motor noises audible from the eastern coast of the Cotentin. The Admiral (Rieve) reports ships located by radar off Cherbourg. Everything seems to indicate a large-scale operation.'

But HQ replied: 'CinC West does not consider this to be a large-scale operation.'

At 0300 hundreds of vessels were reported to have been seen by the naked eye off Port-en-Bessin. Soon the S-boats were ordered out to patrol in the Bay of the Seine and between Dieppe and le Tréport.

At 0330 a report came from 84 Armeekorps to Seventh Army which was much more precise and alarming: 'Important glider landings from 0325 in the neighbourhood of Bréville to the east of the Orne and of Grandcamp. It is probable that landing craft are there also. Situation at Grandcamp is confused. Probably landing craft there, too. HQ of the commander of 91st Infantry Division attacked by enemy troops in battalion strength. Communications with Sainte-Mère-Église cut. Battery Rive-Bella partly damaged by air attack.'

At 0400 von Rundstedt's HQ asked Hitler for permission to use 12th SS Panzerdivision and the Panzer Lehr Division against the parachutists. Hitler was not woken and OKW refused.

At 0430 the first S-boats sortied from Le Havre.

At 0535 as day broke the coastal batteries opened fire at the invasion fleet.

The first accounts of the powerful Allied naval bombardment came through.

Finally at 0645 Seventh Army told Rommel's staff: 'The depth of the aerial landings in the region of the Orne and in the southern Cotentin seem to indicate a large-scale attack. The aim of the coastal bombardments is not yet clear. They seem to be a measure of protection in concert with actual attacks at other points. Our air and sea reconnaissance since dawn has not discovered anything new.'

In fact by this time naval landings had already commenced and if the recce missions had found nothing new it was because they had been repulsed by Allied aircraft and ships before being able to reach the areas

concerned. Finally the news of the landings proper did not get through till 0800 for Omaha and 1100 for Utah. The Germans had been thoroughly mystified, and would continue to be puzzled during the following weeks, asking themselves if this really was the main landing.

View of an American LST carrying British troops and lorries. The white star, originally an American insignia, was marked on all Allied vehicles during the invasion as a clear and simple identification feature. The landing craft in the LST's davits are LCVPs, whilst emerging from behind the aftermost set of these, on the left of the photo, is a British LCI(S). The three large single funnelled ships look rather like American attack transports, numbers of which served in the Royal Navy. (IWM)

Recognisable by their odd, cut-off bows, a
number of Fairmile-designed LCI(S)s move in
towards the French coast. (IWM)

A line of LCTs in the Channel, plus an old
raised quarterdeck engine aft British coaster.
The latter is immediately below the barrage
balloon. The twin machine guns out of focus in
the foreground, and the wash, would seem to
indicate that this was taken from a fast-moving
coastal forces boat, most likely an ML. (IWM)

# 5 The American Landing on Utah Beach

HMS *Black Prince* entering a British port attended by two tugs. The two twin 5.25in turrets forward and the vertical masts and funnels identify her as a cruiser of the 'modified *Dido*' class. (IWM)

IN THEIR FINAL APPROACH the Americans benefited from the fact that the large radar station on the Pointe de Barfleur had been destroyed by aerial bombardment. This must not be forgotten as one of the factors behind the nocturnal approach. Between midnight and 0500, 1,056 British heavy bombers attacked the ten principal German batteries and all the communications behind the beaches. There were more results from the latter point of aim, as there were very few direct hits on the casemates.

## The American preparations off the Cotentin

At 0229 the flagships of Force U, USS *Bayfield*, anchored about 11 miles off the coast. The landing was planned for three hours later, to be simultaneous at both Utah and Omaha. The three British beaches would be attacked a little later, because of the need for

the tide to be higher on that part of the coast with its rocky approaches.

At this time of the morning the minesweepers were the nearest vessels to coast, as always working flat out. It is good to record how well their work was done; only two ships were lost to mines during the crossing, the destroyer *Wrestler* and an LST.

From 0200 eighteen American and sixteen British minesweepers were at work off the beaches. They were not only clearing the access routes for the landing craft to within a mile of the beach, but also freeing the large areas where the fire support ships were to manoeuvre and shoot from.

Unfortunately the Germans had laid delayed action

mines which would not be armed, or come up to their positions, until after several sweeps or ships had passed. This was done to such an extent that there were always some mines to be cleared in the sector which in the end were to cause more losses to the Allied navies than any other means, including the shore batteries. Indeed even fifty years after the battle they are still being swept by the French navy.

## The fight with the German coast defence guns

With the numbers of German guns (110 of over 75mm) installed on the Cotentin coast and reported by aerial reconnaissance, the Americans knew that they could not reduce them all to silence in the preliminary bombardment. General Bradley therefore fixed priority targets. To silence them the destroyers would have to approach within 5,000 yards of the coast, whilst the cruisers and battleships stayed at about 11,000 yards.

If the larger ships had a swept area to manoeuvre in, the same was not the case with the destroyers, confined within narrow channels. They therefore were ordered to moor opposite their targets. This certainly made them more vulnerable to return fire, but avoided the dangers of the redoubtable delayed action mines. Numbers of the larger ships also anchored.

The plan, which was not always followed, as we will see, laid down that at H hour minus 40min the secondary batteries of the *Nevada* and *Quincy* and the main batteries of HMS *Enterprise* and the destroyers *Hobson* and *Shubrick* would open rapid fire on Utah Beach. At H-10 the main batteries of the two larger American ships would, in their turn, fire on the beach. Then, when the landing craft had almost reached the beach, the commander of the leading wave of the assault would fire a black smoke flare. This was the signal for the warships to change their aim and fire further inland or on the flanks of the assault zone.

At 0140 the ships assigned to the bombardment took

The American battleship *Arkansas* firing her 12in guns at German positions is background to the bow of a British LCT(4) proceeding in to the beach. Just as we have previously seen pictures of British soldiers aboard American LSTs, so many American soldiers were carried to battle aboard British landing craft. The wartime censor has cut off the upper parts of the battleship's spotting top and masts by retouching, hiding the radar aerials mounted there. (IWM)

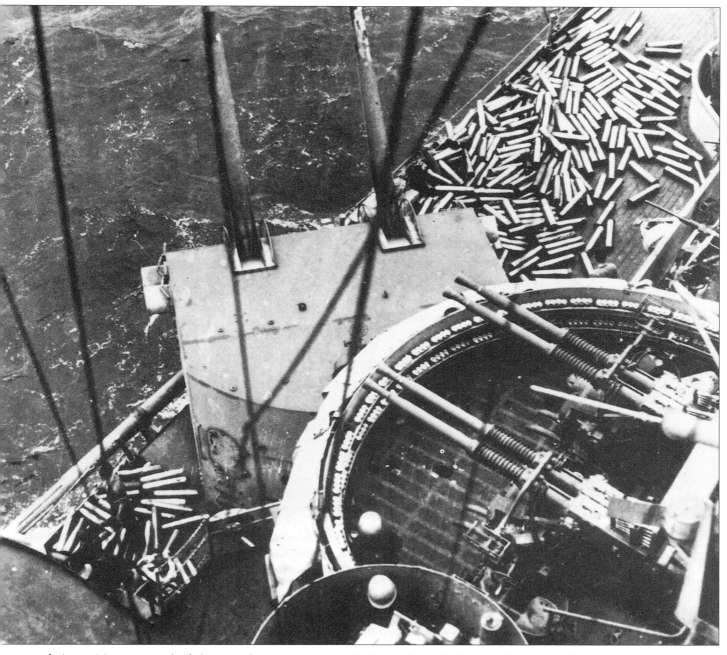

Deck scene aboard the *Nevada*, with a quadruple Bofors gun over a twin 5in turret. Notice the impressive total of cartridge cases surrounding the latter, which tells its own story of the fierceness of the naval bombardment. (DITE)

up their positions, several of them anchoring, giving them time to adjust their fire control instruments. In the end, though, it was the Germans who fired first, since a battery opened up on the destroyers *Fitch* and *Corry* at 0505. Twenty minutes later American reports indicate that a heavy German battery at Saint-Vaast-la-Hogue opened fire upon several minesweepers only 3,500 yards offshore. In fact the Germans had no heavy guns at Saint-Vaast; it seems probable that the shells were from one of the batteries of La Pernelle, a small village above la Hogue.

The cruiser HMS *Black Prince* immediately replied, and naturally attracted return fire. Soon the firing became general upon the heavy ships of Force U, which were naturally the favoured targets. At 0536 Admiral Deyo, their commander, decided to open fire upon the chosen targets without further delay. At 0610, as planned, aircraft laid a smokescreen between the ships of Force U and the shore. Unfortunately the aircraft intended to screen the *Corry* was shot down and soon the destroyer was the only target visible out to sea.

A group of American LSTs come into the beach with their bow doors opening. The calmness of the sea and the clearness of the sky make it likely that this picture was taken on D-Day itself, probably off Utah Beach. The balloons were towed to discourage low-level raids by German fighter-bombers. (IWM)

The German batteries therefore concentrated their fire on her. To avoid this she was manoeuvering at full speed in the narrow channel available to her, when she set off a mine. The damage was very bad, the ship being nearly broken in two and her engine rooms flooded. Lieutenant-Commander Hoffman tried hard to get his ship out to sea, but with all steam pressure lost she came to a stop within four minutes. The only answer was to take off her crew, and the destroyers *Hobson* and *Fitch* came to the rescue. Losses amounted to thirteen killed and thirty-three wounded.

## The attack as seen by the Germans

Without giving it in full it is interesting to see the eye-witness account by artillery Captain Ohmsen, the commander of the battery at Saint-Marcouf. This was the best armed of all in this sector, with its three Skoda 210mm cannon.

The beginning of the Allied attack was the air raid at 0130 lasting about 35min. This knocked out his flak battery and killed several soldiers, though the guns themselves remained intact: 'Direct hits on the garrison billets in the village of Saint-Marcouf. Heavy losses of effectives.'

At nearly the same time American parachutists appeared, which did not simplify the defenders' task. The alert had obviously been given: 'Until dawn, state of alert. In the morning mist enemy ships were seen at sea. About 0600 the three guns opened fire. Immediate enemy reply, with fire directed, from the first salvo, at the interior of the battery. The enemy was soon concealed behind a smokescreen. Targets changed several times. About 0800 a cruiser of about 6,000 tons was hit. Battery fire remained on target. During this phase one gun was hit and put out of action. The

Despite appearances this Czech 210mm gun being surveyed by two American soldiers was actually put out of action by Allied naval bombardment, together with its two companion pieces in the Saint Marcouf battery. This was not, however, before playing their part in the destruction of the American destroyer *Corry*. (DITE)

remaining two guns continued the fight. Range was 17,000 metres. Shortly afterwards a cruiser was sunk by a hit which broke her in two. Target shifted to a destroyer which was hit on the stern. About 0900 the other gun mounted under concrete was destroyed by a direct hit by a battleship shell in its embrasure. All the gun crew were killed. The gun was no longer usable. With the remaining gun (which was in an open mounting) fire was opened on the area of the landing and several landing craft were sunk.'

This account needs some commentary from what we know from the Allied accounts. First, no American or British cruisers were hit in this sector on the 6th. The 0800 hit must have been on some other type of ship. The cruiser cut in two was clearly actually the destroyer *Corry* whose loss has already been described, and which was actually due to a mine, not a shell. However, at a distance of over 10 miles and under fire the mistake is hardly surprising.

What is astonishing is the accuracy of the warships' gunnery, since the two guns pointing out to sea were silenced by 0900. The Allied warships played their part perfectly, on the one hand attracting the fire of the hostile batteries which therefore left the infantry in their landing craft alone, and on the other hand knocking out these batteries one by one.

## A systematic bombardment

The fire of the heavy cruisers *Nevada* and *Erebus* was remarkably precise, the more so because the targets were often invisible, hidden by trees, hedges, or simply out of sight because of the lie of the land of the northern Cotentin. Anybody who has been along that coast by sea will testify that it is almost impossible to identify where things are ashore. A low and foursquare coastal band in the landing area itself is adjoined to the north by hills where the *bocage* (hedgerows with trees) masks all the important points apart from a few bell-towers which are the only breaks in a sea of greenery.

The British and American naval gunners succeeded in a series of blows in achieving their exceptionally difficult aims. They were helped in locating the hostile batteries by aircraft. Previously such spotting was done by catapult seaplanes carried aboard the ships themselves: Kingfishers, Seagulls, Walruses and the like.

American soldiers, Jeeps, light trucks and a staff car seen aboard an LST approaching the beach. Above the bow ramp can be seen a Rhino ferry equally laden with transport, and beyond that and to the right an LST(5). (IWM)

However these had all been landed before the operation; their slowness and lack of manoeuvrability gave them little chance of surviving the inevitable heavy flak. As a result modern fighters were used for spotting instead: Mustangs, Spitfires and Seafires. A total of five RAF and four Fleet Air Arm squadrons were used. All except seventeen American pilots were British. The majority had only the shortest training in working with gunners, but they completed their task perfectly.

Flying from the airfield at Lee on Solent, the fighters were in pairs. Above the targets one would keep an eye for hostile aircraft whilst the other would do the spotting. After 45min it was necessary to return to England because of the short endurance of these fighters, but their reliefs were already to hand. Therefore six aircraft had to be in the air at any one time for a particular target; two on the way to Normandy, two coming back, and the last pair over

the German battery.

Besides the aircraft, spotting for the navy was also done by SFCPs (Shore Fire Control Parties). Groups of observers were disembarked with the 4th US Division at Utah, whilst the paras of 101st Airborne had nine observers with them.

The effectiveness of the bombardment is well shown by the case of the destroyer *Shubrick*, which was in contact with her SFCP from 0635 - only 5min after the landings began. Twice the observers on land signalled that the ship was firing much too close to American troops. This error was explained when the navigators of the destroyer realised that the American assault waves had been swept over a mile south from where they should have been.

At 0704, a battery situated besides Grandcamp, that is to say to the east of what the Americans called the estuary of Carentan, opened fire on Utah Beach. *Shubrick* immediately silenced it, but it opened fire again, having changed its target, as the destroyer was near-missed. After a 25min duel the German guns fell silent for good, doubtless out of action. This battery must have consisted of field guns belonging to an infantry division as the Germans had no coastal artillery in this sector. At 1026 the *Shubrick* was relieved by the *Glennon* after firing 440 five-inch shells. It is significant that the latter destroyer only received one appeal from the infantry for support during the rest of the day; proof, if any was needed, of the success of the Utah landings.

This combat with shore artillery near Grandcamp did not only concern the *Shubrick*. In fact the infantry signalled several times that hostile shellfire was coming from the southeast, and was the most accurate the Germans produced. Soon three other ships joined in. These were the destroyer *Herndon*, the old cruiser HMS *Hawkins*, and the Dutch gunboat *Soemba*. The Dutch

GIs loading aboard LCI 539 (identifiable from the stencil on the back of the crewman in the foreground) from an LCVP for the Channel crossing. (IWM)

opened accurate fire, thanks to the spotting of an observer landed with the Rangers at Pointe du Hoc. The *Hawkins* meanwhile took on a 150mm battery and another of 75mm guns, both situated southeast of Grandcamp. They were neutralised during the course of the morning.

As for the *Nevada*, she was supporting the dangerously scattered paratroopers in the German rear. The fire of her 14in guns was formidable, and dispersed several enemy counterattacks. She even wiped out a group of old tanks of French origin which were about to come into action. She fired a total of 337 shells from her main armament and 2,693 five-inch during 6th June, which was a record. In comparison the *Tuscaloosa* was a pale imitation, with 487 eight-inch shells, and only 115 five-inch. However it seems to have been this ship which silenced the Morsalines battery of four ex-French 155mm guns. This was not without its tight moments, one German salvo landed less than 300 yards from the cruiser.

As for the monitor *Erebus*, it was she who achieved the direct hit on casemate No 2 at Saint-Marcouf. At 1830 the last gun in this battery was finally destroyed, but it is not known whether this was by *Erebus*, *Black Prince* or one of the Americans.

By the evening of 6th June Allied counter-battery fire had proved to be completely successful. This is in contrast to some other attempts of the same type, noticeably the famous attempt to break through the Dardanelles, which ended in disaster. This time, thanks to careful planning, much preparation and sensible use of airpower the Allies had won easily without the least loss to the bombarding ships from the shore artillery. This despite the fact that, especially in the Coastal batteries proper, the Germans were good shots. Their failure off Utah was due to a whole series of unfavourable factors. The air raids of the night had not destroyed any guns, but they had killed some of their crews and, especially, had destroyed much of the communications network. Reduced to their own resources the batteries declined in effectiveness. Also the Allied success owed much to effective spotting both from the air and on the ground.

Utah Beach at high tide seen from behind a German anti-tank ('Pak') gun identifiable from the writing on the shield as a 75mm. Two bulldozers and a the first of a line of amphibious DUKWs comes into shore. Further out and to the left is what looks like an LST (5), and in the background is a long l

...d on the beach; behind them a Rhino ferry is offloading lorries and what looks like the small tracked vehicle known as a 'Weasel'. On the right of the picture ...ters and larger cargo ships. (IWM)

## The Utah landing

Whilst the warships took on the defences, the immense landing fleet began its final preparations. For their own safety the big transports, the LSIs and others, remained outside the range of most of the coastal artillery. They lowered their landing craft at about 11 nautical miles from the beach, at which distance only the Saint-Marcouf guns were in effective range.

The LCVPs were lowered first. For a while they bashed against the sides of the LSIs whilst their troops embarked, then they began the journey to the beach. Then came the moment when the LSTs and LSIs also got under way. The wind was still blowing at Force 4, gusting to 5, on the Beaufort Scale. The sea was far from calm especially further out from shore. As the shore grew nearer so the waves diminished, thanks to the lee provided by the Cotentin peninsula. The departure line proper extended from the Saint-Marcouf Islands to the Cardonnet bank. There the craft were organised into twenty-four successive waves, which were spaced out over a period of 6hr.

Utah Beach was divided into two, Green to the north and Red to the south. A large HQ ship controlled each of these two beaches, aided by two LCC (Landing Craft Control), converted MLs each equipped with a small radar set and radios in order to guide the assault waves.

At the same time as the first wave of assault craft went in, for the first time in an amphibious operation DD tanks (amphibious tanks with Duplex Drive) were put into the water from their LCTs. Each of these eight LCTs carried four tanks which were to be disembarked 5,000 yards from the coast, in order to reach the beach at the same time as the infantry.

The LCTs were guided in towards the Cardonnet Bank by two subchasers - PC 1176 and PC 1261 - after reaching the transport zone at 0430. At 0542, just after crossing the bank, PC 1261 hit a mine and sank immediately. Fifteen minutes later it was LCT 597's turn to strike a mine, and she rapidly sank with her four tanks.

These two catastrophes delayed the LCTs, to the extent that Lieutenant Richer, commanding the remaining PC, decided that the tanks should not be put into the water as planned, but that they should be taken most of the way to the beach. The LCTs continued towards the coast, avoiding hits from shore artillery despite forming a conspicuous target compared to the small LCVPs. Less than a mile from the coast the ramps were lowered and the twenty-eight DD Shermans plunged into the relatively calm water immediately offshore, and proceeded without problems to the sand, floating thanks to their raised 'skirts'. Had they been launched further out it is likely

that many, if not most, would have been lost in the sea that was running.

All hell now broke loose on Utah beach. The 276 B26 Marauder medium bombers of the Ninth US Air Force, dropped 4,400 bombs on the German positions, most of which landed beside their targets, whilst four LCGs armed with 4.7in guns opened fire at short range on the beach defences. Meanwhile the cruisers and battleships continued to pound their targets. When the LCVPs were at 7,000 yards from the shore seventeen LCT(R)s began to unleash their salvos of thousands of rockets in a fearsome display of light and explosions.

This hurricane of fire soon covered the coast in a thick cloud of smoke, which masked the few landmarks visible to the naked eye. Radar was of little use, either, for, as we have already seen, the coast here was entirely flat. A strong current displaced the pilot boats, without them being aware of it; nobody had the time or opportunity (thanks to the smoke and overcast) to make an astronomical fix with a sextant. The LCC therefore started from a line some 1,500 yards south from the intended one. As the landing craft were themselves steering by prismatic compass, without taking account either of the current, or of the deviation of the compasses themselves, the error grew and the wave beached over a mile south of their intended destination.

## On land!

At 0630 twenty LCVPs crunched simultaneously onto the beach, exactly at the planned time. The ramps came down and the men waded through about 100 yards of shallow, calm, water, not much more than a foot deep, before reaching the sand and sheltering behind the dunes. There was no enemy fire, but the officers were unhappy because they did not recognise the terrain at all, despite having studied maps and pictures for day upon day. It was finally General Theodore Roosevelt himself, a volunteer for the first wave despite his age, who discovered the reason for this, and worked out the exact location of the troops.

A photo taken aboard an American LST off Utah Beach; close alongside is the after part of an LST(5) (labelled CTU 381). Behind that is a Rhino ferry ferrying vehicles ashore. Beyond are merchant ships. (IWM)

It remained to decide what to do, whether to continue the landing at the same spot, or whether to direct the subsequent waves to the beaches originally designated for the purpose. A simple observation at sunrise showed General Roosevelt that the Germans held the original target much more strongly than the beach where luck had swept the landing craft. The German pill-boxes were superbly sited to take that original beach under enfilade. So he demanded and obtained by radio the cancellation of the original plan. The following waves followed the original one and soon the new beaches were identified by huge flags and by coloured lights, etc., to mark Tare Green and Uncle Red.

The following assault waves came at intervals of ten to twenty minutes. The second wave landed the engineers who were to blow up the obstacles placed by the Germans, which here were neither numerous nor mined. In an hour and a half a band 700 yards wide was totally cleared, and this was widened to 1,600 yards in the afternoon. This work was not done without losses as the Germans had begun to react with more accuracy. Four US Navy engineers were killed and another eleven wounded.

The landings continued without great problems during the morning, at least until unfounded rumours of a violent fight on Green Beach made Admiral Moon slow down landings there, a delay which lasted for two hours. Soon, however, observers on PC 484 apprised the admiral that 'the obstacles were no longer obstacles' and the flow of landing craft began again.

## Aboard the landing craft

Thanks to the numerous accounts of soldiers and sailors we have an idea what men felt like at the moment of landing. Midshipman Kenneth McCaw RNVR, the first lieutenant of a British LCT destined for Utah Beach, tells us this about the last minutes before reaching the beach: 'We foregathered about 10 miles off the beachhead, and at H-Hour got our signal to proceed - we were scheduled to go in one hour after H-Hour. The sea was rough. We had a US padre aboard who held a short service and the scene with the soldiers' heads sticking out from under tarpaulins as they joined in the prayers and hymns was a moving experience. When the right distance from the beach we let our kedge go. Finally the sushing as we touched the beach, and down went our door. The Jeeps with trailers had great difficulty in getting ashore as the waves made the trailers tend to float away, but finally they all made it. A DUKW going ashore alongside our lot hit a mine and went up in the air. When all were off the craft we wound the door laboriously up and beat a quick retreat.'[1]

An LCI commander tells us that his vessel was towing a kite balloon, which had the effect of drawing enemy fire, the more accurate because the LCI could not beach properly, finally grounding after five tries in water which was too deep for the soldiers to find a footing. Finally the small vessel managed to land her troops, by which stage enemy fire was coming dangerously close. He ordered the cables cut and the balloon disappeared skywards, whilst the German gunners looked for another target.

## Complete success

In spite of the aforementioned slight delay on Green Beach the landing went forward in the best possible way. The big transports discharged their cargoes rapidly into numerous barges, Rhino ferries and DUKWs. Thus the *Empire Gauntlet* was able to leave for England at 0830, and *Dickman* and *Barnett* at 1243. All three were back at Portland by midnight.

The unfortunate convoy U-2A(1) whose late recall on the 4th and failure to get back into harbour we have already mentioned, arrived at the right time and place except for seven vessels out of fifty LCMs, thirty-seven LCTs and twenty-three smaller craft.

At 1800 the Americans had already landed 21,328 men, 1,742 vehicles and 1,695 tons of matériel at Utah. A better start for the invasion could not be wished for.

Ashore operations were going well. The 8th Infantry

Regiment had rapidly taken possession of the beach, and pushed forward inland, taking a number of prisoners. The defenders, who belonged to the 709th Infantry Division, were far from being élite soldiers. They were relatively elderly or not of German origin, and therefore disinclined to kill or die for a cause which was not their own. The gunners of the division fired whilst the Americans were at a distance, but surrendered before they came to close combat.

The men of the 4th US Division were also clearly helped by the work, certainly disordered but also essential, of the two airborne divisions dropped in the enemy rear.

Chaos was such amongst the ranks of the Germans, particularly as a result of the aerial and naval bombardments, that the news of the American landing did not reach General Dollman, commander of Seventh Army, till late in the day on the 6th. The situation was confused, besides, by the American paratroops, scattered over many miles of the interior. So no coherent counterattack was possible on the 6th. For example the commander of the 91st Infantry Division, returning from a wargame exercise held at Rennes on the previous evening, found himself amongst a group of American parachutists when approaching his command post. He was rapidly killed in the fight that ensued. On the evening of the 6th the 4th Division had linked up with a part of the 82nd Airborne and had reached the main road between Carentan and Sainte-Mère-Église. The bridgehead formed an arc 10 kilometres from the coast. The losses of 4th Division were very light, only 197 killed, wounded or missing.

## A well established position

Certainly the American bridgehead in the southern Cotentin, whilst deep, was not completely cleared of the enemy. However the absence of any serious German reaction was a good augury.

Thus Force U had not been disturbed during the day by German naval units based at Cherbourg. Alerted at 0309 the fifteen S-boats certainly sailed, but turned back at daybreak because of bad weather. According to Admiral Krancke this was without sighting a single Allied vessel. This, however, poses a number of questions, when you consider that hundreds of LCTs, much less well adapted to anything of a sea, had made the long crossing from England without suffering unreasonably from the weather. Why were the S-boats, which were excellent seaworthy craft, even if they were also redoubtable rollers, unable to continue their mission? Their crews would probably have said that any major enemy operation was impossible in such weather. Also on 6th June, three destroyers

[1]Paul Lund & Harry Ludlam *The War of the Landing Craft,* London, Foulsham & Co. 1976 p173.

Probably taken from the bow ramp of the LST of the previous photo (the merchantman on the right of the line of ships in the background looks very much like one that appears in the first picture), this shows troops and vehicles being loaded aboard a Rhino ferry. The joining pieces, and the sloping ends of the caissons can be seen to the right foreground, whilst on the left the helmsman in his steering shelter enjoys a quick cigarette. The Rhino ferries had an impressive capacity, but could only be used in comparatively calm conditions because of their low freeboard and unhandiness. (IWM)

based at Royan received orders to sail for Brest for a forthcoming operation, a mistake given the total Allied naval superiority.

Finally, thirty-six U-boats based at Brest, Lorient, Saint-Nazaire and la Pallice received orders to hold themselves ready to attack, but they did not do so this day.

It was mines which caused the greatest damage, especially those laid on Cardonnet Bank. They were the cause of the loss of the destroyer *Corry*, three LCTs, two LCIs and PC 1261. Given the enormous resources used by the Allies this was a fairly light loss.

During the night the Luftwaffe intervened above the bridgehead for the first time, thanks to the departure of Allied fighters after nightfall. This episodic and small-scale attack caused no damage to the Americans, either to the troops ashore or to the numerous vessels afloat.

The advance inland was sufficiently rapid to permit the 9th Engineer Command to put into use a temporary track for the landing of priority supplies as from 2115 of the day of landing itself.

At midnight the situation was perfectly in hand. The 4th US Division, whose baptism of fire this was, had attained all its objectives. The landing at Utah Beach had therefore succeeded. The race between reinforcements to the bridgehead and the movement of the German reserves had begun. The Allies could only win if they retained the initiative.

Seen from the bow ramp the Rhino ferry proceeds away towards the
beach. This is a good view of the two huge outboard motors with their
'Z' drive (driving through two right angles). Notice the little dinghy
attached alongside the left-hand motor. Behind the ferry is another
LST. (IWM)

# 6   Bloody Omaha

Photographs taken during the landing on Omaha Beach are very rare for obvious reasons. Robert Capa took some hundred shots at the risk of his life, only to lose them through a mistake in development. This photo was taken a little later and shows the dreadful devastation on the beach with the debris of obstacles mixed with wrecked LCVPs. The nearest has lost its ramp. In the distance are some LST(5)s. (IWM)

EVEN AT THE DISTANCE of several miles there was no similarity at all between the two American landing beaches of Utah and Omaha, and this applied as much to the valour of the defending troops as to their landscape. Besides Utah was covered by a strong concentration of shore batteries, whilst there was nothing at Omaha, apart from the famous guns of Pointe du Hoc, which caused an attack that proved unnecessary.

## A beach at the foot of a cliff

For holidaymakers who nowadays walk along the Normandy coast the difference between Utah and Omaha Beaches is considerable. On the Cotentin coast the low four-square totally flat hinterland is only varied to the north where hills offer views out to sea. On the other coast there is a continuous line of yellow and brown cliffs, separated from the sea by a narrow coastal band covered with wild grass and dunes, then a beach which uncovers to about 300 yards' distance at low tide.

From the sea Omaha looks as monotonous as Utah, but for different reasons. Here it is the uniformity of the cliffs that is striking. The several routes of access up the cliffs are difficult to differentiate. The villages, situated on the other side of the cliff, are hard to identify except by their church towers. There is a disquieting impression of hostility, whilst Utah evokes no response with its low and almost invisible coastline. Contrary to what the Allied general staff believed before the invasion, Omaha was not defended by the same

The support group approaches Omaha Beach, led by USS *Texas*, behind her is the British cruiser *Glasgow*, followed by *Arkansas* and finally one of the two French cruisers, *Montcalm* or *Georges Leygues*. (IWM)

error of intelligence was one of the gravest committed on D-Day, together with the famous adventure of Pointe du Hoc.

The arrival of the 352nd ID coincided with heavy activity in placing obstacles on the beach. The gentle slope of this was covered with obstacles organised in three lines. The first, submerged nearly all the time, were what the Germans called 'Element C' or 'Belgian stable doors'. These were iron frames, 2½ to 3m high, with mines attached, upon which landing craft were supposed to break themselves.

Twenty yards further inshore, the second line consisted of wooden stakes assembled in triangular form and pointing seawards. A third of these obstacles were crowned with a mine. The final line was formed of obstructions made of three rails or iron bars attached at right angles. Finally the few routes down to the beach were shut off with concrete pyramids. The inner limit of the beach was shut off by a thick band of pebbles, an anti-tank wall and a deep barbed-wire entanglement. Behind, the waste land whose breadth varied from place to place from 150 to 300 yards, was defended by numerous machine-gun nests, trenches, and shelters for 75mm or 88mm guns. Besides these, two little settlements consisting of small holiday villas, had been converted into strongpoints by the Germans. These were Hamel-au-Prêtre and Les Moulins, where the houses which limited defensive fields of fire had been razed to the ground. If the numerous aerial reconnaissance sorties had adequately disclosed the beach obstacles, the majority of the bunkers from which the beaches were taken into enfilade had not been detected. According to the Americans the German defences at Omaha were the worst their troops had to meet in this war, worse even than the Japanese ones at Iwo Jima, Tarawa or Peleliu.

infantry division as the British sector, the mediocre 716th, but by the excellent 352nd, a unit which had arrived in mid-March (and not just before the invasion, as is often believed).

In fact the 352nd ID occupied the western half of the cliffs with one regiment, whilst another was held in reserve at Bayeux with a battalion nearby. The eastern half of the cliff line was held by the 716th ID. Thus the Americans had to confront two regiments in all, with a third close by in reserve, where they only expected to confront one regiment of poor quality. This

## Successful but insufficient naval protection

From the first hours of 6th June the fleet deployed with no difficulties. The Germans had laid no delayed-action mines in this sector, so the areas intended for the manoeuvering of the bombardment ships were clear after being swept. These ships consisted of the two

One of the rare pictures taken of Omaha during the battle, probably in the afternoon. The bow on the left is probably of a wrecked LCI(L). For some reason the censor has touched out two small areas on the picture. The low line of cliffs is obvious. (IWM)

veteran American battleships *Arkansas* and *Texas*, and three cruisers, HMS *Glasgow* and the French *Georges Leygues* and *Montcalm*. There were also three American destroyers and three small British 'Hunt' class destroyers. The big ships were just over 6 miles off the coast, the destroyers stationed 5,000 yards offshore.

The bombardment commenced at 0550 according to plan. In order to preserve the effects of surprise it was only to last 35mins, rather little time. The *Texas* opened fire with her 14in guns on the battery at Pointe du Hoc, digging enormous craters and obtaining several direct hits on the casemates, which remained strangely silent. At the same time the destroyer USS *Saterlee* took on the machine-gun nests which covered the point, whilst HMS *Talybont* bombarded the radar of Pointe de la Percée at close range; USS *Thompson* seconded her in taking on the machine-gun nests on this point, and for this task approached the coast to within a mile or so.

*Texas*' secondary batteries were pounding the western access to Omaha beach, which led to Vierville. The aim was to level the anti-tank wall and destroy the German positions. This was an enormous task for a single ship in so short a time, even if she was helped by a destroyer and an LCG.

At 2,000 yards to the east, the beach access route leading to Saint-Laurent was bombarded by the destroyer USS *Carmick*, whilst LCT(R) 423 fired her thousand rockets at the hamlet of Les Moulins. This little group of houses received particularly careful treatment as Americans feared it was a real entrenched camp. So the *Arkansas* expended several powerful broadsides upon it from 0552. HMS *Glasgow* was treating the wasteland around the settlement in similar manner.

The eastern route off the beach leading to Saint-Laurent is overlooked by a vast meadow, where nowadays the American military cemetery is situated. The defences round here were taken on by the *Georges Leygues* and the destroyer HMS *Tanatside*, then by the thousand rockets of LCT(R)447.

The last access route, the furthest east, leading to Colville, was bombarded by three destroyers and three LCT(R)s firing a thousand rockets apiece.

*Montcalm*, accompanied by an American destroyer,

A poor but historic snapshot, showing the battleship *Texas* hammering the Pointe du Hoc. (DITE)

was firing on Port-en-Bessin, then on several other targets further from Omaha Beach, in order to tie down defenders and prevent them intervening in the battle that was to follow.

During the naval preparation phase there were no hits on any warships by hostile artillery. It was true that there were no shore batteries in this sector apart from the enigma of Pointe du Hoc. The Allied bombardment was above all designed to wipe out the infantry defences especially machine-gun nests and trenches.

At 0600 the noise of the naval bombardment was added to by the passage of hundreds of bombers. These were the 480 B24 Liberators of the Eighth US Army Air Force whose 1,285 tons of bombs were intended to pulverise German beach defences.

The heavy four-engined bombers actually passed over Omaha, but not a bomb fell on its target. Because of the thick weather the aviators had received orders to delay 30sec in releasing their bombs in order not to risk hitting the landing craft then approaching the beaches. The pilots therefore attacked blind, without attempting to sight their targets through clouds which were less thick and continuous than forecast. This bombing failed totally, all it did was to tear up fields and kill livestock inland, without killing a single German.

This failure had serious consequences, because the 35min naval bombardment, despite its successes, was not able to end all German resistance. Morison, the official historian of the American navy, thinks that it reduced the enemy's resistance by a half, or even two-thirds. It did not affect numerous well sighted guns in casemates sited in enfilade, and impossible to see from the sea. They were ready to intervene in the battle, as were many troops who had sheltered from the bombardment in deep bunkers, and who re-appeared when it was over.

## Two assaults for nothing

The American staff feared that two obstacles threatened to compromise the landings at Utah and Omaha. These were respectively the islands of Saint-Marcouf and the German battery on Pointe de Hoc.

The islands of Saint-Marcouf, off the Cotentin coast, were situated exactly on the axis of the start-line of the assault waves destined for Utah. Perhaps the island further offshore on which was a round fortress tower, dating from the mid-nineteenth century, sheltered a German garrison. It was certain that there were no heavy guns capable of damaging the warships, but they might be able to sink landing craft whilst they crossed the Cardonnet Bank, and, worse, might spot for the shore batteries on the Cotentin.

Therefore a landing by Rangers was planned for the early hours of 6th June, before the landing craft had arrived. Two small groups of men landed on the offshore island and the inshore island. They found nothing but mines, thousands of anti-personnel mines, which caused some casualties. There were no Germans.

The menace of the coastal battery on Pointe du Hoc was much more unsettling. Six ex-French 155mm guns, well placed on the promontory, were not only capable of taking the entire length of Omaha Beach in enfilade, but also of firing on the backs of the soldiers landing at Utah. The Americans considered this the most dangerous battery in Normandy.

We have already found out what the 250 fourteen-inch shells from USS *Texas* did. But that would evidently not be enough to obviate all risks, so Bradley decided to send 200 Rangers commanded by Lieutenant-Colonel James Rudder. The mission was particularly risky, because a cliff about 100ft high would have to be climbed under machine gun fire and grenades from the defenders. An intelligence officer snorted: 'It can't

The huge craters left by the 14in shells fired by *Texas* are evident in this photo of Rangers and German prisoners. The characteristic shape of the point itself can be seen in the upper right of this photo. (DITE)

be done. Three old women with brooms could keep the Rangers from climbing that cliff.'[1]

However, the operation actually happened. The 200 men embarked aboard six LCAs equipped with rocket grapnels, capable of lifting rope ladders and lines to the top of the cliff. This allowed men to climb the equivalent of a ten-storey building. These means were augmented by light sectioned ladders, and by great 100 ft turntable ladders, taken from the London Fire Brigade and mounted aboard DUKWs.

The crossing in a heavy sea passed badly. Ceaselessly waves broke over the LCAs and the soldiers were forced to bail with their helmets. Even this did not always work and one of the craft sank, though her occupants were saved.

The Fairmile motor launch which was guiding the little flotilla mistook the target and steered towards Pointe de la Percée. This was an understandable error

[1]Morison Vol.XI p 126

A view taken of Omaha beach from the German defences on the cliff top. Discharging onto the beach below are (left to right) a British LCT, a group of LCMs and two LCT(5s), another LCM (all these American) and finally what is probably another British LCT. (IWM)

as both points look exactly the same from the sea. Fortunately Lieutenant-Colonel Rudder spotted the mistake and himself changed the direction of the force. This confusion had consequences, because the landing craft had to turn around. This was a difficult and dangerous manoeuvre for these rather unseaworthy craft, which then, even worse, had to struggle against the eddies and strong current of the race of la Percée. The Germans on the point of the same name profited by opening a heavy fire on the LCAs and DUKWs almost at their feet and unable to make much headway against the current. A DUKW was sunk, and HMS *Talybont* went to their help; her shells forced the Germans to take shelter.

Finally, 35min late, the Rangers arrived by Pointe du Hoc and ran ashore at the foot of its eastern face. The Germans only fired feebly, thanks to the fire of USS *Saterlee* and the Fairmile. They continued to throw grenades over the top of the cliff, and they wounded

fifteen. The dozen yards of beach was too uneven for the DUKWs and their extending ladders to be used. However the famous grapnels worked well and half an hour after the landing 150 Rangers were at the top of the cliff.

They took advantage of the support of the two vessels in order to make themselves masters of the casemates, only to discover that the only 'guns' present were wooden telegraph poles! At this stage the defenders began to re-appear from the depths of their bunkers, and a long process of mopping up began. This did not come to an end till the next day. Nonetheless Rudder's men managed to reach the Grandcamp to Vierville road and establish a roadblock, whilst sending out patrols further afield. By chance one of these found in a field four of the six 155mm guns they had been supposed to find at the Pointe du Hoc. They were pointing at Utah Beach, with plenty of ammunition, but there was no-one to defend them. In fact the Germans had withdrawn them from the point until all the casemates were completed. The Rangers spiked these guns, and returned to their small bridgehead, where the situation rapidly worsened. No reinforcements arrived until after an entire night of arduous combat, and they were not relieved until about 1130 on 8th June by infantry landed at Omaha in equally bad conditions.

## The disaster of the amphibious tanks

Omaha Beach, divided into three large sections (Dog, Easy and Fox), extended for just under 4 miles. It was attacked simultaneously by eight battalions belonging to the 29th Division's 116th Infantry Regiment, and the 1st Division's 16th Infantry Regiment. This meant eight companies per regiment in the first assault wave, each with its own objective. H-Hour was fixed, as it was for Utah, at 0630. This was an hour after low tide in order to avoid the majority of obstacles which would be above water at this stage. At 0633 fourteen demolition teams were to land, in order to open breaches. These were to allow the landing craft in subsequent waves to come in with the tide without risk of impaling themselves on the *chevaux de frise* and other obstacles. The second wave was not planned to arrive till 0700, then subsequent waves would follow at ten minute intervals until 0930.

Precise timing was important because of the distance the craft had to come (11nm) and also the state of the sea and the number of vessels of all kinds involved. The start line was fixed at about 4,000 yards offshore.

The infantry was to land precisely at 0631, whilst the DD tanks were intended to start their work ashore five minutes earlier. These amphibious Shermans, which were a British development, did not inspire full confidence amongst the American staff. They decided that the tanks should be launched between 6,000 and 1,000 yards from the coast, if conditions were favourable. If conditions were unfavourable their LCTs were to take them right up to the beach, the final decision of what to do being left to the commanders of each landing craft, in the purest American tradition.

In the western sector, given the sea state, it was decided not to launch the tanks. The leading LCTs waited for other vessels of the same kind which were each loaded with two ordinary Shermans and a bulldozer tank, then proceeded to the beach where they arrived at H minus 1min precisely. Then twenty-eight DD tanks landed alongside fourteen standard Shermans. Altogether a not negligible total of forty-two tanks landed at the western end of Omaha. The

Over the ruins of a German field gun, destroyed in its bunker, two DUKWs can be seen, and the stern of a coaster. (DITE)

German riposte was not long in coming. In a few minutes two LCTs were ripped apart by shells and several tanks had been set afire.

To the east there were far worse developments. Launched 5,000 yards from the beach, the DD tanks found it difficult to cope with the waves breaking over their pneumatically raised flotation skirts. A good number had gone down even before reaching the departure line. The others continued at all costs, and foundered in their turn. In the end precisely two reached Fox Green Beach under their own power, closely followed by the three carried aboard LCT 600 whose commander had judged it best to continue to shore. Thus only five of the DD Shermans planned to land on the eastern part of Omaha reached their objective.

## The first wave pinned down

Losses amongst the LCAs and LCVPs were nowhere near as severe, but the sea state, the current, and enemy fire produced general confusion. Units mostly arrived more or less on time on the beach, but in a great mish-

After the drama of its taking, Omaha Beach became the scene of frantic round the clock activity. Here a lorry in the foreground is operating the nearest barrage balloon. Other lorries, a Weasel (tracked amphibian), Jeeps, trailers, tracked transporters and even a cafeteria-waggon can be seen on land. Beached barges and LSTs are in the shallows, whilst further out are a line of cargo vessels. (IWM)

mash of such a nature there was hardly any control by the higher command once the first wave had touched down.

When the ramps went down the soldiers jumped into water three to four feet deep. Woe to the wounded; their heavy equipment dragged them down to a watery death.

The luckier, and more numerous, soldiers, who emerged unharmed from the water, then had to cover 200 to 300 yards of open beach before reaching the very meagre shelter of the anti-tank wall and the pebble bank. The majority of the casualties were sustained at this stage. Very many officers were killed or wounded, which did not help the organising of troops who were already well scattered.

Starting with the westernmost, let us see what

happened to the units of the first wave.

Company A of the 1st Battalion, 116th Infantry, reached that good beach, Dog Green, at 0635 aboard six LCAs. One of these hit a submerged obstacle and sank with many men. Another, loaded with Rangers, was hit five times and was lost with all hands. Three LCAs managed to disembark their men behind the shelter of a smashed LCT, but the men could not manage to cross the fire-swept beach and sheltered behind the beach obstacles. As the tide rose so they found they had to move to other shelter, and the Germans did not neglect their opportunities so, by the end of the day, losses had reached 66 per cent.

To the east three companies, embarked in eighteen landing craft, were lost wherever they tried to land. The men of Company G were suddenly offered the opportunity of being masked by the smoke of a fire in the wasteland, and managed to reach the shelter of the anti-tank wall without appalling loss. Companies E and F did not have the same luck and were decimated as they landed, in total confusion. The DD tanks, numerous in this sector, were unable to come to their aid, and were forced to advance, almost alone, towards the exits from the beach.

In the eastern sector, the landings of the 16th Infantry Regiment were even more disordered. The men who reached land opposite the place where the American cemetery is now were hit, one after another. Companies E and F of the second battalion were literally massacred in front of Exit E3, taken from the side by two guns, one 75mm and one 88mm. On Fox Green the situation was even worse, because men could not even shelter behind the anti-tank wall, which did not exist in this sector. All they could do was to obtain some cover behind the pebble bank. Here two German guns took them in enfilade. It was hardly surprising that company E lost its captain and 104 men from a total of 180 during the morning of the 6th.

The hell that was Fox Green is well summed up by the list of survivors of those who reached it from early in the morning: a single, unique DD tank, several standard Shermans, about 400 totally dispersed men and a group of naval engineer troops.

As for companies L and I, they were lost along the beaches. One of them had nearly landed in the vicinity of Port-en-Bessin before reaching Fox Green an hour and a half late.

The situation was even graver because the American troops had failed to establish a continuous front. Instead, two large stretches of beach were completely deserted. Only two out of eight companies had landed where they were supposed to. There was little the others could do, with most of their officers put out of action, except wait for reinforcements in the shelter of the anti-tank wall or the pebble bank.

Despite all their courage the demolition teams could only imperfectly fulfil their role. Two teams were wiped out by direct hits, but the twelve others did excellent work. Unfortunately they did not have the time to mark this effectively. So it was not until the next tide that the cleared channels could be properly used.

## Subsequent waves land in an inferno

At 0700, to plan, the second wave of LCAs and LCVPs reached the beach. The current swept them all eastwards, but to an acceptable extent as the troops landed more or less where intended. Once again the troops were swept by very accurate fire, but there was less obvious disorder than half an hour earlier. The arrival of senior officers from 0730 permitted the beginning of reorganisation. The losses were also not as heavy, because the waves followed each other at ten-minute intervals and the choice of targets offered to the Germans was greater, and therefore more men survived to reach the shelter of the anti-tank wall.

After the eighth wave larger vessels started to arrive, LCIs, LCMs as well as many DUKWs. LCIs 91 and 92 were hit and set on fire at almost the same moment, which caused heavy losses. The two vessels burned on the beach for hours.

At 0800 the situation was even more critical because not a man, a vehicle or a tank had yet been able to leave the beach. An hour later the Navy Beachmaster in charge of the beach signalled to the ships offshore to stop all offloading of vehicles.

At this moment it is clear that Bradley's staff, looking at the situation from out to sea, began to get seriously worried. The reports which reached them were overwhelming, and the appearance of the beach itself, viewed through binoculars, was very far from encouraging. According to his memoirs, Bradley briefly considered abandoning the Omaha landings and transferring all the troops to Utah, a decision which would have had catastrophic consequences for those troops already landed. Besides, could Utah have absorbed such an extra load? What would have become of the junction with the British?

General Huebner, the commander of the 1st Division, had difficulty in hiding his uneasiness from his men, but Admiral Hall, responsible for the assault on Omaha, reassured his colleagues that landing beaches under enemy fire always looked chaotic.

This chaos is well described by the commander of LCI Group 28, in the eastern sector of Omaha, Lieutenant Wade, USNR: 'Enemy fire on the beaches was terrific - 105mm, 88mm, 40mm, mortars, machine guns, mines - everything, apparently, .... Very few shells fell to seaward. The enemy would wait until the craft lowered their ramps and then cut loose with everything they had. Someone was lucky to get ashore with an FM set [radio-telephone] and was sending back instructions and ordering the craft in. He was doing a marvellous job. Destroyers were almost on the beach themselves, firing away at pillboxes and strongpoints. Rocket boats and gunboats did not faze the enemy in the least; they were too far underground. The soldiers, the battleships and the destroyers did the good work. It seems a miracle this beach was ever taken.'[2]

## The situation begins to improve

Early in the afternoon the LCIs which had been steaming in circles for three hours waiting to find gaps between the obstacles, moved forward again. The tide had been ebbing for half an hour and the *chevaux de frise* were appearing again. However this also meant that if unloading was not very rapid the LCIs would remain stuck on the beach, offering marvellous targets to the Germans. So it was decided to organise a ferry service of small craft, LCAs and LCVPs, from the larger vessels to the beach. It did not take the enemy long to notice this new arrangement and open fire on it.

At this stage aboard the flagship tension was at its highest, because Force B, which was bringing the reinforcements for Omaha, was now late in arriving. Should Bradley divert it to Utah or the British beaches or, if the Good Lord so willed it, would the landing begin to succeed?

The first encouraging news about Omaha arrived at 1137; Germans were beginning to surrender indicating

Although this view was taken some days after the battle Omaha Beach, seen from the cliffs at low tide, is still covered by debris. On the beach from left to right are an LSI(L), a wrecked LCVP, an LST(5) which looks as if it has been hit in front of the steering shelter, an LCVP with its bows pointing out to sea, an LCM, and two more, apparently wrecked LCMs. The nearer of the two seems to have lost its bow ramp, and has probably been pulled up to where it is now, which may be what the lorry alongside the other is trying to do. (IWM)

A view of the maritime coming and going off Omaha, looking towards the land. In the foreground is the after superstructure of an LCT(5), above it a Rhino ferry, and to the right an LCM. Immediately behind these another LCM and two LCVPs. Behind these still are a couple of armed trawlers, British LCTs, an LST and several coasters. (IWM)

a possible reversal of fortunes. Just before midday it became evident that American soldiers had climbed the cliff and a message indicated that the village of Vierville had just been captured by an outflanking movement. At almost the same time the village of Saint-Laurent was reached, though the Germans obstinately held on there till nearly 1600.

Though Vierville was captured the exit from the beach was still under the fire of Germans holed up in a fortified building. At 1300 the great guns of *Texas* put an end to this. By 1630 all the exits from the eastern part of the beach were in American hands, and progress along the tops of the cliffs could be followed through binoculars.

At 1705 the situation was sufficiently clarified for General Gerhardt, commander of the 29th Division, to leave the escort destroyer *Maloy* in order to install his HQ ashore.

The engineers went to work with more and more results and by 2000 a fifth exit from the beach had been created by the use of bulldozers. During the afternoon the intensity of the battle had definitely diminished as the last German strongpoints succumbed one after another. Tanks in increasing numbers left the beach for the interior. The divisional artillery alone could not be made available. It had been put aboard DUKWs and mostly lost in the wrecking of the majority of these amphibians, overloaded for such a heavy sea. Only one battery could be got into action on the 6th itself.

Five complete regiments were ashore by nightfall. The Atlantic Wall had been well and truly breached, and the beachhead was about 6 miles deep. It extended from southwest from Vierville to east of Colleville, though there were several islands of German resistance, some even on the beach. In Colleville the defenders fought with the energy of despair.

## Why was there such a change?

We have seen that throughout the morning the position of the Americans on Omaha remained almost

An American LCT(5) offloads a great crowd of troops from its jam-packed deck. The bridge was offset on this type because they had stern ramps, and could load from the stern as well as the bow, and could act as a bridge between a larger landing vessel and the shore. (IWM)

untenable. Then a little after noon the position was markedly changed. Why?

There were several reasons. The first was doubtless a German error of interpretation. From 0600 the Seventh Army had been aware of an extraordinarily intense naval bombardment between Grandcamp and the mouth of the Orne, but General Dollmann had at first believed it to be a diversion. General Marcks of 84 Armeekorps had not warned him about the landings on the Calvados coast until 0900, and then insisted that the Allies were more threatening on the coast near Caen; that is in the British sector. Whether it was for this reason, or because the reports from his troops made him believe that the Americans could be pinned down indefinitely on Omaha Beach, General Kraiss of the 352nd ID committed the error of sending his reserve regiment off towards the British beaches, instead of throwing it into battle at Omaha, where it could no doubt have continued to hold the Americans on the beach for many hours more.

Kraiss was in any case hesitant. At 1100, on the basis of more recent information, he ordered one of his reserve battalions to turn around and go to Colleville which was being threatened by the Americans.

At 1335 there was a new and contradictory report. Kraiss believed he could state that the Americans around Colleville had been beaten and the Omaha bridgehead could be considered to have been liquidated!

At the end of the afternoon Kraiss sent off a more alarming signal. His strongpoints had been outflanked by an enemy who had reached the line Colleville-Asnières.

Finally, at midnight, forced by the urgency of the situation, Kraiss came personally to Marcks' HQ, in order to tell him that his entire division was engaged in battle, that it was suffering heavy losses, and that though it could continue to hold for the next day, it had to be reinforced with the maximum urgency. Marcks replied that he had no reinforcements available at all.

The errors of the German high command were

therefore one of the causes of the final American success. But how can the abrupt reversal of the situation on the beach at the end of the morning be explained, a reversal that lies behind Kraiss' hesitations? There is only one answer, and that is the fire of naval guns, notably that of the destroyers, which came close to grounding to help the infantry.

## The navy works miracles

We have already seen the effect of gunfire from the destroyers *Satterlee* and *Talybont* during the attack on Pointe du Hoc. The ten other destroyers present off Omaha did not stay inactive during the first difficult hours of the landing. It was just after 0800, thanks to the unfortunate direction taken by events, that the destroyers were ordered to fire at will at targets of opportunity at the sole responsibility of their captains. At 0900 the orders were made more precise still. The destroyers were to approach the beach as closely as possible to fire point-blank at the German positions.

The task of the ships was not easy. The shore control parties that worked so well at Utah were in no state to do so at Omaha. Many of the men were killed, and most of the radio sets lost. This did not prevent the destroyers performing well.

For example Lieutenant-Commander Ramey's USS *McCook*, besides destroying several guns which enfiladed the beach from behind Pointe de la Percée, managed to capture an important group of German soldiers! The event is unusual enough in naval history to bear recounting in detail.

About 0930 the destroyer engaged two guns mounted on Pointe de la Percée and reduced them to silence after five minutes. The first was blown into the sea, the second hit by direct fire. For the rest of the day the *McCook* approached closer still to the coast engaging targets as they were sighted in the absence of contact with her SFCP. The fire was so precise that at 1625 a group of soldiers appeared on the cliff with a large white flag, making unintelligible lamp signals. For nearly an hour the group tried to communicate with the American destroyer, then Ramey began to believe that the Germans wanted no more than to cause the destroyer to cease firing for as long as possible. He therefore signalled them that fire would be resumed immediately, and immediately got the answer 'cease fire!'. Ramey then ordered the Germans to approach the Pointe du Hoc in order to be made prisoner. Rather than flee to the interior the Germans accepted and surrendered to the Rangers.

For the whole day the destroyers worked wonders in order to help the infantry. Some, like the *Carmick*, approached to only 900 yards from the beach. At such a short distance the effect of their broadside on machine gun nests and other German pockets of resistance was totally devastating.

During the afternoon the destroyer *Emmons* received orders for an almost impossible mission from Admiral Bryant. This was to dislodge German observers by destroying the tower of Colleville church without destroying the rest of the building, which dated from the eleventh century. The first eleven shots missed the tower, the twelfth shook it and the thirteenth hit the tower full on, knocking part of it into the cemetery and part onto the nave, which came down with it.

The USS *Baldwin* was the only ship of Force O to be hit by hostile artillery. At 0820 she was hit by two shells fired by a battery situated to the east of Port-en-Bessin. The two projectiles exploded on impact and did not penetrate the interior of the vessel, so damage was minor and nobody aboard was wounded.

If the destroyers' achievement was extraordinary, compensating for the absence of surviving American tanks on the beach, the heavier ships did not remain idle. Their task was easier than the destroyers' because they had at their disposal teams of Spitfires similar to those over Utah Beach. The *Texas*, despite her draught, was ordered to close the coast, and then let fly several devastating broadsides, especially on the access route to Vierville.

The two French cruisers distinguished themselves by the accuracy of their fire, though their position, close to Port-en-Bessin, prevented them firing on Omaha Beach itself. The *Montcalm* fired no less than 174 152mm shells, and the *Georges-Leygues* even more. Their targets were mostly German batteries, many of them mobile.

When General Gerow established the HQ of V Corps on Omaha Beach at about 2000, the first message he sent to Bradley aboard the *Augusta* was one of thanks to the navy, without whom the assault would have failed: 'Thank God, the United States Navy was there!'

This photo was taken off the junction between the British and American sectors, not far from Port-en-Bessin. It was taken aboard an American LST, and shows (a little down from the bow Bofors gun) the lift used to take vehicles from the upper deck to the tank deck and vice versa. In the middle of the picture a Rhino ferry has a number of what appear to be British ambulance lorries on board, plus a DUKW. Beyond this are LSTs, and above the LST's bow what is probably a 'Hunt' class destroyer. (IWM)

# 7    The British Landings

An impressive view of HMS *Ramillies* firing her main armament against the German batteries around the mouth of the Seine on 6th June in a rough sea. (IWM)

THE BRITISH SECTOR included the British beaches; Gold in the west and Sword in the east, with the Canadian Juno Beach in the centre. Although the three sections formed a continuous sector, the landing zones were separated by coastal reefs, very numerous between Juno and Sword, with the Essarts de Langrune and the Isle of Essarts, well known to fishermen, just off the Calvados coast. At this place the rocks uncover at low tide to about a mile off the coast.

## Great differences from the Americans

The British made a more important amphibious effort than the Americans, because their assault area allowed the simultaneous landing of three divisions:
   - At Gold, the 50th (Northumbrian) Division.
   - At Juno, the 3rd Canadian Division.
   - At Sword, the 3rd British Division.

Besides this the 6th Airborne Division was projected into the German rear to the northeast of Caen, principally to seize a defensive flank to the east of the Orne. This was the zone most open to a German counter-offensive, as it was closest to the important reserves in the north of France.

This produced a more difficult situation for the British than for the Americans. The former had to fight in front of Caen, the city which the Germans considered as the pillar of their defence in Normandy, and which became the area of the fiercest German counterattacks.

The proximity of the capital of Normandy was therefore a handicap to the British, as was the closeness of Le Havre. Certainly its defending batteries did not have the range to disturb the invasion fleet, but this great port was one of the chief bases of S-boats and torpedo boats, which would intervene in the battle from 6th June on.

The actual layout of the coast itself was very different from that of the American beaches. Even if Gold had some similarity to Omaha, though with gentle undulations in the place of cliffs, Juno and Sword were radically different. At Sword the coast was covered with houses and bungalows, with the small seaside towns of Luc and Lion-sur-mer. At Juno, Courseulles and Bernières were similar small holiday resorts, but the habitations were in more clearly defined groups, with certain parts of the beach being unbuilt-up dunes. In both cases the coast is low with numerous church towers the only landmarks.

Three of the four twin 15in turrets of HMS *Warspite* fire upon the Villerville battery (close to Honfleur). (IWM)

## The fleet approaches

Forces G, J and S crossed the Channel with no more difficulty than the Americans had experienced. Two small vessels had crossed before the rest. These were the midget submarines X 20 and X 23, with crews of five men each. They had left Portsmouth 72hr earlier, thanks to the delaying of the landing. Rather than return to England they had carefully checked their positions by periscope observations and then lain on the bottom offshore. The crews had waited patiently in extremely cramped and uncomfortable circumstances. At 0500 on 6th June they surfaced and each showed a green light, visible only from out to sea, one marking Juno and the other Sword.

Thirty minutes later the fleet of warships opened fire on coastal targets. A new intensity of naval bombardment was reached, which the Americans would then surpass later in the same month whilst crushing the Japanese defences of the Marianas.

The German response from the numerous shore batteries remained very weak: 'almost negligible' according to an official British account. Several shells were fired at the transports, but none hit. There were no aircraft attacks on the ships. However the German navy did put in an early appearance.

## The only naval battle of the day

Three torpedo boats were sent on a reconnaissance mission from Le Havre, sailing at 0430. These were the T28, the *Jaguar* and the *Möwe*. Each was from a different class, all were basically small destroyers. The oldest was the *Möwe*, launched in 1926, before the Nazis came to power. Based on a First World War design she had a full load displacement of 1,290 tons, was 85.7m long and had a top speed of 33 knots. She was armed with three 105mm guns and six torpedo tubes. She would be sunk on 15th June by an air raid on the port of Le Havre.

*Jaguar* was launched a year later, slightly larger (89m long) and a knot and a half faster (34.6 knots). Like her predecessor she had a crew of 127 men, and her armament was identical, as was her fate.

However the T28 was one of the latest German vessels of this kind. She was of the 'Type 1939' (sometimes known to the Allies as the 'Elbings' as they were all built by Schichau at that port) and was launched in 1943. Full load displacement was 1,754 tons, length 102m and top speed 32.5 knots. Her armament consisted of four 105mm, four 37mm, and twelve 20mm guns plus six torpedo tubes. She had a complement of 206 men. She managed to survive the war, and was delivered to the British who handed her over to the French in 1946. She was renamed *Le Lorrain*, and served her new masters until July 1959.

Another view of the battleship *Warspite* firing three turret salvos at what must be close to the full elevation of 30 degrees, and therefore at long range. The small ship off her bow looks like a tug. (IWM)

After they had quitted their base these three ships sailed to the west, entering the smokescreen laid by Allied aircraft to mask the view of the Le Havre shore batteries and conceal the movements of the Allied fleet. Emerging from the smoke the Germans discovered this huge armada with astonishment. This did not prevent them seizing the opportunity of such a concentration of targets, and they rapidly launched all eighteen torpedoes carried before disappearing back into the smoke and to their base. Given the numbers of ships in such a small area of sea it is both surprising, and a small miracle, that only one torpedo found a target. This was the Norwegian destroyer *Svenner* (a transferred member of the British recently-built war emergency 'S' class). She was hit amidships, broke in two and sank immediately. Another torpedo near-missed the HQ ship *Largs*, the flagship of Rear-Admiral Talbot.

## Duel with the Longues battery

Just as we have given a detailed account of the action between a mainly American force and the Saint-Marcouf battery, it is interesting to do the same with the struggle between the battery at Longues and other Allied heavy ships.

During the night of the 5/6th June, ninety-nine heavy bombers attacked the battery, but here, as elsewhere, the 604 tons of bombs exploded behind their target, killing seven French civilians.

The personnel of the battery were therefore on guard well before daybreak. It was doubtless for this reason that the Allied fleet was soon reported, and the battery opened fire at 0537 some 20min before full day. Ten salvos were fired at the destroyer USS *Emmons* with no results, then the Germans shifted their fire to the battleship *Arkansas*, the best target visible. But she was too far off and the shells fell short in the water, whilst the old American battleship replied with full vigour, firing no less than 20 twelve-inch shells and 110 five-inch.

Under this deluge of fire the battery preferred to cease firing to the west and shift round to the east where numerous targets had appeared. By chance the German gunlayers chose the *Bulolo*, Headquarters ship and flagship of Force G, which was at anchor over 12,000 yards from the battery. From 0557 several shell-splashes appeared around *Bulolo*, whose crew hastily up-anchored to distance her from the shore. Meanwhile the cruiser *Ajax* closed the battery to reply. At about 11,000 yards she fired 114 six-inch shells and at 0620 the Longues battery ceased fire.

This ceasefire was only temporary. Abandoning targets out at sea the battery then fired on one side at Omaha and on the other at Gold. Under the circumstances only two out of the four guns,

guns, those at either end of the battery, could be served. The fire on Gold was taking effect and *Argonaut* came to the aid of *Ajax*, firing twenty-nine 5.25in shells whilst the latter despatched thirty-six rounds of 6in, with what British accounts describe as diabolical accuracy. It appears to have been a classic example of what a ship could do against a shore battery, given the difficulty of assigning the origin of particular hits when more than one ship is firing at the same time.

It is certainly sure that three out of the four guns of this battery were put out of action during the day. However this achievement must be shared. *Ajax* may indeed have been the most accurate bombarding ship, but we have already seen that *Arkansas* had already fired an impressive number

The 'S' class destroyer HMS *Scourge* photographed in the Solent. The round cylindrical structure to the left of the picture is one of the Victorian seaforts there, whilst the line of black objects in the water are the buoys supporting the net defence. (IWM)

of shells against the battery, and she was not the only other ship to engage it, as both *Georges Leygues* and *Montcalm* also fired on it. It was the former in fact which was the first to do so, at 0537. In mid-afternoon the fight with the battery was principally the concern of *Ajax* and the two French cruisers. At 1700 *Ajax* actually signalled *Georges Leygues* by searchlight to cease firing on Longues as that battery was 'reserved' as her target. No doubt her spotting was being confused by the French salvos. The French ship did not stop, and at about 1900 claimed two direct hits.

At the end of the day, the German battery finally and permanently closed down. When British infantry came on the scene on the morning of 7th June the gunners surrendered without any resistance, led by the

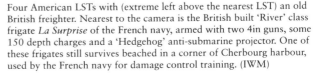

Four American LSTs with (extreme left above the nearest LST) an old British freighter. Nearest to the camera is the British built 'River' class frigate *La Surprise* of the French navy, armed with two 4in guns, some 150 depth charges and a 'Hedgehog' anti-submarine projector. One of these frigates still survives beached in a corner of Cherbourg harbour, used by the French navy for damage control training. (IWM)

Despite the (borrowed?) duffle coat the cap of this British officer speaking into a radio or loud hailer microphone on the bridge of a small warship looks as if it is khaki. (IWM)

commander of the battery, as Bertil Stjernfelt has recounted.

## The landing on Sword Beach

Sword Beach was considered as the most exposed of all the beaches, thanks to the closeness of the cities of Le Havre and Caen. It had also the most difficult of the seaward approaches. On the western side were the rocks near Bernières which were uncovered at high tide. On the eastern loomed the great sandbanks of Merville, to the east of the mouth of the Orne. Precise navigation was therefore vital, hence the presence of a midget submarine 7,000 yards offshore.

The proximity of the coastal batteries at the mouth of the Seine had little real effect on the approaches to Sword. Only one vessel, an LCI, caught fire after being hit. Other damage to landing craft was minimal as far as the artillery was concerned.

Because of rocks uncovering at low tide, H-hour was fixed quite a bit later than for the two American zones. This gained another 1hr 45mins of flood tide. The double advantage of the delay was to permit easy passage over the reefs, and to offer the naval guns extra bombardment time. On the other hand the tide seemed to gain faster than forecast (had the planners checked their tidal calculations?), and the first row of German obstacles was already covered by water when the landing craft reached it. It was therefore out of the question to try to avoid these invisible obstacles and many craft were damaged on the 'Element Cs' and 'Hedgehogs'. This did not have particularly severe consequences as the German response was weak, as Admiral Talbot himself wrote: 'The air was full of our bombers and fighters, and of the noise and smoke of our bombardments. The enemy was obviously stunned by the sheer weight of support we were meting out.'

A DUKW amphibious lorry reverses into the sea from the ramp of an LST. The helmets of its crew are of British type. A couple of armed trawlers pass in the background. (IWM)

## Frenchmen and tanks on the coast

Away from Sword Beach proper, two LCIs put down the 171 French marines (*fusiliers-marins*) of 4 Commando under Lieutenant de Vaisseau Kieffer. They captured the town rapidly, though with heavy losses, and then crossing the Caen canal and the river Orne, joined up with the British parachutists scattered around Merville the night before.

At almost the same moment the forty DD tanks of the 13th/18th Hussars, intended for Sword Beach, entered the water. There was a rough sea and the tanks were launched some 5,000 yards from the beach. Out of forty, thirty-two reached the beach at about 0730. At least two of them were sunk in collision with the LCTs bringing the engineers' tanks to the beach. However their fire was vital for silencing the guns which had the beach in enfilade.

The infantry began to land at almost the same time. Unlike the events at Omaha the landing at first went forward very well, except for the more or less grave damage caused by the submerged obstacles. Several LCAs were lost on their return trips to the LCIs offshore when the landing ramp, caught on an obstacle, suddenly fell off. The very choppy sea off the beach would then cause immediate foundering. On the beach itself the demolition teams rapidly accomplished their task, as did the numerous DD tanks. But as time passed the German reaction grew in intensity. Mortar fire became particularly troublesome.

## German counterattacks

At 0930 eight German twin engined Junkers Ju88 bombers appeared above Sword Beach. Their bombing was inaccurate and only caused light damage. This was the only German bombing raid made on the 6th, though further raids took place the

This picture appears to show members of the crew of a British LCI (H) about to drop one of the four bow gangways to allow the commandos waiting behind to land on Sword Beach. A number of vehicles are already gathered on the beach, including DD Shermans (recognisable by their collapsed flotation skirts) and probably the engineer's BARV (beach recovery) tanks and other specialised armour. (IWM)

An LST disembarking the tanks of 13th/18th Hussars on Hermanville Beach between Lion-sur-Mer and Riva-Bella. The smoke is from a smoke screen, not the vessel burning, despite appearances. (IWM)

These unfortunate soldiers of the 3rd Division are having to wade out of deep water on to Sword Beach, having been landed from an LSI(L) clearly handicapped by its comparatively deep draught. It looks as if this group are the last to land, and the LSI appears to be winding up its landing gangways and trying to withdraw backwards into deeper water. (IWM)

they had in this sector the only armoured division close to the beaches, the 21st Panzerdivision. It had been put on alert by von Rundstedt from daybreak, as was the 1st Panzerkorps. During the morning Hitler forbade any movement of the SS armoured corps, but authorised action by 21st Panzerdivision. That unit had already been fighting the British parachutists who had jumped into an area held by one of the Panzergrenadier regiments.

At 1000 the division passed to the command of 84 Korps, which held the coast. It was then readied for attacking the parachutists to the east of the Orne. But at 1300, because of the news of the Sword landing, General Marcks, commander of 84 Korps, ordered 21st Panzerdivision to attack to the west of the river, towards the Allied bridgehead. The change of objective produced a further delay and when the Panzers finally attacked at around 1600, they were rapidly halted along the canal by the men of the 3rd Division and their M 10 tank-destroyers. But this equally had the effect of putting a stop to all British progress.

A little more to the west a battalion of Panzergrenadiers made a deep thrust to the north and nearly reached the sea itself between Sword and Juno, thereby cutting all land communication between the British and the Canadians. But this wedge forced into the British lines could not serve at all as a starting point for an attack on the beaches themselves. Naval support was on the alert and any sighting of tanks was greeted by 6in or even 15in shells from *Warspite*.

In these conditions the first German counteroffensive on any scale finished without appreciable results. In the evening 3rd Division's bridgehead reached about 4 miles inland. The Panzergrenadiers of 21st Panzerdivision had prevented it linking up with Juno, but on the other hand it was already linked at Ouistreham and Bénouville with the large pocket occupied by the parachutists of 6th Airborne.

## Juno, the Canadian beach

The seas breaking on the Essarts de Bernières and on the rocks of Ver-sur-Mer were so rough that H-hour was put back 10min at Juno Beach. Here the first assault waves reached land at 0755, nearly an hour and a half after the Americans. This delay, as at Sword, had the consequence that the landing craft had to beach

following night. As for German fighters, their only appearance was when the ace Pips Priller led a patrol consisting of himself and one other Focke-Wulf Fw190. In all ten German aircraft against nearly 4,000 Allied machines, a completely different situation from two years earlier when the Luftwaffe competed on equal terms with the RAF over Dieppe.

At 0943 the entire assault brigade had landed on Sword Beach, only 18min later than its timetable laid down. However the two following brigades, which were to disembark shortly afterwards, were held out to sea, because the battle was not developing favourably. Whilst the landing craft of the first wave came back out from the beach declaring 'It's a piece of cake', the situation was worsening by the end of the morning. The two follow-up brigades could not be landed before the afternoon. When the exits from the beach were finally cleared it was getting too late to march on Caen, which should have been reached on the same day if things had gone according to plan.

It soon became evident that advance was not possible, because the Germans had not remained passive. In fact

amongst the German obstacles and not in front of them as had been intended. There were occasional losses, but the obstacles were very scattered. Twenty out of twenty-four LCAs which had carried one assault battalion were destroyed on these obstacles whilst going back out to fetch more troops.

The officer commanding the LCTs carrying the DD tanks considered the sea too rough for his charges, so instead ordered his large landing craft into the beach itself to land the tanks with greater certainty. One group of DDs were launched 800 yards out, however, without suffering loss. They arrived on the beach just after the infantry and immediately engaged the guns taking the latter in enfilade. They were followed about 10min later by the rest of the Sherman DDs. This slight delay had troublesome consequences because the demolition teams were pinned down for several long minutes and were unable to destroy the obstacles already mostly submerged by the tide. These would cause extra difficulties for the following waves until the tide ebbed.

The cruisers and destroyers continued to work miracles in silencing German guns. The cruisers HMS *Diadem* and HMS *Belfast* took on the batteries situated inland. Meanwhile the eleven destroyers hammered the coastal defences. This stopped most of the shelling and greatly aided exploitation towards the interior.

LCAs landing French Canadian soldiers of the Chaudière Regiment on Juno Beach near to Courseulles after the initial action had died down. The tank on the extreme left is a DD Sherman, whilst the nearest tank in the centre is a Churchill with the characteristic shape of the 95mm 'Petard' spigot mortar of an AVRE (Armoured Vehicle, Royal Engineers). (IWM)

Unfortunately not all the guns were destroyed, and they opened a renewed fire on the following waves. Thus No 48 Royal Marine Commando, which landed just after the waves of Canadians, was subjected to intense machine gun and mortar fire. Their LCAs, despite their reinforced hulls, were severely damaged by the submerged obstacles and shell bursts, causing appreciable losses. All the surviving machine-gun nests on the beach itself came back to life as the marines appeared. The commandos were soon pinned down and it needed intervention by the destroyers to free them.

By the end of the morning, the beach and its access routes was cleared and activity redoubled in intensity. The consolidation forces arrived from out at sea in large ships which anchored and offloaded the 7th Armoured Division and part of the 51st (Highland) Division.

Inland the Canadian advance met little opposition. At the end of the day the bridgehead was some 4 miles

At Saint-Aubin-sur-Mer, at the eastern extremity of Juno Beach, the Germans mounted a vigorous resistance to the attack of the Royal Marine Commandos of the 4th Special Service Brigade. Numbers of landing craft, like the LCT and LCA seen here, were damaged and thrown up against the water's edge. The banners by the damaged wall were erected by the British engineers to indicate the direction to follow for craft approaching from the sea. (IWM)

deep, but armoured patrols had reached the main road (Route Nationale 13) between Caen and Bayeux, at nearly 8 miles from the coast. The day's operations had cost the Canadians 335 killed and 611 wounded.

## Gold Beach, the westernmost in the British sector

At Gold, the western British beach, the coast is relatively wild, with few habitations apart from the village of Asnelles and the hamlet of La Rivière. The coast was held by the 716th Infantry Division, a static unit of low morale, a good third of whom were Ukrainian or Polish.

The preliminary bombardment was by the cruisers *Ajax, Argonaut, Emerald* and *Orion*, plus the Dutch gunboat *Flores*, assisted by thirteen destroyers. They were to have a fierce struggle with two strongpoints, but the initial bombardment went off successfully; the only opposition came from the battery at Longues, as already described.

The sea was rough, the LCTs carrying the amphibious Shermans were pushed forward almost to the shore in order not to lose any of these tanks in the fierce chop prevalent off Gold.

The infantry landings began punctually at 0725. The leading elements of the 50th (Northumbrian) Division easily swept aside the majority of the enemy defences, except at Asnelles and La Rivière, where the battle lasted all morning. However the landing was not very rapid, because the beach was absolutely covered in obstacles. There were more than 2,500 along some three miles of foreshore, weighing a total of 900 tons. Because of the storm winds the tide rose more rapidly than forecast, or rather its rate of flooding was greater than that laid down in the tide tables. As a result at Gold, as at the other British beaches. the obstacles were to a great degree already submerged when the landing craft beached, which produced a number of shipwrecks. Fortunately hostile fire was not intense and the infantry did not have to disembark in a hail of bullets.

It was not actually till noon that the British infantry finally debouched from the beach, after having to fight very hard with the enemy, especially around Asnelles, a little straggling village held by the men of the 352nd Infantry Division, the same as at Omaha Beach.

The choppy sea did not make the disembarking from an LCI(S) like this, near Saint-Aubin, particularly easy. Here a heavily loaded commando falls off the gangway. (IWM)

## The struggle for Asnelles

As elsewhere the preliminary air bombardment failed totally, the bombs falling at random inland. The landing craft gunboats and rocket projectors were also very far from accurate. This was partly because their fire control officer had been wounded just before the assault.

When the British infantry disembarked it soon encountered the Germans in the bunkers and fortified houses of Asnelles. Losses remained moderate, however, because of the support of the Sherman DDs and the Churchill AVRE tanks of the Royal Engineers. The latter in particular, with the other specialised tanks (called 'funnies') saved the British many casualties in their landings. The Americans, perhaps, might have had fewer losses had they not spurned the aid of such specialised armour. However on this occasion they could not make the attack on Asnelles any easier. The tanks which tried were knocked out one after another. The destroyers were called in but it was difficult to land shells on targets which were so well concealed. Besides, their 4.7in or 4in shells were inadequate to pierce the thickness of concrete on the bunkers.

Finally, at about 1600, the German defence began to weaken. Tanks supporting one another began to achieve several decisive hits and the intensity of German fire diminished. The AVREs with their 'Petard' spigot mortars firing huge demolition charges, opened up at point-blank range on the bunkers and silenced them. The advance towards the west could begin again, but it went no further than Arromanches, whilst the British should have joined up with the Americans from Omaha that evening.

One of the classic images of the landing, still at Saint-Aubin, with the marine commandos landing from LCI(S)s. Two men struggle with a motor scooter. (IWM)

This picture must have been taken late on the 6th or even the next day. It is high tide and men of one of the later waves struggle ashore from LCI(L)s. The small space left between beach and sea wall is crammed with men and vehicles. (IWM)

Troops from the 50th Division land upon Gold Beach. One of those burdened with a bicycle has just fallen off the gangway of the nearer LSI(L). Beyond the further one is the bow of an LST(4). (IWM)

## The Ukrainians of La Rivière

Whilst the Germans fought to the end at Asnelles, the same did not happen at La Rivière, the principal strongpoint of the eastern sector of Gold Beach. Early in the morning an 88mm gun managed to destroy two engineer tanks, a Churchill AVRE and a minesweeping Sherman 'flail'. But another Churchill managed to get close making full use of 'dead ground' and fired point-blank at the embrasure. The German gun was silenced. It was then nearly 1000 and this incident provoked the rout of the Ukrainian troops. At the lighthouse of La Rivière, the defenders came out carrying white flags, and the British discovered the body of a German officer, no doubt killed by his own men, even if they claimed it was suicide. The taking of the lighthouse had bad consequences for the German coastal artillery, because the British found an observation post there, probably linked to the batteries at Longues and Grayes. The latter, situated only 800 yards from the beach, was abandoned before the end of the morning thanks to the surrender of the Ukrainians. It had lost one of its 120mm guns to a direct hit from the cruiser *Orion*, but it had also caused some losses to the landing craft.

On the evening of 6th June, the beach-head at Gold had a varied appearance. Towards the south the 50th Division had nearly reached Bayeux, its objective for the day. On the other hand to the west No 47 Commando was far from its target, Port-en-Bessin. Decimated and isolated, it had lost all its radios and nearly all its LCAs; it was to require 36hr to outflank Port-en-Bessin and then take it.

This did not prevent the bridgehead looking solid on the evening of 6th June, especially because a link had been made with the Canadians from Juno.

## The effect of the naval bombardments

The conclusions that can be drawn from the results of naval bombardment in the British sector are equally valid for the American.

Doubtless the Germans were best placed to judge

Gold Beach on the 7th at Hamel near Asnelles. The clear-up has already begun. Beach obstacles have been moved out of the way, and the two bulldozers (one armoured) are resting. The A/A tank on the right has lost its tracks (one in the foreground), but its Bofors gun is still manned. In the background are the ubiquitous LSTs. (IWM)

A damaged Jeep and a DUKW which looks as if it had set off a mine are pictured here on Sword Beach. The craft half-hidden by spray is a ramped, powered, landing barge coming through the surf to beach. Behind her is an LCT apparently heading out to sea. (IWM)

for themselves the effects of the bombardment. General Dollman, head of Seventh Army, sent Rommel a message on the evening of 6th June which had much to say about the power of ships' guns: 'The guns installed in open positions had been deterred before coming into action by the enemy's preliminary naval bombardment. The coastal artillery were most often put out of action by direct hits on the casemates. Counterattacks ... in the neighbourhood of the coast had suffered very heavy losses because of the fire of enemy warships.'

It is not impossible that Dollman was even exaggerating the effects of the bombardment a little, in order to explain the reasons for the failure of his troops. In fact direct hits were not that frequent. At Houlgate battery, for example, two guns, which were inside casemates, only received one direct hit from a very heavy shell out of the 218 fifteen- and sixteen-inch shells fired at it by *Nelson, Ramillies, Roberts* and *Erebus*, on D-Day and the following days. At Bénerville, neither of the two guns under cover was hit, despite the repeated firing of 16in and 15in shells (284 in all), and also fifty-six 6in projectiles, by *Rodney, Warspite, Ramillies* and *Roberts*. It was only the battery at Longues that was hit twice by shells which passed through the embrasures of two of the casemates. An excellent success, but owing much to luck, the sort

of luck that comes with the expenditure of large quantities of ammunition. In the American sector, too, the firing on the Saint-Marcouf battery had also been very effective, but had not succeeded in completely silencing the guns.

After the landing the Admiralty had a study made of the counter-battery fire of the fleet. The report showed that it was relatively easy to silence a battery in an open position with no concrete protection. It was, however, very difficult to wipe it out completely. We have seen several times on D-Day German batteries reduced to silence for several minutes or even hours, then opening fire again. The problem was even more difficult with artillery in casemates, since only a direct hit could put these out of action.

On the other hand the effect of the bombardment on neighbouring troops was marked. For men well protected in thick bunkers, like those who served the coastal artillery, the effect was negligible. It was evidently considerable, however, on men in trenches or other shallower protection.

In any case it is wrong to believe that only direct hits by naval guns are effective. Just like aerial

Despite this damage from a direct hit or a mine, this LST managed to cross back to England in a terrifying 15hr voyage, but was in such a state that she had to be scrapped. (IWM)

bombardment which quite simply did not destroy any coastal battery because the few bombs that actually hit did not have the penetrative power to pass through the concrete, the shells of the fleet which dug huge craters on the outskirts of the batteries did not directly cause the loss of a single gun. However they cut telephone lines and broke all communications with the outside world, making any co-ordinated fire virtually impossible. Thus the battery at Longues, certainly deprived of its means of communication, could only fire at a very slow rate.

This lack of liaison is certainly one of the reasons of the failure of the German coastal defence guns. These, despite the incredible number of targets, had not been able to do more than to contribute to the loss of a single American destroyer and a few dozen landing craft. No spotting worthy of the name had been done, whilst the teams of Spitfires and Mustangs had done a splendid job of directing Allied fire.

## The balance sheet at midnight, 6th June

At the end of D-Day it was evident to the Allied command that the landing had succeeded, at a cost slightly less than forecast: 4,300 soldiers on the British side and about 6,000 for the Americans. This comprised killed, wounded and missing (the majority of the latter prisoners). These figures are the total for all the assault divisions; that is to say, five infantry and three airborne divisions. Taking into account the total numbers engaged and the strength of the German defences, these losses could be considered light. There are enormous discrepancies between areas. For example on Utah Beach the 4th Division only lost 197 men, whilst on Omaha the losses exceeded 2,000. In general the parachutists suffered worse than the infantry, because of the way they were dispersed.

To succeed in landing five, or eight, divisions, was certainly not sufficient. Now they had to be supplied with munitions and food, whilst at the same time building up the number of divisions engaged without delay. It was necessary to exploit the initial successes without leaving the Germans with time to pull themselves together.

In this respect, also, the situation seemed rather favourable. Thus by midnight on 6th June an impressive total of men had been landed, despite all the delays, especially at Omaha. The precise figure was 132,715 men. For matériel we only have the British figures, but they, too, were impressive: 6,000 vehicles (900 of them tanks or other armour), 240 field guns, 80 AA guns, 280 anti-tank guns. The number of tanks and armoured vehicles is particularly amazing, for at the same moment the only German armoured division present, 21st Panzer, had no more than 140 tanks, the majority of which were of poor quality.[1]

The only weakness as night came on the 6th was in the supply of munitions. Expenditure had been, as always, greater than had been foreseen.

We do not have precise figures from the Americans for 6th June, but by the evening of the 10th no less than 62,550 men, 4,133 vehicles and 9,986 tons of matériel had been landed on Utah Beach alone. At the same date the Americans had five infantry divisions, two airborne divisions, and one armoured division in Normandy, an impressive total.

The losses of warships were also low. On the day of the landings itself there were only two relatively important vessels lost, the American destroyer *Glennon* and the Norwegian destroyer *Svenner*. Besides these, several minesweepers had been sunk, blown up on the

[1] The 21st Panzerdivision was the exception that proves the rule. All the other German armoured divisions to be engaged in Normandy had excellent equipment. Their tanks were mostly much greater in individual fighting power than their Anglo-American equivalents.

weapons they were trying to clear. Landing craft losses were relatively low, in all respects lower than anticipated by the Allied planners. However, many had been damaged by the heavy seas and even more by the German defences. In the British sector the total of damaged LCAs and LCTs reached 258. It was slightly less in the American sector, the LCVPs being better seaboats than the LCAs, the beach obstacles having been avoided at low tide, and only two divisions having been landed instead of three.

In this picture taken on 7th June we can see a group of British LCTs waiting at low tide for the sea to return to unbeach. The nearest vessel contains a load of German prisoners. The next has a shell hole above the first 'T' of the inscription 'All looters will be shot'. Two armoured bulldozers and a couple of DUKWs can be seen on the beach, with a column of lorries behind. (IWM)

A group of German prisoners under British escort pass a beached
American LCI near Ver-sur-Mer. (IWM)

# 8  The Artificial Ports

One of the 'Corncobs' scuttled as blockships for the 'Gooseberry' breakwaters was the *Alynbank*, a merchantman which had been converted to an auxiliary anti-aircraft vessel. Her 4in guns had been removed, but their positions are still visible here. (IWM)

MOST TOURISTS VISITING the Normandy coast today doubtless believe that there was only one artificial port. Actually there were two, one off Omaha Beach, the other off Arromanches. The storm of 20th June totally destroyed the first, to such effect that there is no visible trace left. However the port of Arromanches, though it has been literally eroded over the years, still has numerous remaining parts which are visible, even at high tide.

## Failure of the bubble port

From the beginning of work on projects for landing in France it seemed that no existing port would be captured intact. The tragedy of Dieppe in August 1942 only underlined this sad reality. However, in order for the landing to have a chance of succeeding it was essential that the front-line units should not only be supplied, but also continually reinforced. Logistics were the key to success. In order to maintain the flow of

supplies at a high level the transport and landing vessels had to be able to land hundreds of tons of matériel, of munitions, etc per day. How could all this be done, in the knowledge that the Channel coast was badly sheltered, that the weather never remains good for more than a few days on end, and that storms follow one another in a pattern of about one a month? These storms were a true menace, because there was not only the risk of ships being flung ashore, but also, even in the most optimistic of cases, when actual damage was limited, there would, nevertheless, be a total cessation of the arrival, unloading and return of the supply ships. As all gaps in the arrival of supplies risked a loss of the initiative, this could mean the resurgence of the Germans.

General aerial view of the Arromanches Mulberry in full use. To the right is the breakwater partly formed from the concrete 'Phoenix' units, partly from blockships. In the centre of the port is a long jetty made of many Lobnitz pierhead units and connected to the shore by the floating pontoons known as 'Whales'. Around and between these elements the ships and craft come and go in large numbers. (IWM)

This was so alarming that during long months in 1942 the planners indicated that no port meant no invasion attempt. Commodore Hughes-Hallett's splendid statement in 1943 about taking a port with the invasion force has already been quoted. But in what form?

The first British suggestions were generated by the Admiralty's Department of Miscellaneous Weapons and Devices, which picked up the far-fetched idea of an American swimming-bath proprietor called Brasher, who had observed that the river Hudson was calm in certain spots, even in the most violent storms. In trying to understand this astonishing phenomenon, he discovered that the calm areas corresponded to the places where thousands of air bubbles came to the surface, escaping from tunnels under the river.

In 1916 Brasher experimented with a bubble-breakwater in Florida, made of pierced pipes through which compressed air was blown. The technique proved too costly and complicated to be put into operation, so the project was abandoned. However it interested a writer who recorded it as a curiosity in the pages of the *Scientific American*. A member of DMWD discovered the article in an old issue of this journal, and the project was put to the test in 1943.

In the absence of anything better, and despite the obvious cost, work was initiated on this far-fetched project. The first trials in a pond at Kensington, were perfectly successful. The bubbles effectively undermined waves and made them disappear. It only remained to try the system on a realistic scale. If that worked, the imaginative picture of the creation of a large port off the Normandy coast protected from bad weather by millions of bubbles might become a reality.

Sadly for this striking vision, what worked perfectly at 1:50 scale in a London pond, obstinately refused to function at all at full size. It was not, incidentally, the technique itself that was at fault. However at that date the available technology was not adequate to install a gigantic pipe system and keep it supplied with air at sufficient pressure. Besides, sand would rapidly jam the orifices, and the compressed air would then tend to raise the pipes and break them. The questions of how to transport the equipment and keep it in place remained unanswered for the trials were abandoned.

Another apparently bizarre idea which was developed at this stage was a huge aircraft carrier made of reinforced ice known as 'pykrete'. Named *Habbakuk*, this would have been several times the size of the largest liner and virtually unsinkable. Large scale trials were reasonably successful, but the overwhelming scale of Allied air superiority removed any need there may have been for a floating airfield of this nature as part of the support of the invasion, and no more came of it.

## Mulberries and Gooseberries

It is difficult to establish the exact paternity of artificial ports of the kind used off Normandy, and an attempt to do so would fill a book of this size. It came, in fact, from the putting together of numerous new ideas, many of which came from Mountbatten's Combined Operations Headquarters. One of the best descriptions is given by the official historian of the US Navy: 'In their final form two artificial harbours were produced, both built by British labour; 'Mulberry A' for the American beaches, and 'Mulberry B' for the British sector. Any ship approaching a Mulberry would first encounter a floating breakwater composed of 'bombardons', floating steel structures, to break up wave action. Next came the 2,200yd breakwater of thirty-one concrete caissons called 'phoenixes', each as tall as a five-storey house, to be towed across the Channel and sunk. The phoenixes formed a sea wall on two sides of an artificial harbour about two square miles in area, equal to that of the harbour of Gibraltar, and big enough for sever Liberty ships and twelve smaller vessels to moor. Within each harbour were three 'whale' pontoon-shaped runways anchored at their seaward ends to the 'Lobnitz' pierheads, named after the engineer who designed them to rise and fall with the tide. This combination would enable LSTs to unload at any stage of the tide, and provided their wheeled cargoes with a one-way road for rolling ashore.'

The long line of scuttled merchantmen forming a Gooseberry are seen from aboard an old excursion paddle steamer turned into an auxiliary A/A vessel (see the aircraft-style perspex machine gun turret). (IWM)

Besides the two Mulberries, five other smaller and simpler ports were planned. These were the 'Gooseberries', which consisted of a line of blockships ('Corncobs') scuttled parallel to the coast to afford protection, albeit limited, to the landing craft of various sizes. One Gooseberry was planned for each landing beach, and they were all put in place, with a great degree of success. All the photographs taken after the landing showing beached LSTs, also have in the background a line of semi-submerged blockships.

## Difficult construction

After four years of war, the efforts of construction and ingenuity demanded of Great Britain were enormous, and its industry was scarcely able to cope. Thousands of men, almost all over the country, worked on Project Mulberry, without

A photo taken at the same time as the previous one, with the same LCVP (347) in the foreground. Probably taken during the scuttling of the Gooseberries, hence the activity aboard. Also alongside the line of blockships are a DUKW, an MFV (Motor Fishing Vessel) and at least two tugs holding the sinking vessels in place. (IWM)

Two old cruisers in the line of scuttled blockships. The nearer is the Dutch *Sumatra*, the further the 'D' class HMS *Danae* (IWM)

knowing much about what they were making, and still less about the full picture. In fact everything was kept very compartmented; everyone worked on a small part of the project, in order to restrict the danger of information getting out.

This was made easier by the fact that responsibility for the different elements was divided between the War Office on the one side and the Admiralty on the other. At the beginning, around mid-1943, the sailors and the soldiers were still disputing over who should have overall control. The Admiralty noted that it had always had control over taking charge of and repairing captured ports. The War Office replied that this would

not be a captured port. In the end it needed a decision taken at Chiefs of Staff level to end the bureaucratic bickering. It was, logically, the Admiralty which was in charge of the design and functioning of the artificial ports. However the War Office controlled the construction of both the reinforced concrete caissons and the diverse elements of the 'Whales' or floating pontoons.

The most characteristic element of the Mulberries was, without doubt, the type of floating caisson called Phoenixes. With an average length of 180 feet they displaced between 2,000 and 6,000 tons. The construction did not, in itself, pose too many difficulties. However these enormous cubes took a lot of space, and their storage was achieved by an original method. They were sunk off shallow beaches, which uncovered at low tide. Shortly before the landing the army refloated them, not without difficulty as the pumps they had at their disposal had not sufficient capacity and an appeal had to be sent to the Navy, which was only too pleased to show off its ability to the footsloggers.

The War Office also threw itself on the Admiralty's mercy over the difficult problem of the Bombardons, the floating breakwaters, whose cruciform structure appeared to be dangerous in cases when the moorings broke. In this particular case the War Office was right, as we will see the Bombardons rapidly became dangers to navigation.

The other key element of the artificial port were the Whales which allowed LSTs to discharge their vehicles directly onto a floating road. After a certain amount of groping in the dark a successful answer was discovered in mid-1943, and a full scale trial was made with one and a half miles of floating quay. As the results were satisfactory the War Office ordered another ten miles of quay and fifteen pierheads, the ends of the quays which floated up and down on articulated arms according to the level of the sea. For several months the War Office was rather worried about the slowness of the building of these items, but by June 1944 an adequate number were available.

The forecast of the time needed for construction was three weeks, and capacity was intended to be 7,000 tons of matériel a day. Between them, therefore, Mulberries A and B would therefore make possible the landing of 14,000 tons daily. This would equal five million tons per year. It was intended, however, to stop using the artificial ports once Cherbourg and other large ports were liberated and cleared.

The two cruisers seen from a little further away. The line of scuttled ships gave shelter to heavily laden and not very seaworthy craft like the two DUKWs seen here. (IWM)

## Gooseberries reinforce the Mulberries

Towards the end of 1943, some senior officers at the Admiralty became concerned at the potential of the Phoenix caissons to survive the storms which rage in the Channel, and especially in July. Could these huge concrete cubes survive the short wicked waves which were quite capable of sweeping over big stone jetties. As doubt remained about the solidity of the caissons under extreme conditions, Admiral Tennant proposed the use of block ships to make solid breakwaters. These block ships were old worn-out vessels, stripped and heavily ballasted. They would be sunk in a line which would then give shelter. Admiral Ramsay was enthused by the idea. In January, therefore, the plan was modified by the inclusion of a 'Gooseberry' per landing beach. Two of these were alongside, and an integral part of, the two Mulberries, whilst the three others were placed, respectively, at Varreville (for Utah), and at Courseulles and off Ouistreham for the British sector. To make these five breakwaters, fifty-five old cargo ships (twenty-three of them American) were requisitioned, and also four old warships. Two of these were old battleships, the French *Courbet* and the *Centurion* which the Royal Navy had converted to a

Four Phoenix caissons have been placed in line here; a fifth, in the background, is being pulled into place by a tug. The Bofors anti-aircraft guns on each unit are already manned. The soldier looking uncomfortable on the bridge of ropes may be transferring to another unit, or another vessel, from the army-manned salvage vessel in the foreground. (IWM)

This photo of a Phoenix unit was taken on 12th June, before the Arromanches Mulberry was operational. The line of ships in the background are blockships, as their lowness in the water indicates. The ship on the extreme right of the photo is probably the British cruiser *Hawkins* or her sister *Frobisher*. (IWM)

This strange caisson is a Lobnitz pierhead unit. The four 'spuds' - the pillars on which it floats up and down - are in the lowered position. It appears to be in place off Arromanches, but still awaiting its floating jetty. Notice the rapid launching life-raft on the ramp on the nearest corner. (IWM)

A Lobnitz unit being manoeuvred into place by tugs onto the end of its Whale jetty. The other end of this floating jetty would reach the shore. The pillars on the Lobnitz are in their highest position. **(IWM)**

radio-controlled target ship between the wars. The other two were cruisers, HMS *Durban* and the Dutch *Sumatra*. The *Courbet* was the only one of these 'Corncobs' not to make the voyage across the Channel under her own power. She had to be towed like the

Phoenix caissons. All the others, assembled in Scottish ports, sailed well in advance of the invasion. Some had to leave on 28th May, since they were scarcely capable of 6 knots! Their first destination was Poole harbour, where they assembled into a convoy for the Channel crossing. Their arrival was planned for the evening of 6th June, to put the Gooseberries in place immediately and to give all the shallow draught vessels shelter of some kind from the start.

## A deepwater port

The diverse elements of the Gooseberries and Mulberries between them created a port, or rather several ports of different depths. The Gooseberries were sunk in water of 2½ to 3 fathoms. The draught of vessels taking advantage of their shelter could not be more than 12ft to 15ft. Inside the vast semi-circle formed by the Phoenix caissons, depths reached about 30ft, which was enough to allow use by large ships. The Bombardons were moored on the 10 fathom line, a depth of some 60ft. In comparison the access channel to the port of Le Havre is today only dredged to the permanent depth of 15½m (about 50ft).

The port of Arromanches, Mulberry B, inside the shelter of the Phoenix caissons, could accommodate 7 deep-draught vessels, 20 coasters, 400 tugs and other auxiliary vessels, and 1,000 small craft, DUKWs or LCAs. The space between the Phoenix caissons and the Bombardons offered extra capacity. The Bombardons began to be put in place on the 7th, and their installation completed on the 12th (Mulberry A) and 13th (Mulberry B). At first these were very effective, even if only a single line was moored instead of the two experimented with at Weymouth. On the 14th the two new barriers stayed in place despite a

rough sea. The Bombardons hardly moved and in their shelter the choppy waves were no more than 1½ft high, whilst outside the swells broke in plumes of spray about 20ft high. It was therefore undeniable that the system worked; but how strong was it?

A Whale jetty under tow. Road units are placed on individual floating pontoons stayed with wire rope. The difficulty was to combine sufficient flexibility with adequate strength so the articulated structure moved with the tides and the waves, but did not tear itself to pieces. As a tow for a tug the structure must have been a nightmare. (IWM)

## The question of towage

As they were completed the Phoenixes were assembled in the Thames and off Dungeness, where they were carefully sunk in sandy or muddy bottoms with gentle slopes such as at Selsey. The parts of the Whale pontoons were assembled at Dungeness and Selsey, also in the Solent. Finally the Bombardons were collected in the port of Portland.

At the time of the landing, several convoys of the total of 400 separate structures which made up the two harbours had to be brought together. The total weight of the structures was in the region of a million

and a half tons. No fewer than 10,000 men were involved in the towing and positioning; 160 tugs, mostly of American origin were requisitioned for this task - but the number was not adequate for transporting all the structures in one go.

## The beginnings

The first convoys left England on 6th June. These consisted of the 'Corncobs' for the Gooseberries, and also of Bombardons and Phoenixes.

Work commenced at Omaha on the 7th with a detailed investigation of the best positions to sink the Corncobs and Phoenixes. Lighted buoys were placed

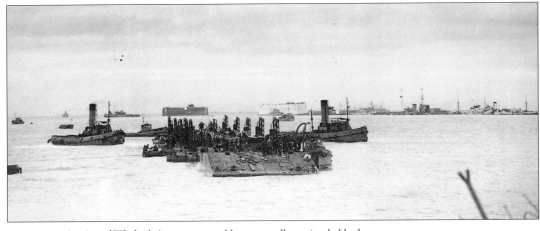

A string of Whales being manoeuvred by two small tugs (probably the 'war emergency' type known as 'TIDs') and two motor launches, plus what looks like a DUKW. Behind is the row of blockships, Phoenixes and a much larger tug. (IWM)

An end-on view of the offshore end of a Whale jetty under construction off Arromanches. (IWM)

June. This was the moment when an LST came to the end of a Whale pontoon and began to offload thirty-eight vehicles which were ashore within 38min only, with much less work, worry and problems than if they had been landed via LCMs or LCTs. Eleven LCTs unloaded in like manner on the 16th and 17th June, in an average time of 1hr 4min, as against 10hr to 12hr had they been offloading directly onto the beach. The gain of time was therefore considerable.

## Getting up to cruising speed

From 17th June a second floating quay was put into operation, and the third was being completed when the storm struck.

The timetable was almost identical in the British sector. The Phoenixes began to be sunk in place on the 9th, whilst the first parts of a Whale pontoon were being assembled. At the end of ten days, that is on 16th June, the Bombardons were in place and half of the Phoenix breakwater installed. It is stated that the American Mulberry was operational sooner than its British equivalent. All this was not achieved without loss, mostly due to bad weather. Two tugs, two Phoenixes and five Whale tows were lost in the Channel. On 12th June Admiral Tennant forbade any night crossings with Phoenixes, whilst Whale tows were only allowed to cross in calm conditions with little wind.

Therefore, for the first two weeks, apart from at Omaha, landings were made with only the shelter of the Gooseberries and the two lines of Bombardons at Arromanches. At Arromanches itself work took longer than at Omaha, so that no vessel had been able to use it before the terrible storm of 19th, 20th and 21st June (see Chapter 9). It is enough here to state that Mulberry B could not start work until 29th June, to reach a daily total of 6,000 tons landed from 8th July. The floating quay for LSTs did not start being used until 19th July. This then permitted a clear increase in unloading, which then surpassed 7,000 tons a day, reaching a record of 11,000 tons on 29th July.

The retarding effect on plans was therefore important, especially because of the storm. The ports ought to have been operational from D+14; the one at Omaha actually began on D+10, but the storm then threw everything into question again. As for

in the chosen places. The first Corncobs arrived the same day and three were scuttled before nightfall. This work was somewhat disturbed by German artillery which took these old ships for troop transports.

At Utah Beach the blockships were put in place on the 8th, again under German artillery fire. The Germans claimed a ship sunk that day, which was in fact a Corncob deliberately sunk by its crew!

On that same day the first Phoenixes arrived off Omaha, and were sunk. It was simply a matter of opening several valves to let in water. The task was more difficult with the Corncobs, because it was essential that the blockships went straight down, exactly where they were intended to go. They were heavily ballasted and fitted with explosive charges placed in all compartments and set off simultaneously.

On 10th June Omaha's Gooseberry was complete, a day before Utah's. Work having been carried on at high speed, Mulberry A was operational from 1630 on 16th

Arromanches, that port only received its first cargoes on D+23, and did not reach its true 'cruising speed' until 8th July, that is D+32. The planned total of 7,000 tons per day was only rarely reached or passed, and between 20th July and the end of August the average was fixed at 6,000 tons daily.

## The debate on the usefulness of the Mulberries

After the war several historians, mostly American, but notably the Australian Chester Wilmot, questioned the real usefulness of the Mulberries. They made the clear and implacable statement that whilst the British managed more or less to secure their daily 6,000 tons at Arromanches, the Americans managed a much more important daily volume directly across the beaches without any help from an artificial port after the destruction of Mulberry A. They landed 15,000 tons a day at Omaha and 8,000 at Utah, a total of 23,000, four times as much as the British one.

Wilmot wrote: 'Undismayed by the destruction of their artificial harbour, the Americans applied to the development of the Omaha and Utah anchorages their tremendous talent for invention and organisation. In defiance of orthodox opinion they beached coasters and unloaded them direct into Army lorries at low tide. ... during July the Americans here handled more than

This view of the inshore end of one of the Arromanches Whale jetties shows how the road units linked the flotation pontoons. (IWM)

twice the tonnage which passed through the British Mulberry.

'The achievement has led to the suggestion that the vast expenditure of effort and materials on the artificial harbours was in fact unnecessary, and that the same build-up could have been achieved with a few more landing craft and ferries. .... [this] ignores strategic and psychological factors of great importance. When the Overlord plan was drawn up there was no shipping to spare, and no evidence that a large cross-Channel invasion could be maintained over open beaches. Strategically the 'possession' of Mulberry gave the planners freedom to choose a landing area well away from the heavily fortified major ports; psychologically it gave the Allied High Command a degree of confidence without which the venture, which seemed so hazardous, might not have been undertaken.'[1]

Several other witnesses, including some senior British officers, tend to show that the role of the artificial port had been somewhat over-estimated. So Captain Harold Hickling, Royal Navy, Chief of Staff to Tennant himself, has declared that the Mulberries' contribution to the supplying of the Allied armies in Normandy was

[1]Chester Wilmot *The Struggle for Europe*. Collins, London, 1952

This aerial photo of the eastern end of the Arromanches Mulberry very clearly shows the breakwater effect of the Phoenixes in keeping the inner anchorage calm. Notice the floating crane on a square pontoon in the middle of the picture. The settlement in the background is Asnelles. (IWM)

A closer aerial view of part of the Arromanches Mulberry. The line of Phoenixes has been bolstered by others brought from the shattered Mulberry A. One Liberty ship and a British war-emergency cargo ship (*Empire Perdita*) are moored to buoys inside the line. (IWM)

Looking towards Arromanches along a Whale roadway makes it evident how easily vehicles could roll ashore once disembarked. (IWM)

The pier end of the roadway. Alongside the Lobnitz are a couple of US Coastguard launches, and a row of tugs behind. A coaster on the other side is mostly concealed by the structures of the pier. The ship on the right of the photo is an LSI. (IWM)

The shoreward end of the Whale roadway is being protected by stones piled up by British soldiers. [IWM]

landing would have been doubtless delayed much longer.

It is almost certainly the case that the money, the manpower and the industrial capacity requisitioned for the construction of the Mulberries could have been better employed in the building of a larger number of landing craft (though manning them would have been a problem). However at the moment the decision was taken to use artificial ports there was no other choice possible.

Despite all their imperfections, the Mulberries remain as the very symbol of the landings. The numerous remains always visible out to sea from Arromanches show that numerous structures, planned to last for merely a few months, are still there fifty years later. This is proof of a good design and of particularly robust construction.

The description of Mulberry B by Gerald Pawle[2] is a tribute to the British achievement: 'When it was finally completed on D plus 40 the harbour at Arromanches was a truly remarkable enterprise. Two miles long by a mile broad, it was maintained by a force of over 5,000 officers and men of the Royal Navy, and a fleet of hundreds of specialised craft, including port-construction ships, boom-defence vessels, tankers, ferries, floating cranes and floating docks. The harbour was defended against air attack by nearly 200 Army guns as well as the guns of the fleet; on the Eastern flank two miles of nets acted as a trap for infernal machines, long range torpedoes, one-man submarines[3], and drifting mines.'

only 15 per cent of the total. This small figure is confirmed by a report of the Allied staff which states that the landing would probably have succeeded without artificial ports. As to Admiral Hall, commander of Force O, he did not hesitate to declare that the Mulberries had consumed more steel and manpower than they were worth.

Of course all the British did not share this opinion. Roskill prefers not to enter into the debate, though the Admiralty report to the War Cabinet gives the average tonnages landed at Omaha and Utah given above. It is perhaps significant that the ratio of vehicles to supplies landed was higher in the British sector.

On the other hand the American General Bedell Smith, who admits the figure of 15 per cent, also states that 'this 15 per cent was vital'. Gerald Pawle's *The Secret War* gives a point of view which seems to reconcile the views of the partisans of both viewpoints. He recognises implicitly that the artificial port of Arromanches did not have the turnover hoped for, but notes that the Allies lacked landing craft when the Overlord plans were being drawn up and that the possibility of creating an artificial port appeased the fears of the high command that grew from the impossibility of capturing a large port intact. Had they not had the possibility of taking a port with them the

[2]Gerald Pawle *The Secret War* Harrap. London 1956 p 286
[3]The attack by the German special units with their 'human torpedoes' and midget submarines did not start until July, which is why it is not dealt with in this book.

# 9    The Storm

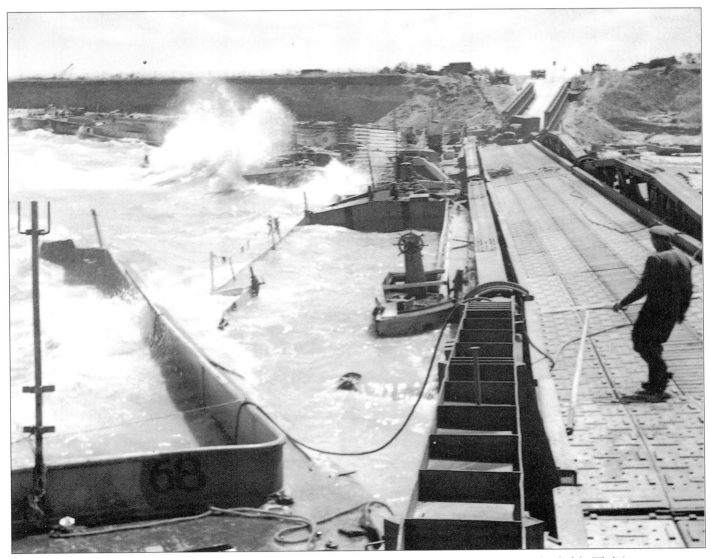

The classic image of the storm. The shoreward end of the Whale jetty at Asnelles is battered by two semi-submerged barges, thrown against it by the waves. Other barges have been driven ashore in the background. (IWM)

HISTORIANS OF THE landing have all described the storm that raged from 19th to 22nd June 1944 off the Normandy coast as the worst at that time of year for forty years.

Though it is certain that the storm had devastating effects, it is necessary to state that the wind did not blow as strongly as one might imagine. According to the American navy's meteorological observations made off Omaha Beach the wind blew at a maximum of 27 knots for several hours at the end of the day 20th June. On the Beaufort Scale this speed of 27 knots is the upper limit of Force 6. It therefore would not raise waves any higher than 10ft. The author of this book has been in several squalls of between Force 6 and Force 7 whilst sailing in a small 5.5m sailing boat in the vicinity of the Saint-Marcouf islands. I can testify that, if these conditions are not very agreeable, they are at least manageable by most boats. But it happened that in June 1944 the majority of the craft surprised by the

Another view of the same scene as shown on the previous page. The line of barges thrown ashore stretches into the distance. (IWM)

A closer view of the two swamped barges. The nearer one appears to be lashed to the jetty. (IWM)

storm were of clearly inferior seaworthiness to a sailing cruiser, and suffered more from the impossibility of finding refuge. Besides, the wind was blowing at Force 5 or more for over three days.

## Keeping to the plan

When the storm struck the Normandy coast, the operation of supplying the divisions engaged in the battle for the bridgehead was proceeding well. By the evening of 18th June the Americans had disembarked 314,514 men, 41,000 vehicles and 116,000 tons of supplies on their two beaches. The British had done much the same in their sector, with 314,547 men, 54,000 vehicles and 102,000 tons of supplies. These figures were less than had been forecast, but this was happily compensated for by the good news that the losses were clearly less heavy than forecast, both in men and matériel.

For example, the Americans had disembarked by then five divisions of infantry and one armoured division over and above the two airborne and three infantry divisions landed on D-Day itself.

Also on the 18th Mulberry A at Omaha began to function, whilst the Arromanches one was still being assembled. The weather had never been particularly clement since 6th June, but no storms had appeared. These were in any case rare in this part of the Channel in June. On three of the five beaches the only available shelters at this date were the blockships of the Gooseberries, which only gave protection to shallower draught vessels. At Arromanches the Bombardons were in place, and the Phoenixes partly so. It was Omaha which was the most complete. The Bombardons had the advantage of offering a much bigger sheltered area than did the Gooseberries, but they were intended to resist winds of up to Force 6 and no more, because of their method of fastening. They were bolted together, and not riveted or welded. Of course they could resist more violent winds, but only in the form of squalls of limited duration. For several hours no-one knew what would become of the Bombardons. One of their designers, Mr Lochner, had asked the Admiralty to place explosive charges on the anchor chains at one end of each Bombardon, in order to allow them to be put before the wind instead of across it in the case of a bad storm, but because of lack of time or means nothing had been done. There was, therefore, a risk that the Bombardons would become unbolted and disintegrate, but this had been judged acceptable by the Admiralty and the War Office, whilst the other elements of the artificial port, notably the Whale jetties and the Phoenix caissons, were not expected to resist winds of more than Force 8.

Probably the same jetty as in the previous pictures, but seen from dry land looking out to sea. It seems to have broken loose (or perhaps merely had not been completed?). Three ramped barges can be seen close inshore on the other side of the jetty. The shipping further out seems less affected by the storm. (IWM)

## Good weather at last

On Sunday 18th June, the weather became noticeably better and the barometer remained high. Admiral Tennant, who was responsible for the placing of the Mulberries, wrote that the 18th ended with, 'a marvellously calm summer's evening, so calm that I could see ripples running on the water as far as the horizon.' A consequence of this was that his staff ordered the despatch of no fewer than twenty-three tows across the Channel, intended to reach Normandy on the 20th. On the French coast, as well, the weather was set fine. Roskill describes the day thus: 'Furthermore on Sunday 18th June the weather appeared to have taken a turn for the better; for the sun shone on a calm sea and the barometer was steady. Indeed the beaches, black with men and vehicles, the landing craft busily plying to and fro, and the forest of masts in the off-shore anchorages produced an atmosphere which a Cockney naval commando was

heard to describe aptly, if nostalgically, as "like Margate on a Bank Holiday".' [1]

Alas, it was the calm before the storm. During the evening the barometer began to fall, but not too heavily before early morning on the 19th when it suddenly dived. At the same time the wind began to blow with force from the north-northeast, that is from the English shore. Therefore the Cotentin peninsula offered no shelter, and the storm could blow across the full width of the Channel. This was not a squall, but a continuous depression, and the waves began to break without hindrance upon the Gooseberries and Bombardons installed off the Normandy beaches.

## An uncommon storm

At first sight the storm lasting from 19th to 22nd June

[1] Roskill Vol III pt 2 p 63

These damaged pontoons look rather like parts of a Rhino ferry. The houses in the background are part of the settlement of Arromanches. (IWM)

1944 was not of unheard-of violence. It remained remarkably stable around Force 6, with some gusts reaching Force 8. The relevant data from Omaha Beach are of interest.

| Date | Hour | Wind Direction | Wind speed | Waves |
|------|------|----------------|------------|-------|
| 19th | 0100 | NNE | 13 knots | 2ft |
| " | 0700 | NNE | 19 knots | 6ft |
| " | 1300 | NNE | 22 knots | 6½ft |
| " | 1800 | NE | 21 knots | - |
| 20th | 0100 | NE | 19 knots | 6½ft |
| " | 0700 | NE | 23 knots | 7ft |
| " | 1300 | NE | 21 knots | 7¾ft |
| " | 1800 | NNE | 27 knots | 7½ft |
| 21st | 0100 | NNE | 26 knots | - |
| " | 0700 | NNE | 25 knots | 7½ft |
| " | 1300 | NNE | 19 knots | - |
| " | 1800 | NNE | 17 knots | 7ft |
| 22nd | 0100 | NNE | 16 knots | 7½ft |
| " | 0700 | NNE | 15 knots | 5½ft |

Note that the average speed in knots on the Beaufort Scale is as follows:
Force 4 = 11–16 knots
Force 5 = 17–21 knots
Force 6 = 22–27 knots

It is equally to be noted that the height of the waves corresponded to a rough sea. A heavy sea is one where the waves reach over 7½ft and that height was only reached around mid-day on 20th June.

All these figures agree in making it clear that this

storm was nothing extraordinary. It is difficult to believe that this was a rare meteorological event which had not happened for forty years previously.

However, as we will see, the damage was horrific. The only valid explanation lies in the wind *direction:* north-northeast. This struck directly upon the beaches, blowing across the Bombardons, the Phoenixes and the blockships, instead of taking them head on, on the bow, if one can talk of the bow of a square structure like the Phoenix caissons. The waves were certainly not very high, but in the Channel the seas are particularly short and wicked, and the repeated blows of a bad chop are often more destructive than the effect of a long Atlantic swell.

## Convoys overwhelmed

The first to be struck by the storm were the convoys crossing the Channel. The troop transports, LSIs or LSTs did not suffer too much, even close to the coast, because they could always go out to sea, whilst awaiting calmer weather. However the twenty-three convoys of towed Mulberry structures had no way of escaping the storm. One by one the tows broke loose and the Whale pontoons broke up. The Lobnitz pierheads and Phoenix caissons capsized, sometimes taking their tugs with them when the cables were not cut fast enough.

The Mulberries in position were submitted to a rude testing, as the storm produced a strong sea of powerful waves, which increased the amount of water breaking over the piers and Bombardons, straining their anchor cables even more. There was less danger to the Phoenixes as they were already on the bottom. Only the crews of the anti-aircraft guns based on them could spare the time to appreciate this. The caissons which remained afloat were themselves real dangers if they broke loose and their 6,000 tons crashed into ships or port structures situated close at hand.

But no one thought that this awful weather would last, given the rarity of such a storm in the month of June.

Another aggravating factor was the absence of any accurate warning. There was no gale warning, or even information about strong winds. This was so much the case that not only were the convoys out to sea taken by surprise, but also the multitude of small and medium sized craft working off the beach around the LSIs, LSTs and LSDs.

Towards noon on the 19th all ferry services departing from England were suspended. Unloading operations continued off the Normandy coast until about mid-afternoon, then they, too, were stopped.

This extraordinary picture shows the British destroyer *Fury* aground off the cliffs to the west of Arromanches. In front of her is the cruciform shape of a wrecked Bombardon, behind her the bows of an LCM(1). The destroyer had hit a mine on 21st June. Damage was not really severe, but she lost all power, and the storm did the rest. She became a constructional total loss and had to be broken up. (IWM)

## Mulberry A breaks up

When the sea began to grow rough, the landing craft and numerous small boats took shelter behind the blockships of the Gooseberries, whilst the amphibious DUKWs drove up onto the beach. The larger vessels whose draught was too great for them to take advantage of the Gooseberries were rapidly put in a difficult position. Anchors dragged, and collisions of a greater or lesser degree of violence were frequent. The increase in the storm and above all its length caused more and more serious damage from the afternoon of the 20th. Numerous LCTs, barges and all sorts of launches were driven onto the coast and destroyed on the rocks.

After thirty hours of storm, some of the lines of Bombardons suddenly broke loose and these cruciform structures were tossed about in all directions, with devastating effects for all they smashed into, whether caissons or ships.

Mulberry A off Omaha Beach, much more advanced than its equivalent at Arromanches, suffered enormously. Some blockships were knocked out of their positions and settled down, the current digging the sand from under their hulls. In spite of her impressive size the old British battleship *Centurion* broke in two. With the disappearance of the Bombardons and a proportion of the blockships, the port at Omaha rapidly became untenable. On 20th June a big American salvage barge and five LCTs began to hammer harder and harder against the central floating pontoon, already heavily mistreated by the waves. To avoid the worst Captain Clark ordered the vessels to go out to sea immediately, but the crews were not much inclined to do so. The LCTs had only two little anchors, of little help if one tried to moor outside harbour. Also their reserve of fuel was insufficient for them to stay out to sea, still less to get back to England.

The scene which then took place on the Whale pontoons was incredible. The American sailors who were trying at the risk of their lives to save the port became furious and tried to chase off the LCTs whose blows were inflicting increasing damage on the articulated pontoons. Insults and injuries were insufficient; shots were even fired at the LCTs, without the latter budging, however. They therefore continued their slow work of destruction.

In order to try to save the jetties the Fairmile launches of the port were used to deflect the numerous craft which were adrift. In this crashing about they were soon themselves rapidly sunk or abandoned to such an extent that only one remained by the evening of the 20th. A single tug was still active. It was the last and could do no more than pull back the numerous vessels of all sorts which were about to crash into the floating pontoons.

The situation became graver still with the end of the day when several tows of Phoenix caissons came over the horizon. These were intended for the central breakwater, which still presented a large gap in the middle. The arrival of these 6,000-ton monsters, totally impossible to manoeuvre in such weather, was most unwelcome. Captain Clark ordered them to return to England, but with the wind blowing from the north-northeast the tugs were quite incapable of competing with the elements to return across the Channel. Nothing more could be done except to sabotage the newcomers and throw them ashore.

These losses of Phoenix caissons were added to those caused by the blows given by the Bombardons which were pivoting on their chains and beating against the concrete cubes. Out of the thirty-five 200ft Bombardons laid before the storm, no fewer than twenty-five were disintegrated by the waves, and finally thrown upon the coast together with hundreds of hulks.

When the wind finally began to drop on 22nd June, desolation, to use the very words of General Bradley, reigned at Omaha. The damage was such that it was hopeless to try and reconstruct Mulberry A. All that could be hoped for was to re-establish the Omaha Gooseberry. Admiral Kirk finally decided to transfer the intact parts of Mulberry A to Arromanches, where the port had suffered much less.

## The storm in the British sector

It seems that the wind had been slightly less violent at Arromanches, the reasons for which are difficult to establish, even if some authors talk about the shelter offered by Cap de la Hève at Le Havre.

It may be that the reason Mulberry B survived was, quite simply, that it had not been completed, and therefore did not have to serve as a refuge for hundreds of vessels, mostly more or less out of control, and did not have to withstand the same punishment.

On 19th June unloading operations continued off the three British beaches, because it was necessary that the flow of supplies should not cease. The DUKWs managed to offload a number of cargoes, but their individual loads were certainly much reduced, and they were only used for urgent tasks, that is to say landing ammunition for the troops at the front. Everyone hoped that the storm would be short, given the time of year. But the several craft that risked ferry trips between the coast and the ships moored out to sea, often destroyed themselves when approaching the beaches and soon the majority of action ceased. It was no longer a case of unloading come what may, but of survival.

The destroyer HMS *Fury* struck a drifting mine at 1045 on the 21st. With her machinery stopped she was driven ashore. Other ships broke their anchor chains and found themselves tossed on the waves. If they could not get their machinery under way rapidly, they were lost. During the night of the 21/22nd June, a call directed at certain vessels caused a certain amount of terror: 'If the vessel approaching you is No 269, she carries 3,000 tons of ammunition.'

When the storm slackened from the morning of the 22nd, the same scene of desolation extended along the three British beaches: 'But the scene revealed on the beaches might well have daunted the stoutest hearts. Upturned broken-backed boats and craft lay everywhere, sometimes actually piled on top of each other by the force of the waves. Lorries, guns, Rhino ferries and all manner of equipment had been strewn in hopeless confusion, while at the water's edge came in a vast flotsam of wreckage - and of dead men.' [2]

The precise number of victims of the storm is unknown, but the British Official History of the War at Sea cites the figures for lost vessels: 800 ships and craft lost in both British and American sectors. It was a grave loss, the more so because so many of the vessels lost were the small craft ferrying between the landing ships and cargo vessels and the shore. Nevertheless the worst had been avoided thanks to the five Gooseberries, without which the landings and the craft involved would have been relentlessly wiped out. Much more than the Mulberries, it was the Gooseberries which had probably save Operation Overlord.

## Unloading begins again

Morison gives several interesting figures on the unloading done by the Americans before, during and after the storm. The best figure achieved before the 19th was 9,008 tons at Omaha and 5,736 at Utah. The worst figure during the storm was 494 and 865

[2]Roskill Vol III pt 2, p 64

tons respectively on the 22nd. Finally the best score for the whole month was 14,869 and 8,171 tons respectively on the 29th. It is very interesting to see that the destruction of Mulberry A had not caused a fall in the unloading at Omaha, rather the opposite, it would seem. This was principally due to the enormous effort made just after the storm in order to win back the lost time and tonnage. In fact, the almost total interruption in re-supply had forced the staff to reduce the ammunition allowance to front line troops. The danger was then so real that on 22nd June it had been decided to transport ammunition by air, thanks to the thousands of Dakotas (Douglas DC-3s) available in Britain. The first squadrons arrived over Normandy at the same time that the sun reappeared.

In the British sector the interruption of supplies had been nearly identical. Here on 21st June fourteen LSTs came to unload on the beach at Juno. During the three days of storm the average tonnage disembarked at the port of Arromanches was in the neighbourhood of 1,800 tons per day, whilst the beaches took about 1,600 tons daily, clearly in greater quantities than the American beaches, but nonetheless still insufficient. Apart from the delay in the landing of troops - three British divisions were still in their transports on 22nd June when they should already have been about their tasks in the bridgehead - the delay in re-supply is estimated at 105,000 tons and 20,000 vehicles for the period involved, and despite the means used to pile them up, this deficit was not overcome till the 26th. Happily for the Allies the Germans were unable to profit from this delay in supplies by counterattacking.

Special measures were taken by the British naval staff to put damaged craft and harbour structures rapidly back into service. Teams of the best specialists were rapidly formed in Britain and rushed to Normandy, whilst numerous repair vessels crossed the Channel to work on the hundreds of craft thrown ashore. The majority were repairable, and soon some of the fleet considered to have been lost were moving about again off the beaches and in Mulberry B, which welcomed its first cargoes on 29th June.

At almost the same moment the pipe line - PLUTO -

The small beach at Arromanches is covered by the debris from the storm, bits of Whale pontoons and a ramped barge. The stone sea wall also shows signs of damage. However activity has started again, a DUKW full of soldiers is coming out of the water. (IWM)

came into service and delivered a daily total of 8,000 tons of fuel starting at the beginning of July.

Thus the storm had not managed to break the flow of Allied supplies completely, nor even to cause the troops on the ground to lose the initiative.

# 10  Cherbourg and the German Riposte

HMS *Glasgow* suffers a direct hit exploding in the starboard hangar. Four minutes later another 105mm shell hit the after superstructure. Meanwhile destroyers are laying a smokescreen in the background. *Glasgow* remained ready to steam and to fight. (IWM)

WHILST THE ALLIED TROOPS were fighting in the Normandy interior, enlarging the bridgehead, the purely military mission of the fleet had not yet come to an end.

It had become more difficult, because it was no longer a question of firing on easily identifiable targets along the beaches, but of defending the extensive maritime lines of communication against attacks from submarines, surface vessels and even aircraft. This task was the more difficult because there was no longer an element of surprise. Meanwhile the need to support the troops ashore had not come to an end.

## The Germans reorganise

It might be difficult to get the German divisions up to the front line, long and dangerous for U-boats to penetrate to the Bay of the Seine and near-suicidal for the German surface forces to deploy from Le Havre or Cherbourg. On the other hand it was easy and speedy to get together an aerial force to attack the Allied fleet. In consequence it was the Luftwaffe which was ready to move first.

Its two raids of 6th June were pitiable efforts, but other sorties were made by the Luftwaffe that day, 319 in all, and all the rest of them failed to reach the beaches. On the other hand the gathering of nearly a thousand aircraft on the airfields of Northern France, the Paris area, and central France was an exploit that few would have thought the Luftwaffe capable of at this stage in the war. However this achievement was at the cost of other fronts, of Italy, and particularly of the Fatherland, whose cities were left much less well protected. Besides, it was largely fighters that were gathered. They could not do much against the replenishment ships, even the Focke-Wulf Fw190 fighter-bombers. The two types best fitted for the fight against the fleet were the Junkers Ju88s adapted to carry torpedoes, and the Heinkel He177s with their unconventional and unreliable layout of four engines in coupled pairs driving two propellers. These fragile giants carried the redoubtable glider bombs. The other bombers were most often used to carry mines. The most dangerous of these were what were known to the Allies as 'Oyster' mines. They were set off by the pressure-wave of a passing ship. These mines were near-impossible to detect and even harder to sweep with the technology of the day. However they had the disadvantage that they could only be used in shallow water.

The night of the 6/7th June was calm. No German aircraft intervened effectively in the American zone. Over the British zone protection was the task of six squadrons of Mosquito night-fighters. There, too, the Luftwaffe had no successes; not a ship was hit.

## Glider bombs

On the night of 7/8th June the Luftwaffe made about a hundred sorties against the Allied fleet. At exactly 0152 the US destroyer *Meredith* was hit by a radio-controlled glider bomb, launched by an He177, which hit near the waterline. The destroyer, which was patrolling about 3½ miles off the Saint-Marcouf Islands, soon lost all power and began to drift slowly. At 0250 her crew abandoned her, rather prematurely as she did not sink. For the whole day of the 8th the destroyer *Jeffers* tried to save her, but unsuccessfully. Finally the *Meredith* broke in two on the morning of the 9th, and rapidly disappeared, so fast that she nearly dragged the tug down with her which had no time to cut its cables.

The other Luftwaffe raids were not so successful, despite their large number. There were 1,683 sorties against the Allied fleet in the first week of combat. On 10th June a Liberty ship, the *Charles Morgan*, was hit by a bomb off Utah Beach. Although the stern was nearly torn off, the ship was saved.

The *Ramillies* enveloped in the smoke from her 15in guns off the Calvados coast. The upperworks behind her look like those of the *Frobisher* whilst the ship on the left is probably a more modern British cruiser, the *Mauritius*. (IWM)

The Luftwaffe also attacked in the British sector, by day as well as by night, at least in the first days after the landing. The HQ ship HMS *Bulolo* was struck by a bomb at 0600 on the 7th. Fire broke out aboard but was fairly quickly extinguished with only light loss.

At 0515 the next day the frigate HMS *Lawford* was sunk by another aerial attack. The nocturnal attacks produced fewer direct hits, but the German bombers dropped mines which caused noticeable losses. On the night of 12/13th June a torpedo dropped by a Ju88 caused the loss of the destroyer HMS *Boadicea*. On 23rd June, HMS *Scylla*, the flagship of Admiral Vian, was blown up by a mine and had to be towed to England. Then the destroyer *Swift* was sunk on the 24th. On the following days two small ships and the transport *Derry Cunahy* were sunk off Sword with serious loss of life amongst the soldiers aboard.

## Mines, a redoubtable enemy

Mines therefore represented the most important danger to the Allied fleet, whether laid by minelayers before the invasion or dropped by the Luftwaffe during it. We have seen a destroyer lost on the 6th itself. The next day it was the troop transport *Susan B.Anthony* which exploded in the approaches to Omaha and sank rapidly. Happily numerous landing craft were close and the troops could be saved. LCI 496, for example, took aboard no less than 436 men in a quarter of an hour.

On 8th June the American destroyer *Glennon* was steaming towards her firing position off the Saint-Marcouf Islands when she set off a mine a little after 0800. The explosion was so great that a sailor on deck was thrown up some 40ft before falling into the water with both legs broken. To avoid panic and premature abandoning ship, Commander Johnson, her CO, told his men, through a loud-hailer, to keep calm. The ship wasn't going to sink, everybody was to stay aboard, damage control teams were in the process of containing the leaks. Then he asked help from ships in the vicinity. Half an hour later the minesweepers *Staff* and *Threat* came up. One took the *Glennon* under tow whilst the other swept a channel in front.

The crew believed themselves to be safe, but then a German salvo fell only a couple of hundred yards off the stern of the destroyer. A cruiser nearby, doubtless HMS *Black Prince*, riposted at two batteries suspected of firing these shells, but two other salvos then exploded very close to the *Glennon*.

The destroyer escort USS *Rich* then approached, asking by signal if any more help was needed. With the two minesweepers already helping Johnson replied in the negative, warning that the DE should distance herself whilst taking the utmost precautions against mines.

Turning round the stern of the *Glennon* the DE began to move away when she hit a mine. Three minutes later a second opened a gaping hole in the stern of the *Rich*, then a third mine exploded alongside the forecastle. The ship was devastated; an eye-witness describes it as a holocaust, with bodies hanging from the masts, in the debris of the funnel, and even on the gun barrels. When the *Rich* sank a man suddenly appeared on the surface, certainly the last survivor. PT 508 rushed forward to save him and a line was thrown, but the survivor yelled in a strong and astonishingly calm voice that it was no good, he had no hands left to grab the line. The commander of the PT boat immediately jumped into the sea to save him, but too late, the unknown man had sunk.

In 15min the USS *Rich* had sunk, taking with her 79 men killed out of 215, with 73 wounded.

Whilst this was going on the *Glennon* was facing new problems. Taking on water she was beginning to founder, and it was impossible to pull her forward or to disengage from her. The *Staff* therefore took aboard most of the destroyer's crew and moved off. Those who remained aboard tried to lighten the stern of the vessel by emptying tanks and jettisoning the depth charges. A tug, the *Kiowa*, came to the rescue, preceded by two sweepers who set off another two mines, proof of the way the area was infested.

Despite all the *Kiowa*'s efforts, the *Glennon* remained desperately low in the water. The crew was nearly all evacuated at nightfall, then next morning sixty men went back on board to continue the salvage attempts. These were as useless as those of the previous day. On the morning of the 10th the crew was getting ready for new efforts when a German salvo from the Quinéville battery fell several yards from the ship. The enemy artillery then found the right elevation and the second salvo hit *Glennon* amidships, destroying her engine room. This time it was impossible to save the ship, the more so because the third salvo was almost as accurate. The *Glennon* was therefore abandoned, but remained afloat until 2145 when she suddenly turned over and disappeared. She had lost twenty-five killed and thirty-eight wounded.

These losses were the worst suffered by the US Navy as the result of mines, but they were not the only ones. On 7th June the minesweeper *Tide* hit a mine on Cardonnet Bank and sank several hours later, whilst under tow. LST 499 was badly damaged by a mine, and the British hired netlayer *Minster* sank from hitting one off Omaha. But the danger diminished in proportion to the enlargement of the swept channels by the sweepers. Up to 3rd July 261 mines were destroyed by the US Navy alone, whose minesweeping forces present were considerably smaller than those of the Royal Navy.

The problem posed by pressure mines, laid in considerable numbers by the Luftwaffe from 11th June, was finally answered when one of these Oyster mines fell intact into Allied hands. Immediately examined in detail it revealed its secrets. Laid on the bottom, where it was impossible to sweep, it was set off by the pressure waves caused by passing ships. But below 4 knots speed the displacement of water by the ship's passage through it was not strong enough to be detected by the mines, and they remained inert. All ships, therefore, received orders not to go over 4 knots whilst proceeding in shallow water, and this finally put an end to the losses.

## The Royal Navy versus the Kriegsmarine

If the US Navy suffered from mines, especially in the Utah Beach sector, the British were especially disturbed by the S-boats and other small surface craft used by the Germans out of the port of Le Havre and other bases to the north of the Bay of the Seine. All in all during the period from 6th to 30th June mines cost the Allies seven destroyers (four of them American), two minesweepers (both US) and ten naval auxiliaries.

The appearances made by the S-boats were not really very conclusive, but almost every night there were exchanges between British and German patrol craft. These rarely resulted in the destruction of a vessel, but they prevented the Germans from reaching the Allied convoy routes. The first skirmishes in mid-Channel saw the S-boats sinking LSTs 376, 314 and 715, with six smaller craft. The destroyer USS *Nelson* was hit in the stern by a torpedo, but survived to be scrapped in 1968. We have already seen that the Norwegian *Svenner* was sunk on 6th June.

On the night of 9/10th June two coasters carrying munitions were sunk, whilst the next day HMS *Halstead* was hit by a torpedo which tore off her bow. She was towed back to Portsmouth.

The Germans experienced great difficulty in getting any results from their raids, because the RAF sought out the S-boats without let-up, by night as well with patrols of Bristol Beaufighters. The approaches to the ports were ceaselessly overflown by Coastal Command Wellington bombers, which attacked by the light of flares which particularly picked up the foam of the boats' wakes. Any damaged boat trying to return to base at reduced speed had no chance of survival if caught out in daylight, thanks to the incredible Allied air superiority. As a final step the Allies themselves were also laying mines to protect their routes. Thus on 7th June S 139 and S 140 set off mines off Barfleur. On the 11th in the same area two other S-boats (S 136 and S 137) were sunk by the destroyer HMCS *Sioux*, the destroyer escort HMS *Duff* and the 'Hunt' class Polish destroyer *Krakowiak*.

Allied aircraft also took their toll. On 13th June aircraft of 143 and 236 Squadrons of Coastal Command surprised a German flotilla off Le Touquet and sent three S-boats and an R-boat to the bottom. These were losses much too heavy to be compensated for by the rare successes against the immense Allied fleet. The menace and annoyance of these guerilla raids nonetheless led Admiral Ramsay to ask for massive raids by Bomber Command against the S-boat bases.

## The RAF strikes

The first blow was against Le Havre, attacked just before nightfall on 14th June by 221 Lancaster and 13 Mosquito bombers (the latter presumably being the pathfinders). The raid came in two phases, one at the end of the afternoon, the other at twilight. Success was complete in both cases. The port was hit by some 1,230 tons of bombs, which sank or destroyed three torpedo boats (*Falke*, *Möwe* and *Jaguar*) and ten S-boats (S 84, 100, 138, 142, 143, 169, 171, 172, 173, and 187), one R-boat and 17 patrol boats and sweepers. This was for the loss of a single bomber. No 617 Squadron (the 'Dambusters') attacked with twenty-two Lancasters carrying the immense 12,000lb

HMS *Rodney* appears to be firing one gun at full elevation from each of her three triple 16in turrets (all of them before the bridge) at targets inland from the bridgehead. The salvos from her and her sister *Nelson* had a terrifying effect on German attempts to counterattack, all of which crumbled in the face of such fire. **(IWM)**

'Tallboy' bombs, which according to the reports of the defenders, caused considerable damage. Despite the general accuracy of the bombing, which achieved its objectives well above expectations, no less than 700 houses were destroyed in the port, and 76 French civilians killed, especially in the Nôtre-Dame district. But this time the menace represented by the S-boats was reduced to nearly nil.

For good measure, Bomber Command attacked again the next day, this time over Boulogne with 155 Lancasters, 130 Halifaxes and 12 Mosquitos. The results were noticeably similar, with the destruction of seven R-boats, of S-boats Nos 178, 179 and 189 plus a dozen patrol vessels. French civil defence considered this raid as the worst to hit the town since the beginning of the war and 200 civilians were unfortunately killed. Only one Halifax was lost.

The German Admiral Krancke noted in his war diary that the results of the two raids were catastrophic: 'The naval situation in the Bay of the Seine has completely deteriorated. It will be impossible to start the planned operations with the forces that have survived.'

Krancke was forced urgently to demand reinforcements. A flotilla of S-boats was transferred from the Baltic to the Dutch base of Ijmuiden, considered for good reason to be more secure than Le Havre or Boulogne, but noticeably further from the theatre of operations. This flotilla arrived too late to intervene in the month of June. Allied records show that S-boats had only sunk one destroyer and eight small auxiliaries (patrol vessels, armed trawlers, etc) in that month.

## Naval battle between Brest and Cherbourg

On 7th June aerial reconnaissance by the RAF revealed the presence of four German destroyers at Brest. Three ships had left Royan on the orders of Admiral Krancke in order to proceed to Brest. Admiral Leatham, CinC at Portsmouth, easily guessed this and sent the 10th Destroyer Flotilla to intercept them. This flotilla was under the flag of Commander Jones aboard the destroyer HMS *Tartar*. Four of his destroyers were British, two Canadian, and two Polish.

Between 0127 and 0526 on the night of the 8/9th June the two flotillas of destroyers met in a violent naval battle called by the British 'the night action off Ile Vierge'.[1]

This started on the 9th at 0127 when *Tartar* opened fire at 5,000 yards on the four enemy destroyers. The Germans replied with torpedoes which missed their targets. Soon afterwards the Allied vessels closed the enemy and fired at short range upon the German formation, which broke apart. Two destroyers tried to escape to the north, two back towards Brest. The latter had chosen the better course, though the Z 24 was heavily hit by the Canadian 'Tribals' *Haida* and *Huron*; both she and the smaller (classed as a torpedo boat) T 24 got away. To the north the ZH 1 was hit by *Tartar* and seemed to have broken down. Whilst this was going on the flagship, Z 32, pushed on towards the two Polish destroyers, firing torpedoes which forced the *Blyskawica* to turn aside. Keeping straight on she then met *Tartar* which fired several broadsides which reduced her speed. However *Tartar* was also hit and lost touch, but then sighted ZH 1. With the aid of *Ashanti* she sent the ex-Dutch destroyer (built as *Gerald Callenburgh* and scuttled incomplete in 1940, but salvaged and commissioned by the Germans as ZH 1 in 1941) to the bottom with a torpedo hit. The Z 32, meanwhile, continued to try to escape. However she then ran into the Canadian destroyers *Haida* and *Huron*, whose fire rapidly put her aflame. To save her from certain sinking her captain ran her aground on the Breton coast.

None of the Allied ships were sunk, and the Canadian destroyer *Haida* is still in existence, having been selected for preservation in 1964 and is now moored at Toronto.

---

[1]In *Conway's All the World's Fighting Ships 1922-1946* this action is referred to as 'off Barfleur' - which is the wrong side of Cherbourg, while referring to the Z 32 having gone ashore on the 'Ile de Bas' - a mistake for the Ile de Batz - after being cannonaded by the Canadian destroyers *Haida* and *Huron*.

## The Americans confront the S-boats

If the larger force of German motor torpedo boats were next to the British sector, several S-boats did have Cherbourg as their base. They certainly did not remain inactive. In the night of 7/8th June, five of them left Cherbourg and advanced to near the Saint-Marcouf islands, from where they launched torpedoes at what they identified as destroyers and a cruiser, claiming three hits on their return. However the Allied fleet had no losses during that night.

The next day there was a similar mission with ten of the Cherbourg S-boats. They steered towards the Saint-Marcoufs with orders to lay mines. However, not far from Barfleur, they were spotted on the radars of the destroyers *Frankford*, *Baldwin* (both US) and HMS *Hambledon* (of the 'Hunt' class). These opened rapid fire and drove the Germans back.

Not everything went badly that night for the S-boats, some others found and sank LST 376 and LST 314 both of which were part of a convoy of five under the escort of HMS *Beagle*, surprised in mid-Channel. In the sinkings LST 314 lost half her crew.

On the 11th it was the turn of the large tug *Partridge* to be sunk by torpedo attack, hit whilst towing with four other tugs Whale pontoon elements. Only 10 miles from Omaha, she was hit by a torpedo which sank her in a minute, with the loss of half of her crew, thirty-two men.

Soon afterwards the S-boats took on a convoy of LSTs and hit LST 538, which, however, was able to run herself ashore, where she was subsequently repaired enough to go back to sea.

The following night the American destroyer *Nelson* was hit and had to be towed to England. But this was the last of the Cherbourg S-boat successes. The land fighting was getting dangerously near to the port. On the 17th the Americans cut off the northern part of the Cotentin peninsula   level with Barneville. The evacuation of naval forces commenced soon after, the vessels being shared out between Le Havre and Saint Malo. Meanwhile demolitions began to make the port unusable by the Allies.

## The defeat of the U-boats

Whilst they could have been the greatest menace of all to the Allied fleet, the U-boats were prevented from coming into action thanks to the exceptionally heavy countermeasures taken by the Royal Navy, the RAF and the USAAF.

On news of the landing, the two groups of submarines intended to combat the invasion were put on alert, whilst five schnorkel-equipped U-boats were diverted towards Brest as they were off Iceland on their way towards the USA.

The deployment of U-boats was ordered as follows:
- Nine with schnorkels to place themselves 25 miles south of the Isle of Wight to attack the traffic on its way to France. This was a particularly dangerous mission.
- Seven without schnorkels to deploy at the entrance to the Channel.
- The nineteen remaining U-boats to form themselves into a line in the Bay of Biscay in order to prevent any possible landings on the west coast of France.

During the night of the 6/7th June aircraft of No 19 Group of Coastal Command surprised several of the nineteen U-boats in the Bay of Biscay. U 955 was sent to the bottom and five others were damaged and forced to return to base. However four British aircraft were shot down. After these discouraging beginnings the U-boats received orders to remain submerged for as much of the time as possible, to avoid becoming targets for air attack. This seriously limited their operational capabilities.

On the night of 7/8th June the British obtained more successes against U-boats surprised on the surface at night. A Sunderland flying boat sank U 970, whilst a Liberator of 224 Squadron sank U 629 and U 373 within the space of half an hour.

In the Channel itself the power of the air was shown very clearly. On 9th June a Liberator of 120 Squadron sank U 740 off the Scillies. The next day U 821 was surprised on the surface by four Mosquitos which shot her up and left her dead in the water near Ushant. Shortly afterwards a Liberator finished her off.

These very heavy losses obliged the German high command to recall all the submarines which were not equipped with schnorkels, and therefore could not proceed for long distances submerged. This considerably reduced the numbers available for action.

However on 15th June they were finally rewarded for their efforts. U 767, which had arrived from

Aerial view of one of the 280mm guns of Battery Hamburg in its armoured turret. Thick concrete walls reinforced the protection but, as can be clearly seen here, prevented the gun from firing over a full 360 degree arc. This explains the ability of *Texas* and *Arkansas* to fire from the 'dead arc' and avoid retaliation. Despite this and the awful devastation produced by their shells, they only destroyed one out of the four guns. (DITE)

Norway, sank the frigate HMS *Mourne* off Lands End, whilst U 764 torpedoed the DE HMS *Blackwood* at the Cap de la Hague. U 621, which reached the sector of Utah Beach on the same day, fired several torpedoes at American heavy ships without any hits, but later destroyed an American LST off Barfleur, before returning to Brest.

On 18th June U 767 was sunk by three British destroyers off the Breton coast, and U 441 suffered the same fate near to Ushant under the attack of a Polish-manned Wellington bomber. The Norwegian-based U-boats suffered equally; six were sunk and three damaged during the month of June.

At the end of the month the Allies were less successful, because the second wave of U-boats had learned the lesson of the opening stages of the battle. They only proceeded when submerged at periscope depth, using their schnorkels. On 29th June U 984 achieved a major success by sinking four Liberty ships in one go. The same day another transport, the *Empire Portia*, was

The American heavy cruiser *Quincy* seen from aboard a British warship with her triple 8in and twin 5in turrets trained on the beam. (IWM)

sunk in the same waters off Selsey Bill.

The balance sheet for U-boat operations in June was clearly biased in favour of the Allies, who had been able to prevent the majority of the enemy submarines from reaching the Bay of the Seine. Once there they could have caused carnage amongst the vast number of ships ferrying backwards and forwards across the Channel. This defeat of the Germans could have been foreseen, however, because of the lack of schnorkel-fitted U-boats.

## The advance on Cherbourg

During the month of June the role of the navy was not limited to the protection of the invasion fleet. The most important offensive operation was the bombardment of Cherbourg, in support of the land attack which developed from 22nd June.

In the initial plans it was forecast that the big Norman port would be captured by the Americans on D-Day + 8. At that time (14th June) the Cotentin was not yet cut in two. It would be another three days before General Collins men reached Barneville on the west coast.

On 22nd June, Collins deployed his VII Corps towards Cherbourg. He fielded four infantry divisions, two divisions of parachutists, two tank battalions and two armoured reconnaissance battalions. The assault itself was confined to the three infantry divisions and their armoured support. The details of the battle do not concern us here. It suffices to say that to finish off the 40,000 men defending the fortress that Cherbourg

had become, the Americans lost 2,800 dead and 13,500 wounded. In order to break the resistance of the principal enemy batteries, the fleet was tasked with bombarding them in a major operation on 25th June.

The decision to do this was taken on 18th June, the eve of the great storm. The US Navy, in the person of Admiral Deyo, proposed to Collins that his attack would be supported by the neutralisation of some fifteen heavier calibre batteries (with guns of over 6in) situated around Cherbourg.

As the storm meant that the warships were dispersed over most of the ports of the south of England, the operation was put back for several days. The ships re-assembled in the shelter of Portland on the 22nd. At first planned for the 24th, the operation was postponed to daybreak on the 25th because of the tardy arrival of the battleship *Arkansas*.

After several changes of opinion the army asked Deyo that the bombardment should not begin until noon on 25th June and would only last 90min instead of the planned 3hr. In fact the German pocket of resistance had been considerably reduced - it only measured about a mile in radius; and it was necessary that the navy did not fire on American soldiers. Let us however notice that there remained isolated German defenders on the Cap de la Hague at the west and between Cap Lévi and Barfleur Point to the east.

## The fleet takes position

On 25th June at 0430 the Allied fleet left Portland in two distinct groups:
- Group 1: USS *Nevada*, *Quincy*, *Tuscaloosa*, HMS *Glasgow* and *Enterprise*, with six destroyers.
- Group 2: USS *Texas*, *Arkansas* and five destroyers.

These two groups were preceded by two flotillas of minesweepers, one British and one American, whilst the Ninth USAAF provided aerial protection. On the arrival at about 15 miles from Cherbourg, Deyo received a message from Collins which reduced the role of the fleet even further. This was now to fire only onto objectives assigned by the army. This scarcely pleased the sailors, who had already chosen a number of priority targets. After some discussion Collins left the fleet with three of these, reserving others. He did however authorise the fleet to open fire on batteries opening fire on them, the least he could do!

For an hour the fleet approached Cherbourg behind the minesweepers, with nothing happening. *Quincy* launched a seaplane on a spotting mission. It soon reported that two of the priority targets, on the Cap de la Hague, were totally destroyed, probably by the Germans themselves. This news was hardly encouraging. Had the fleet come for nothing?

At noon, the hour planned for the beginning of the bombardment, nothing had yet happened; no calls from the shore fire control parties, nor even any shells from the German batteries. Finally at about 1205 flashes appeared beside the village of Querqueville and a salvo of four 150mm shells burst close to the minesweeper at the head of Group 1, HMS *Sidmouth*.

## Battle commences

At 1214 Deyo ordered the cruiser HMS *Glasgow* to reply to the battery which was firing at the minesweepers. She opened fire, soon joined by the *Enterprise*. However their shells lifted such a cloud of dust that the spotting Spitfire was not capable of locating the German battery correctly, then of distinguishing the origins of the explosions around Querqueville. Profiting from this relative immunity the German battery placed a number of shells close to the sweepers, to such a point that Deyo ordered them to retire.

During this period the German battery - called 308 by the Americans - shifted its fire to the *Glasgow*. At 1251 a 150mm shell hit, exploding in the starboard hangar. Four minutes later another shell hit the after superstructure. In order to escape this punishment *Glasgow* speeded up and broke off the combat to give herself time to check that she was not badly damaged. Her machinery remained intact so her captain asked to be allowed to regain his place in the line and was given permission so to do.

The duel went on. At about 1300 *Enterprise*'s spotter plane announced that two of the four guns of battery 308 were destroyed. The others continued to fire till 1440 when 308 was temporarily neutralised at the expense of 318 six-inch shells.

Some shoots were fortunately less laborious. *Nevada*, at the request of a SFCP, opened fire on a target situated five kilometres to the southeast of Querqueville. Her fire was very accurate and the soldiers indicated that the 14in shells were burying the enemy. After 25min of firing the soldiers on the spot signalled 'they are showing a white panel but we have learned to pay no attention to that. Continue firing.' Shortly after that

The battleship USS *Nevada* approaching Cherbourg. The ship over her stern looks like HMS *Glasgow*, whilst over her bow is one of the American cruisers. (IWM)

the *Nevada* shifted targets. In all she fired 114 fourteen-inch shells and nearly 1,000 five-inch.

During the period of 90min which had been given to them, all the ships of the fleet, apart from the majority of the destroyers, fired on various targets, without major results; the German batteries were not muzzled. Deyo was fully conscious of this and asked Collins if he wished the fleet to continue firing. After three-quarters of an hour Collins deigned to reply in the affirmative. He asked the fleet to continue firing till 1500, it being then 1405.

The battle was not over at this stage. Battery 308 at Querqueville had returned to life, firing several salvos at the destroyer USS *Murphy*, which received no direct hits, but whose superstructure was swept by dangerous splinters. The *Tuscaloosa* came to her assistance, also two other destroyers and then the cruiser *Quincy*. Their joint fire put a third German gun out of action, but the last continued its undisturbed fire. The *Nevada* was then called in and several 14in salvos finally, it seemed, reduced the battery to silence. In fact it resumed fire the moment the fleet began to leave its position! Thus the efforts of one battleship, four cruisers and numerous destroyers had not been conclusive; no more so, perhaps than the battery itself which had not scored a direct hit throughout the battle.

The calls of the troops on the spot were essentially confined to the batteries placed in Cherbourg or its port, in proportion as the day advanced to the soldiers'

Another shot of HMS *Glasgow* in action on 25th June, bracketed by the splashes from 105mm shells fired by Battery 308 at Querqueville. (IWM)

penetration into the town. The *Tuscaloosa* got two hits on the bunkers of the arsenal, whilst the *Quincy* took on the Fort des Flamands. The *Nevada* also fired on the positions to the west of Cherbourg. In the middle of spouts of water the battleship was the target of several German guns. She, too, received no direct hits, and not a single man was killed, though the shell bursts produced some superficial damage.

At 1525, Group 1 ceased fire for good and left, not without regrets as all the German batteries were not reduced.

## Battery Hamburg and Group 2

The principal German coastal battery in the northern Cotentin was near to Fermanville, a little distance from Cap Lévi. It consisted of four 280mm (11in) guns in steel armoured turrets, protected by concrete casemates and covered by twelve AA guns, not counting the six 88mm guns. It was, therefore, virtually a fortress, whose guns ranged out to 25 miles. However it suffered from a handicap. Intended to defend Cherbourg, it could not fire out to the east at more than 35 degrees.

To finish it off it was decided to place *Nevada* at the limits of her useful range, whilst the *Texas* and *Arkansas* attacked from the east in total immunity, or at least apart from the fact that the two old battleships had to pass in front of the battery to reach their bombarding position.

But the *Nevada* was required for another mission to the west, which meant that the *Texas* and *Arkansas*

would have to parade past the 280mm guns before these had been battered by the *Nevada*. This seemed suicidal, but an airplane signalled that Battery Hamburg had been taken by the infantry, which was false news. So, when Group 2 approached to within less than 20,000 yards from the German guns, those guns suddenly opened fire. Two destroyers were rapidly hit by shells which went through them but did not explode in either case.

The battle then became general. The destroyer *O'Brien* was soon also hit, but this time the 280mm shell exploded inboard, killing thirteen men and destroying the fire control centre.

Shortly afterwards the battleship *Texas* was also hit by Battery Hamburg. The shell exploded in the wheelhouse, killing the helmsman and wounding eleven men, but the ship could be steered from another spot and was therefore able to continue the fight. She soon was hit by another shell, this time a 240mm, which did not explode. The *Texas* took her revenge several instants later when one of her shells hit a casemate, pierced the armour, and destroyed one of the four 280mm guns.

At the beginning of the afternoon the two old battleships were sheltered in the blind arc of the battery, at some 12 miles from the coast, a distance at which the accompanying destroyers could not fire. It was therefore only the two big ships that fought, without obtaining any more direct hits. Battery Hamburg continued to fire, but on other targets.

At 1407 the SFCP of the *Arkansas* indicated that the battery was no more than a mass of debris, to which the spotter plane replied, 'Possibly, but they are still firing.' When Group 2 withdrew after 1502, the battery was still not annihilated, even though it had been the target for 206 fourteen-inch and 58 twelve-inch and no less than 552 five-inch shells. Photos taken after the battle show that the ground was effectively transformed into a series of craters, but the turrets were still intact, with the exception of the one destroyed at 1335 by *Texas*.

This does not mean that the naval bombardment of Cherbourg was useless or ineffective. Certainly few direct hits were registered, on one side or the other, but the fire of the big naval guns had two effects. The first was on the morale of the German troops, already hard pressed by the infantry, and for whom the fire of the battleships and cruisers was particularly trying. The second was that the majority of the batteries were

A German rail gun on a turntable mounting in a concrete emplacement. This is one of the two 203mm guns at Auderville-Laye after the June bombardments. (DITE)

turned towards the sea at the moment of the actual assault by the American infantry, which greatly cut down the loss of the infantry, and for the same reason, greatly helped in the capture of the town, as Collins, Rommel and Krancke were all prepared to admit soon afterwards.

The town fell the next day, 26th June, and the port capitulated two days later, after having been strafed by both PT boats and by P-47 fighter-bombers. Some 39,000 German soldiers were captured, without counting the 6,000 others, entrenched at Cap de la Hague, who surrendered on 1st July. This date is considered by the Americans to represent the end of the Operation Neptune part of Overlord.

# 11 The Consolidation of the Bridgehead

A British coastal salvage vessel is raising a German landing craft used as a flak barge scuttled in the outer harbour of Port-en-Bessin. Notice the tug moored outboard. This photo was taken on 13th June. (IWM)

FROM THE EVENING of 6th June 1944 Allied convoys brought to the freshly conquered beaches thousands of men and hundreds of vehicles. This was in order first to consolidate and then to increase the foothold in France. It was the least impressive and the least glorious phase of Operation Neptune, but the most important after the landing itself.

## The American bridgeheads grow

On 7th June the 4th US Division progressed about a couple of miles northwards, whilst firming out the Utah bridgehead, whilst the scattered parachutists were regrouping. All day the fleet fired on targets designated by the troops on the spot, and equally engaged the batteries at Pernelle, close to Saint-Vaast-la Hogue. In the end the *Nevada* reduced them to silence.

Progress was constant in the Omaha sector, too, on the 7th. The 1st and 29th Divisions were present in the front line, and the former managed to cut the main road (Route Nationale 13) between Isigny and Bayeux. The second had more difficulties in its progression towards the Pointe du Hoc. All day Force O supported the footsloggers, the French cruiser *Montcalm* fired 309 rounds at eleven different targets. During the afternoon General Eisenhower and Admiral Ramsay visited the beachhead. The two men were worried by the large gap which remained between Omaha and Utah, but the Germans were not in a fit state to take advantage of it. Their reinforcements were only able to advance at night, and when the units called up from Brittany arrived in the Cotentin it was already too late; the 29th Division had made its junction with VII Corps, thus joining the two bridgeheads.

The progress continued on 8th June. The 4th Division approached Montebourg, already pounded by *Tuscaloosa*'s guns. Near Omaha the American engineers began to build a landing ramp, where the American cemetery of Saint-Laurent is now. On 12th June the five bridgeheads of the first day were united, linked behind a single front over 50 miles long and about 15 miles deep.

## A million men on 4th July

During this time the unloading of ships proceeded off the two American beaches. On 8th June at 1030 seventeen Liberty ships arrived off Utah Beach, carrying the complete 90th Infantry Division. On the evening of the 9th all these men were landed, with the major part of their equipment. By the evening of the 10th, 62,550 men, 4,133 vehicles and 9,986 tons of supplies had already been unloaded at Utah.

The list below gives the order of the arrival of American divisions in Normandy at both beaches:

Another view of Port-en-Bessin, whose harbour was soon put to work as shown here. An LCT(4) disgorges a lorry with the inscription *'vive la France'* across its bonnet. On the other side of the quay is a small coaster. Behind them one of the ubiquitous ramped barges proceeds out of harbour. (IWM)

| June | Division(s) |
|------|-------------|
| 6th | 1st, 4th & 29th Infantry, 82nd & 101st Airborne |
| 8th | 2nd & 90th Infantry |
| 10th | 2nd Armoured |
| 12th | 9th Infantry (a day in advance) |
| 14th | 79th Infantry |
| 16th | 30th Infantry (3 days late) |
| 21st | 83rd Infantry (9 days ahead) |
| 22nd | 3rd Armoured (5 days late) |

Seven extra divisions landed in July. The millionth Allied soldier arrived in Normandy on 4th July, appropriately on the day of the American celebration of the Declaration of Independence.

This uninterrupted flow of reinforcements can be understood when the impressive numbers of ships arriving each day off the Normandy coast are cited:

- 9 troop transports
- 20 LCIs
- 25 Liberty ships
- 40 LSTs
- 75 LCTs
- 38 British coasters.

From 7th to 30th June the British and American beaches combined received the following number of visits:

- 180 troop transports
- 372 LCIs
- 570 Liberty ships
- 905 LSTs
- 1,442 LCTs
- 788 coasters.

Admiral Ramsay himself declared that during this period the daily tonnage arriving in Normandy corresponded to a third of the capacity of Britain's imports, an astonishing figure if you compare the almost non-existent infrastructure which existed on and behind the beaches that June, with the immense ports of the British Isles, such as London, Liverpool or Glasgow.

## The consolidation of the British beachhead

The three British beaches were all linked with one another from 7th June, and at first the advance south was rapid. Notably Bayeux was captured on the 7th.

The old 'D' class cruiser HMS *Despatch*, converted into a depot ship and armed only with a few anti-aircraft guns. An American-built tug passes her stern, and in the foreground is the stern of an LCA. The photo was taken off Port-en-Bessin. (IWM)

However the larger part of the German reinforcements arrived in front of Montgomery's men to prevent the taking of Caen. The front stabilised very rapidly, therefore, for about a month, with tank battles of great violence, particularly to the west of Caen on ridge 112. During this time reinforcements did not cease to arrive on Gold, Juno and Sword. This last beach was the most dangerous, because the Germans had direct views over it. Their nearest footholds on the Orne were no more

than just over 5 miles distant. Several batteries of 88mm guns were established here in order to fire on the landing craft off Sword.

Thus, on 16th June, LSTs 226, 307, 331, 332 and 350 were all beached during the morning on Sword Beach in order to land their vehicles. They were then taken under fire by the 88s without the least chance of getting off or replying, a peculiarly painful situation. The Germans obtained fifteen direct hits, which was rather few for such large and immobile targets, and none of the vessels were destroyed. They all left with the flood tide, having only lost five killed and 26 wounded.

Consolidation eventually merged with the story of the construction of Mulberry B, which has already been dealt with at length.

## A balance sheet

To draw up the balance sheet of Operation Neptune, that is to say, of all the naval operations in the Channel during the month of June 1944, is in the end fairly easy.

The first point is certainly the incontestable success, in all aspects, of the naval operations:

The transportation of all the invasion forces, despite the bad weather and the difficulties due to the incredible number of vessels, succeeded even more than hoped for, with insignificant losses, whilst completely mystifying the enemy.

The phase of the assault proper was equally a great success. More than five divisions of infantry were landed on 6th June itself, often in the face of savage opposition. The conception of the invasion force, and the execution of the plan, were both shown to be perfectly adapted to the mission.

Naval gunfire support had been an inestimable help, very much more than that of the Allied bombers, at least on the first day of fighting. Later the efficiency of

A typical scene during the consolidation period, with a beached LST unloading a fleet of lorries onto the sand. The photo was taken on 7th June, and the vehicles belong to the British 50th Division, which means that this must be Gold Beach. (IWM)

Craft of all types off one of the British beaches. The picture includes LCVPs, LCPLs and LCT(4)s and (5)s, ship's boats, ramped barges, one MTB/MGB (probably a Fairmile 'D'), a tank barge (the one in the foreground bearing a large notice proclaiming it is carrying petrol) and a barge fitted out as a kitchen to feed the crews of small craft (on the left of the picture, marked by its forest of chimneys with 'H' shaped tops). (IWM)

DUKWs ferry backwards and forwards between these small freighters beached in shallow water and the beach, on which a shell bursts. (IWM)

This photo seems to show two of the ships shown in the previous photo, but here the photographer has come ashore at Arromanches with the group of DUKWs in the foreground, and the tide has retreated even further. The line of blockships can be seen dimly in the distance, and on the left of the picture what looks like a forest of factory chimneys are in fact the pillars of the Lobnitz units of the British Mulberry. (IWM)

tactical air support was of first importance, whilst naval support remained at the same level of excellence. Rommel himself believed this. This, too, had been obtained with very little loss.

The consolidation phase had suffered no hindrance from the enemy. Only the elements slowed the flow of reinforcement for the bridgehead, but not to the point of making the Allies lose the tactical initiative.

The protection of the invasion fleet, and especially the consolidation, succeeded so well that in less than 15 days any threat from German surface forces had vanished. In this field it is well to remember that it was the air forces that had the most terrible effect on the enemy, with the destruction of the S-boat bases of Le Havre and Boulogne, with the putting out of action of the majority of the U-boats attempting to enter the Channel, and finally the sweeping of the Luftwaffe from the sky, making it incapable of intervening in daylight, and limiting it therefore to night attacks which were altogether not particularly effective.

## The losses

The totally positive results of Operation Neptune were obtained with remarkably light losses. The three tables below provide a reckoning:

The first lists all the losses of warships and merchantmen during the period from 5th to 30th June 1944, but excludes landing craft.

| Sunk by | Large warships | Small warships | Merchant ships & auxiliaries |
|---|---|---|---|
| **Mines** | 9 (a) | 7 | 10 |
| **U-boats** | 2 (b) | 0 | 4 |
| **Aircraft** | 2 (c) | 0 | 3 |
| **S-boats** | 1 (d) | 0 | 8 |
| **Artillery** | 0 | 2 | 3 |
| **Accidents** | 0 | 1 | 7 |
| **Total** | 14 | 10 | 35 |

(a) seven destroyers and two minesweepers, (b) two frigates/DEs, (c) one destroyer, one frigate/DE , (d) one destroyer = total of nine destroyers, three frigates/DEs, two minesweepers.

The second table lists damaged ships:

| Damaged by | Large warships | Small warships | Merchant ships & auxiliaries |
|---|---|---|---|
| **Mines** | 12 | 7 | 14 |
| **U-boats** | 2 | 0 | 2 |
| **Aircraft** | 2 | 1 | 4 |
| **S-boats** | 2 | 0 | 2 |
| **Artillery** | 13 | 5 | 10 |
| **Accidents** | 9 | 6 | 29 |
| **Total** | 40 | 19 | 61 |

A Sherman tank called 'Somua' drives onto the beach at Saint-Martin-de-Varreville on Utah Beach. As can be seen from the tricolour flag, the map of France with the cross of Lorraine, this is one of the tanks of General Leclerc's 2nd Armoured Division, which landed in France between 1st and 5th August. (ECPA)

The heading 'Accidents' covers all the normal hazards of the sea, storm, collision, foundering etc. Once again it is worth underlining that it was mines that caused the worst damage.

The last set of tables covers the landing craft. The following figures are taken from Bertil Stjernfelt, do not include LCVPs, and only apply to the British beaches:

On 6th June itself 291 landing craft were destroyed or badly damaged: 131 LCTs, 117 LCAs and 43 LCIs.

Unfortunately Morison does not give the American losses in his splendid work. They must have been similar, insignificant at Utah and very heavy at Omaha. The greater seaworthiness of the LCVP as opposed to the LCA should have saved them some losses.

During the first week of the operation, excluding D-Day itself, losses were as follows:

|  | German resistance | Bad weather |
|---|---|---|
| Craft Sunk | 64 | 34 |
| Damaged | 106 | 106 |
| TOTAL | 170 | 140 |

For the two following weeks the figures were:

|  | German resistance | Bad weather |
|---|---|---|
| Craft sunk | 27 | 118 |
| Damaged | 29 | 297 |
| TOTAL | 56 | 415 |

Finally, at the end of the first month of the invasion the number of craft lost or damaged by the enemy reached 261 as against 606 by bad weather. This was about 20 per cent of the total number engaged. The figure of 606 lost or damaged is close to that cited in Chapter 9: 800 craft and various boats thrown ashore during the storm from 19th to 22nd June. This latter figure includes a number of vessels which were not landing craft, and also numbers of landing craft which

On one of the British beaches the success of the landing is symbolised by the White Ensign flying over the beachmaster's post whilst a coaster, an LCT and an LST lie beached. In the foreground is an amphibious jeep, whilst the two vehicles in front of the coaster's bow are a Bren gun carrier, and the larger shape of a BARV (tank converted for wading and recovering other vehicles in shallow water). (IWM)

were thrown ashore intact. We must not forget that landing craft were designed to beach easily, storm or no storm. Even putting all these losses together one is still forced to state that they remained light. The invasion of a continent only cost the navies involved a total of nine destroyers, three frigates, two minesweepers and around 250 landing craft. Fortunately the toll of human beings was equally slight as far as the navies were concerned. This was an even more amazing achievement when one considers that the Germans were particularly strong adversaries.

# Further Reading

J J COLLEDGE & H T LENTON, *Warships of World War II*. Ian Allan, London, 1964 (Royal Navy only)

K EDWARDS, *Operation Neptune*. Collins, London 1946

L F ELLIS (Ed), *Victory in the West* Vol 1. HMSO, London 1962

B FERGUSSON, *The Watery Maze*. Collins, London 1961

R GARDINER (ed), *Conway's All the World's Fighting Ships 1906-1921* and *1922-1946* volumes. Conway Maritime Press 1985 & 1980

H T LENTON, 'Navies of the Second World War' series, published by Macdonald, London in the 1970s, including volumes on British, American, German, French and Dutch navies

S E MORISON, *History of United States Naval Operations in World War II* Vol XI. Little, Brown & Co, Boston 1957

G PAWLE, *The Secret War*. Harrap, London 1956

A RAVEN & J ROBERTS, *British Battleships of World War Two*. Arms & Armour Press, London 1976

A RAVEN & J ROBERTS, *British Cruisers of World War Two*. Arms and Armour Press, London 1980

S W ROSKILL, *The War at Sea* Vol 3 pt 2. HMSO London 1961

C WILMOT, *The Struggle for Europe*. Collins, London 1952

# Index Of Ships' Names

Page location references in italic refer to illustrations. Abbreviations used in the index are as follows:-